The Green and the Black

Indiana Series in Arab and Islamic Studies

Salih J. Altoma, Iliya Harik, and Mark Tessler,
general editors

The familiar image of Muammar Qadha[fi] as a crazed leader with a pathological ad[-]diction to terrorism has tended to evoke a stereotyped U.S. political response. In an effort to move beyond the "mad-dog" syn-drome as an adequate explanation of Lib-yan foreign policy, leading specialists in Middle Eastern and African politics examine the historical forces, attitudes, interests, and priorities that have shaped Libyan behavior in Africa. Part I probes the de-terminants and motivation of Qadhafi's Af-rican policies. Special attention is paid to the relative significance of ideology and na-tional interest, the role of Islam, and the function of the armed forces in translating Qadhafi's vision into reality. In Part II re-gional case studies focus on the Maghreb, Sub-Saharan Africa, Chad, the OAU, and the Libyan domestic scene as separate, yet interacting, arenas in which Qadhafi's poli-cies have been articulated and tested. A concluding chapter compares the behavior of Libya and South Africa as regional hege-mons. Emerging from this collective analy-sis is a nuanced view of Libyan politics as a complex mix of ideological consistency and tactical shifts: an overarching commitment to Arab unity tempered by opportunism and improvisation. *The Green and the Black* provides students and policy makers with a sophisticated and dispassionate analysis of the circumstances that have inspired, nur-tured, and, more often than not, constrained Libyan adventurism in the African continent.

Contributors are François Burgat, Mary-Jane Deeb, Chris Dunton, William J. Foltz, E. J. H. Joffé, René Lemarchand, Jean-Emmanuel Pondi, Ronald Bruce St John, and Mark Tessler.

THE GREEN AND
THE BLACK

Qadhafi's Policies in Africa

EDITED BY

RENÉ LEMARCHAND

INDIANA UNIVERSITY PRESS
BLOOMINGTON AND INDIANAPOLIS

91-456

© 1988 by Indiana University Press
All rights reserved

Manufactured in the United States of America

Library of Congress Cataloging-in-Publication Data
The Green and the black.
(Indiana series in Arab and Islamic studies)
Includes index.
1. Africa—Foreign relations—Libya.   2. Libya—
Foreign relations—Africa.   I. Lemarchand, René.
II. Series.
DT38.9.L75G74   1988   327.61'206   87-46088
ISBN 0-253-32678-8
1 2 3 4 5 93 92 91 90 89 88

CONTENTS

PREFACE

Dissatisfaction with the mixture of hype and humbug that has come to characterize American attitudes toward Libya is the principal motivation that underlies this collective effort. It is a sentiment shared by most of the contributors to this volume. Our hope is that it may broaden readers' perspectives on an area where American policy has consistently been out of its depth.

American perceptions of Libya tend to crystallize around the all-too-familiar caricature of Qadhafi as a crazed leader whose pathological addiction to terrorism poses a permanent threat to our citizens—an image that is consistent with a certain form of American popular culture, perhaps best exemplified by the *Rambo* series or *Red Dawn*. From this type of representation emerges a dangerously stereotypical view of U.S. relations with the Third World, aptly summed up by Richard Falk: "A complacent America ill-prepared for the coming of the barbarians—Third World terrorists somehow managed from Moscow by psychopathic intermediaries. Against these fiendish enemies anything goes." Seen through these Ramboesque lenses Qadhafi is the archetypical Third World terrorist; against "the mad dog of the Middle East" the application of force is the only sensible response; all other considerations are either irrelevant or misguided.

This book is an attempt to shift the ground of debate beyond the realm of stereotypes and simplicities and to invite a more sophisticated—and dispassionate—enquiry into the dynamics of Libyan policies in the continent. The American fixation on Qadhafi's "mad dog" image has evidently done very little to promote a realistic understanding of the conditions out of which terrorism arises. As several of the contributions to this volume plainly demonstrate, the complex of historical forces, attitudes, interests, and priorities that have shaped Libyan policies is simply not reducible to the slogans and metaphors that have guided American responses. Demonology, in short, is a poor substitute for a careful analysis of the circumstances that have inspired, nurtured, and, more often than not, constrained Libyan adventurism in the continent.

My contribution as editor and coauthor is in part the product of serendipity. While doing research in Chad in the 1970s I stumbled upon Libya and quickly came to realize that there was no point in trying to elucidate the byzantine complexities of Chadian factionalism unless the Libyan connection was properly taken into account. For years the root of the Chadian crisis has been in Libya, and now that Chad lies at the core of the Libyan malaise it is becoming increasingly evident that their destinies cannot be fully dissociated from each other.

In coming to grips with the configurations of Libyan influence in Chad, as well as in other parts of black Africa, I am constantly reminded of the obstacles raised by the arbitrary but nonetheless persistent division of labor between Middle Eastern specialists and Africanists, a state of affairs hardly conducive to a proper appraisal of Libyan-African relations. Not the least of our concerns in this volume is to provide a point of entry for a more sustained and presumably more rewarding academic exchange between area specialists. If nothing else, Qadhafi's propensity to cross boundaries may help stimulate similar moves on the part of academics.

It would have been surprising if, out of our collective efforts, anything like a common consensus had emerged about the wellsprings of Qadhafi's African policies. On that score the present volume holds few surprises. If there is any single truth about Libya it will not be found in these pages. The aim, rather, is to move away from any single set of preconceptions and instead to look at the determinants of Libyan policies from different vantage points. Only through such an eclectic approach can one properly grasp the texture of such policies, their motivations, temporal priorities, and contextual variations.

The idea of a book on Libya first entered my mind in December 1986, when asked to organize a panel on the theme of Libyan-African relations at the joint meeting of the Middle Eastern Studies and African Studies Associations, held in New Orleans. Two subsequent conferences on Libya, held in Stuttgart in April 1986 and March 1987, both organized under the joint auspices of the Defense Intelligence College and the United States European Command (USEUCOM) of the North Atlantic Treaty Organization, helped to further stimulate my interest in this theme and, above all, convinced me of the urgent need to educate the U.S. military as to the realities of Libyan policies in the continent. Meanwhile, a number of contributors were added to the small core of participants to the New Orleans meeting. Maintaining a reasonably effective level of communication between Gainesville, Florida, and such far-away places as Ndjamena, Lima, Yaounde, Aix-en-Provence, Geneva, Paris, and London proved a somewhat complicated but nonetheless manageable enterprise, thanks to the good will and cooperation of our more distant collaborators.

Three of the chapters in this volume have appeared elsewhere: Mary-Jane Deeb's discussion of Libya's national interest appeared under a different title and in a slightly abbreviated version in the _SAIS Review_ (Summer–Fall 1986), vol. 6, no. 2; this also applies to Chris Dunton's piece, published in _West Africa_ (Sept. 1, 1986):1820–22; (Sept. 8, 1986):1873–74; (Sept. 15, 1986):1918–19; and to Bruce St John's contribution, which appeared in his _Qadhafi's World Design: Libyan Foreign Policy, 1969–1987_ (London: Saqi Books, 1987).

In the absence of equivalents in the English language for the Arabic letters _qaf_ (ق) and _dhal_ (ذ) the spelling of Qadhafi's name opens up a wide range of possibilities—no less than 432 if we are to believe the _Sunday Times_ of London. Our choice of Qadhafi is therefore wholly arbitrary, though consistent with the preferred spelling of several press organs, including Libya's _Jamahiriya Review_.

Bill Foltz and Goran Hyden will find here the expression of my sincere gratitude for their judicious commentaries on my concluding essay. While in Aix-en-Provence, François Burgat's help proved invaluable—not only in facilitating my access to the archival gold mine of the Institut de Recherches et d'Etudes sur le Monde Arabe et Musulman, but in sharing with me his admirable grasp of Libyan history and politics. Omar Sefiane was kind enough to translate into French lengthy excerpts from Said Alderhamane al-Hendiri's fascinating work on _Libyan-Chadian Relations_ (Al-Alaqat al-Libiyya al-Tchadiyya). Mark Tessler gave consistent support in addition to alerting me to the Indiana University Press Middle Eastern Series as a possible publication outlet. Last but not least I owe a deep debt of gratitude to Kay Haile for deciphering my normally illegible handwriting and putting the entire manuscript through the word processor with maximum speed and efficiency. For all the blemishes and editorial shortcomings of this book I claim full responsibility.

RENÉ LEMARCHAND

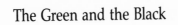

The Green and the Black

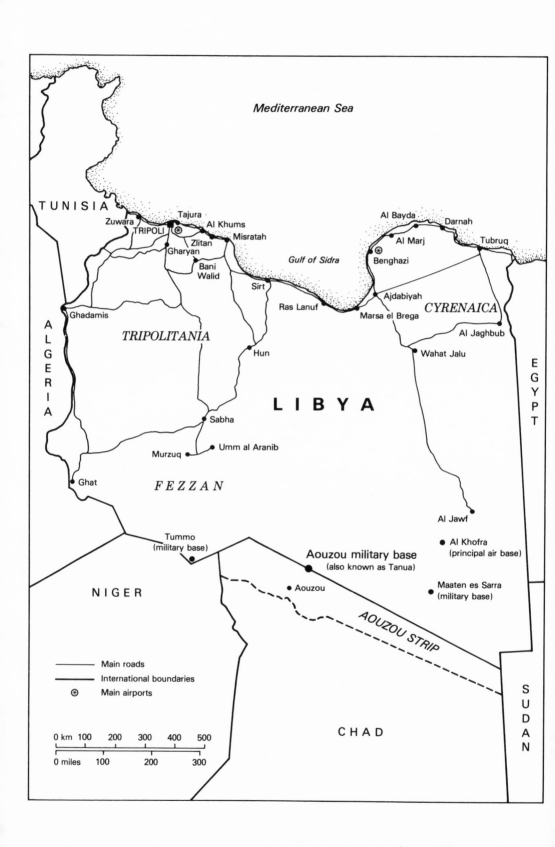

Introduction

BEYOND THE MAD DOG SYNDROME
René Lemarchand

> Qadhafi is a rogue criminal
>
> —Kissinger

> Like all sons of the desert he is a man of stubborn and
> independent character. . . . His mental universe is
> simple and rough, free of those nuances which
> hamper action among settled people. A Bedouin is
> always marching towards a well, discovery of which
> will make the difference between death and
> survival. . . .
>
> —Guy Georgy, former French Ambassador to Tripoli

> The difficulty is that this particular rogue enjoys the
> support and protection of the Soviet Union. . . . If we
> cannot find a way to deal with the Qadhafi problem,
> Western interests and values are likely to suffer the
> death of a thousand cuts.
>
> —*The Wall Street Journal*, October 9, 1981

Qadhafi violates geographical and conceptual boundaries, and the second of these transgressions argues for considerable caution in explaining the first. The image he projects evades all conventional categories of statesmanship and diplomacy. It incorporates the notions of *mahdi* and desert warrior, of pan-Arabist and Islamic reformer, of revolutionary fanatic and compulsive meddler, of mad dog and terrorist. His ability to slip from one category to another does more than create puzzlement; it also gives Libyan foreign policy its presumed singularity.

As the quotes above suggest, most explanations of Libyan foreign policy are reducible to three basic sterotypes. There is, to begin with, what might be called the pathological or idiosyncratic view of Qadhafi's behavior. It brings into focus his brutal and erratic style, the mixture of guile and obduracy that colors his foreign policy, including the "rogue criminal" aspect of his personality. The characterization offered by *The Economist* is not untypical: "His erratic tactics, his conceit, his readiness to use every sort of violence to fulfill his dreams are the stuff of madness" (*The Economist* 1986, 11). If this diagnosis has any merit one wonders whether the tools of political science can usefully compete with the psychiatrist's couch in analyzing Qadhafi's motives.

The culturalist perspective, on the other hand, draws attention to the conditioning effect of his Bedouin heritage and desert environment. It uncovers "the reformist fundamentalism of the Libyan desert" (Zartman and Kluge 1984, 177) and presumably helps elucidate some of his more enduring personality traits ("his independent and stubborn character, his profound religious convictions and his unshakable certitude that God blesses his projects") and tactics ("a Bedouin knows that he must single-mindedly and relentlessly go forward, that he must cover his tracks and change paths in order to fool the enemy" [Georgy 1984, 72]). In the words of Henry M. Schuler, "it is only in traditional Libyan and Bedouin terms that his resentment of Western influences and his advocacy of Libyan expansionism can fully be understood" (Schuler 1981). Though not necessarily irrelevant, at this level of analysis it is a question whether culturalist interpretations can provide as much as a clue for mapping the different routes—and impasses—of Libyan foreign policy, not to mention its successes and failures.

Yet another form of reductionism focuses on "the Soviet proxy" dimension. Attention here shifts to the heavy dependence of Libya on Soviet-supplied weaponry, the visits occasionally paid by Libyan officials to Moscow, and the temporary alignment of Tripoli with the Ethiopian-South Yemen axis as conclusive evidence of a close Soviet-Libyan connection. From this vantage point Libya figures as yet another ominous red spot on the "Kremlin's playground," along with Angola, Ethiopia, and Mozambique—in short as another "Communist, Marxist-Leninist controlled state" (Johnson 1987, 7).

Qadhafi's credentials as a Soviet client are nowhere more firmly established than in the White House. Thus, shortly before the April 1986 U.S. strike on Tripoli, in a move apparently designed to appeal to Ronald Reagan's previous incarnation, a 15-minute color movie prepared by the CIA was reportedly shown on the White House screen to drive home to the viewers Qadhafi's "close ties with the Soviet Union" (Hersch 1987, 22). Whether explicitly or at a more or less subliminal level the "Soviet proxy" fixation is a key ingredient of American perceptions of Qadhafi as a "hate figure."

This comic-strip imagery sets the basic parameters of our universe of discourse about Qadhafi. Out of it emerges a singularly perverse and irrational character whose physical elimination is made imperative by the "mad dog" streak in his personality. Ideally, his family as well needs to be eliminated, for reasons that are deeply imbedded in the ethos of Bedouin culture. As one reliable observer recently disclosed, "the notion of targeting Qadhafi's family, according to an involved National Security Council (NSC) aide, originated with several senior CIA officers who claimed that in Bedouin culture Qadhafi would be diminished as a leader if he could not protect his home. One aide recalls a CIA briefing in which it was argued that 'if you really get at Qadhafi's house—and by extension his family—you've destroyed an important connection for the people in terms of loyalty' " (Hersch 1987, 20). At this level of abstraction the link between cultural stereotypes and public policies leaves one to wonder whether self-deception—to put it mildly—is an exclusively Libyan monopoly.

Only through a basic alteration of our structure of cognition can we begin to talk intelligently about Libya. All too often by consistently mistaking style for substance, tactics for strategy, national interests for ideology, we end up eliminating all traces of coherence from the Libyan record. That the latter shows considerable evidence of brutality is no reason to brush it aside as an aberration. One could indeed argue that there is in this case a certain logic to the use of violence, made all the more compelling by the exceptionally brutal character of Libya's encounter with the West.

Historical Threads

It may be useful at the outset to remind ourselves of a few basic facts about Libyan history—the most salient being that of all the states of North Africa and the Middle East, Libya is the one about whose past we know least. Only recently, thanks in part to the painstaking and pioneering efforts of Lisa Anderson, have we begun to appreciate the extreme complexity of Libya's history under Turkish and Italian rule and the extensive violence that has accompanied its passage from one form of colonial bondage to another. Measured in terms of human statistics this transition has meant the loss, through death or exile, of approximately half the total population of Libya between 1911 and 1943 (Anderson 1982, 44). There is simply no parallel elsewhere in the continent for such massive blood-letting, or for the ferocity it revealed—a phenomenon "unmatched by anything experienced elsewhere in the Arab world" (ibid.). Scarcely more propitious were the circumstances of Libya's transition to independence, in 1951, resulting in something approximating a caricature of the neocolonial state: An aging and pliant sovereign brought back from Egypt by courtesy of Great Britain, the installation shortly thereafter of British and U.S. military bases, generous concessions to foreign oil companies, the maintenance in positions of relative wealth of a sizeable European settler community, and, in symbiosis with this foreign "estate," a political system deeply ensconced in corruption, prevarication, and nepotism. The country acceded to independence with a per capita income of $25 a year and, according to a World Bank report, "an acute lack of technicians, professional people and administrators in every field of activity" (International Bank for Reconstruction and Development 1960, 252).

To an extent seldom appreciated in the West, the indignities and humiliations of colonial rule are an irreducible element of Libya's historical encounter with the West. The Libyan version of the colonial (and neocolonial) situation thus provides an important frame of reference for an understanding of the Qadhafian mind-set. Both his violently anti-Western dispositions and his passionate commitment to a reconstruction of the Arab nation are the product of a uniquely cruel and frustrating historical experience. And so, arguably, is his hypersensitivity to all forms of external interference in the affairs of Libya, a trait that, as Dunton shows, is widely shared among Libyans and deeply rooted in their own recent history.

One could move even further back into the historical layers and detect a parallel of sorts between the social ethos of the Senussiya brotherhood—its reformist, anti-urban, revivalist orientation—and Qadhafi's own political leanings. "In all of these characteristics, the 'Qadhafia' is similar to its predecessor, the latest wave of austere fundamentalist revivalism, seeking to create solidarity across state boundaries" (Zartman and Kluge 1984, 178). Again, there is a striking historical parallel between the nineteenth-century expansion southward into Chad of both the Senussiya and its Libyan-based Ottoman overlords on the one hand, and Qadhafi's relentless efforts to push his way into the Tibesti and beyond, by hook or by crook.

Libyan history, in short, helps us place the Qadhafi phenomenon in a larger context than the stereotypes mentioned earlier; it provides us with illuminating insights into the circumstances that have shaped his perceptions of the West and framed his self-image as prophet and redeemer. And it also leaves a host of questions unanswered.

Thus, if history helps explain his sensitivity to external meddling in Libyan affairs, it sheds precious little light on the fact that he turned out to be, in this and other respects, the worst offender. Furthermore, whatever links can be discerned between the Senussiya and the "Qadhafia," the uncomfortable fact is that he has shown undisguised contempt for the Sufi brotherhood and its ancestral figure, Mohammed Ibn Ali al-Senussi, going so far as to have his grave obliterated. Why this contradiction? And why has the "Islamic archetype which he seeks to embody" (Roumani 1983, 166), and which some have traced to the legacy of the Senussiya, failed to prevent him from entering into alliances with anti-Islamic forces as in the Sudan and Ethiopia?

The answers lie not in history as much as in Qadhafi's highly selective *vision* of history. The Arab nation is the only truly significant historical reality; the persistence in Africa of a state system inherited from the West has no historical validation, any more than do the forms of nationalist self-expression that brought it into existence. Both are the product of Western imperialism, whose impact on the contemporary map of Africa is consistently denied in the name of a higher historical reality, the *umma*, that is, the community of the believers. Reconstruction of the *umma* is the paramount objective; in pursuance of this ultimate goal all means are legitimate.

Dimensions of Analysis

A closer look at the evidence presented in this volume suggests several qualifications to this formulation. To begin with, attention to the *regional contexts* of Libyan policies brings to light significant variations on the theme of Arab unity, with the concept of the Libyan national interest emerging as a major subtheme in the African setting. This is indeed the crux of the argument set forth by Mary-Jane Deeb—to which we shall return in a moment. The *time-frame* within which Libyan policies have evolved represents yet another crucial variable, pointing to significant shifts in the proximate goals and instrumentalities of Libyan policies. Finally, there is the more complex issue of the relationship of Libya's *economic and military capabilities* to the conduct of its African policies, pointing to a persistent gap between ambitions and performance.

Contextual Variations: National Interest vs. Ideology

Africa is only one of several arenas incorporated into Qadhafi's foreign policy mold, and one in which, according to Deeb, the primacy of Libya's national interest supersedes ideology as the prime mover of Libyan policies. Visualizing Qadhafi's foreign policy universe as consisting of five overlapping geographical sectors (North and sub-Saharan Africa, the Arab world east of Egypt, the Islamic world, the Third World, and the industrialized countries of the North), she argues that only in the first, and most notably North Africa, is Libya's policy "primarily determined by its national interest, or at the very least by Qadhafi's perception of Libya's national interest." At this level "ideological considerations, whether Arab, Islamic, or revolutionary play a secondary role" (Deeb in this volume).

The principal merit of the Deeb thesis is to invite a careful reconsideration of the more glaring inconsistencies of Qadhafi's foreign policy options. Even though the concept of national interest may not provide all the answers, the questions she raises are highly pertinent:

> Why did Qadhafi, an Arab nationalist, support Ethiopia, an African, primarily Christian country, against the Sudan (under Numeiry), an Arab country with a Muslim majority? Why did he, a major Muslim reformist, support animists and Christians in southern Sudan against Arab Muslim northerners in the first half of the 1980s? How could a self-styled revolutionary and socialist support and set up unity agreements in 1984 with a traditional, pro-Western monarch in Morocco, whom Qadhafi had previously described as corrupt? (Deeb chap. 2, this volume)

Tessler's answer (in this volume) to the last of these queries is entirely consistent with the thrust of Deeb's argument: "Considerations of national and personal interest provided the principal motivation for the formation of the Arab-African union [between Libya and Morocco]. . . . Indeed, given that the Libyan leader was associating himself with a monarch and a regime he had repeatedly denounced, it may plausibly be argued that the alliance was formed in spite of, rather than in response to, ideological considerations." The national interest argument takes on added plausibility in the light of our own discussion of Libyan involvement in Chad, but appears of little help to explain Qadhafi's military intervention in Uganda (see Foltz in this volume).

That the concept is not without certain limitations in reasonably clear. For one thing, the scope of its applicability (both geographically and analytically) is rather more restricted than Deeb would like us to believe. Whether defined in terms of a "unitarist doctrine" (to borrow Burgat's phrase) or a pan-Arab commitment, ideology is, after all, the principal axis around which Libyan policies in North Africa have tended to revolve. The stamp of the Nasirist conception of pan-Arabism on Qadhafi's vision is unmistakable. His less-than-impressive performance in translating this vision into reality does not detract from its usefulness as a point of reference for analysis and identification. Insofar as the "primacy of the national interest" argument lends itself to empirical verification (of which more in a moment), its relevance appears limited to specific cases and circumstances. And even where this argument seems most compelling, considerations of national interest are not always clearly separable from ideological motivations. Chad is a case in point. Similarly, the case of the Libyan-Moroccan union lends partial support to this contention. As Tessler himself concedes, "The role of ideology should not be dismissed entirely [from discussions of the Oujda Treaty]. It is in part for ideological reasons that Qadhafi opposed the overtures toward Israel made by Hassan in 1985 and 1986" (in this volume).

But what, exactly, are the empirical referents of the Libyan conception of the national interest? The answer is anything but clear. To argue, as Deeb does, that the Libyan national interest is what Qadhafi perceives it to be comes dangerously close to a tautology. And yet, in a fundamental sense, her point is correct. What makes the concept so difficult to handle in this or any other context is that it incorporates a large element of subjectivity. Nowhere does this element loom larger than in the case at hand.

If so, one wonders whether there is any point in postulating the primacy of the national interest *as an alternative* to ideology. Ideology, for Qadhafi, is both a political resource that can be manipulated for a variety of purposes, including promotion of the Libyan national interest, and the organizing principle of his foreign policy. In the latter sense it is almost wholly centered upon the Nasirist notion of pan-Arab unity. There is more to this view, however, than a nostalgic longing for the golden age of the Arab nation. The achievement of Arab unity is seen as a historic opportunity for a "settling of accounts" with the legacy of European imperialism—making it possible for the Arabs to recover what has been taken away from them, that is, unity—but it is also a necessary first step in anticipation of a future confrontation with the new form of imperialism incarnated by Zionism and its American props. Viewed in this light Qadhafi's ideology brings into focus the key dimensions of his foreign policy stance: not just Arab unity but anti-Zionism and anti-imperialism (the latter generally seen as synonymous with U.S. hegemony).

Chronological Discontinuities: The Shift from Diplomacy
to Destabilization

Qadhafi's ability to respond to changing circumstances by constantly recalculating his moves, shifting his partnerships and exchanging one set of tools for another is nowhere more apparent than in the extraordinary swings and contradictions of his African policies. In spite of all this, however, a certain logic emerges from the record. Whether described as pragmatic or opportunistic, it underscores the degree to which Libya's African policies fit the "policy of opportunity" model proposed by Zartman and Kluge: "When the opportunity presents itself, Libya acts. When opposition is too strong Libya effects a strategic withdrawal, but not a change in goals" (Zartman and Kluge 1984, 183).

The consistency with which Qadhafi has pursued his "unitarist" goals is made abundantly clear in Burgat's discussion, and also the radically different pathways and partnerships through which unity has been attempted. Until 1974, "conference diplomacy" was the preferred means by which the posited goal was to be reached. Success in forging Arab unity could not be obtained in any other way. By 1974, however, failure could only be averted by the choice of alternative means.

Qadhafi's diplomatic setbacks since the Tripoli Charter (1969) is another area where consistency is undeniable. None of the six regional unification agreements concluded between 1969 and 1981 went beyond the drafting stage. The Oujda Treaty (1984) temporarily brought Libya and Morocco into a marriage of convenience, only to be dissolved in 1986 amid mutual recriminations.

Table 1 sums up the record of Libya's diplomatic fiascos; what it does not reveal are the reasons behind them or, more importantly, what Qadhafi perceives them to be. Drawing from Ajami's insights, it is clear that his less-than-distinguished performance on the Arab unity scorecard is not just a policy failure; it also reveals the failure of an idea, the bankruptcy of an ideal: "Neither the fire and passion of the Libyan revolution, nor its money could turn history around and revive an exhausted idea. . . . The Pan-Arab idea that dominates the political consciousness of modern Arabs has become a hollow claim" (Ajami 1981, 126).

A totally different construction emerged from Qadhafi's cognitive map, however, pointing to a drastic change of course. Reactionary governments and their external patrons (primarily France and the United States) were now perceived as the main obstacle in the way of Arab

TABLE 1. **Libya's Bid for Regional Unification and/or Cooperation, 1969–1986**

I. *Regional Unification Agreements**

1969	Egypt/Sudan/Libya (Tripoli Charter)
1971	Egypt/Syria/Libya (Benghazi Treaty)
1972	Egypt/Libya
1973	Algeria/Libya (Hassi Messaoud Accords)
1974	Tunisia/Libya (Djerba Treaty)
1981	Chad/Libya (Tripoli Communique)
1984–86	Morocco-Libya (Oujda Treaty)

II. *Cooperation Agreements*

1972	Trade and cultural cooperation	Mauretania
	Trade and investment agreements	Chad
1974	Economic, agricultural and cultural cooperation	Chad
1977	Cultural cooperation agreement	Angola
	Economic and technical cooperation agreements	Ethiopia
1980	Mutual defense accords	Chad
1981	Military and political cooperation accords (Aden Treaty)	Ethiopia/South Yemen/ Libya
1981–86	Bilateral military and/or cultural cooperation agreements	Burundi/Burkina Fasso/ Seychelles/Zimbabwe/ Ghana/Sudan/Mozambique/ CAR/Uganda/Malta/ Djibouti/Togo

*Reference is sometimes made to "mergers" and "federal unions" yet in most instances the distinction appears highly arbitrary given the lack of concern shown by Qadhafi for the procedural and institutional steps intended to lead to regional unification. The tenor of the 1981 Tripoli Communique, announcing the fusion of Chad and Libya, is not untypical: "The Socialist People's Libyan Arab Jamahiriya and Chad have agreed . . . to work for the realization of complete unity between the two countries—a Jamahiriya unity in which authority, arms and resources are in the hands of the people; its foundation is the people's congresses and committees" (quoted in Neuberger 1982, 70).

unity. The awakening of the Arab consciousness presumably requires an all-out struggle against the "enemies of the Arab nation," including the United States, "itself the foremost enemy of Islam and Arabism" (*Al-Zahar al-Akhdar* 1983, November 23). Since the achievement of Arab unity through negotiated phases is clearly not feasible, a radical leap is required to bring it about. Only by striking at the source, against reactionary regimes, can unity be envisaged as a long-term objective.

As Burgat conclusively shows, Qadhafi's perception of the internal obstacles faced by his own revolutionary efforts at home is entirely consistent with his reading for the international situation. The Zuwara speech, in 1973, constitutes a watershed: From then on the "masses" are expected to act as the privileged vector of the socialist revolution; their historic mission, inscribed in the Green Book's Third Universal Theory, is to spawn "popular congresses and popular committees everywhere," thus enabling society to become "its own supervisor" (Harris 1986, 57); meanwhile, "perverts" and "deviationists" must be weeded out. The aim, as Burgat (in this volume) notes, "is to break away from the traditional elites and eliminate

competing centers of authority," which can only be accomplished "by taking Libya into the
adventure of direct democracy." What Burgat euphemistically refers to as Qadhafi's "thoroughly unconventional diplomatic style," is in a sense the normal outcome of his efforts to
extend to the international arena the logic of his 1973 domestic experiment.

Qadhafi's efforts at destabilization are richly documented and require little elaboration
except to note the striking parallel with South Africa both in terms of tactics and strategy, if
not capabilities, a point more fully articulated and qualified in our concluding chapter. A
glance at the roster of Libyan-sponsored attempts at destabilization (table 2) shows the range
of the target areas and the multiplicity of tactics involved. With the exception of Chad, virtually
all of these initiatives took place within a post-1973 time-frame.

As shown by table 2, Libyan destabilization covers a wide gamut, ranging from direct
military intervention on behalf of incumbent regimes (as in Chad and Uganda) to financial
and military support of anti-regime factions (as in the Sudan, Mali, Chad, Niger, and Burkina
Fasso), to which must be added various terrorist activities involving the use of hit squads
and assassination plots (as happened in Egypt, Tunisia, and Chad). Although the choice of
tactics is in part dictated by the circumstances of the target state, a fairly consistent pattern
emerges from the record: It usually begins with bilateral cooperation agreements, designed
to set the stage for a Libyan presence; the next phase involves the recruitment, training, and
funding of political dissidents, and where local insurgencies seem reasonably promising from
the standpoint of Libyan interests every effort is made to provide their leadership with logistical, military, and financial assistance; a possible third stage, most dramatically illustrated
by the cases of Chad and Uganda, takes the form of outright military intervention by Libyan
units (see Foltz in this volume).

Given the drastic change in the perceived identity of "relevant enemies" in the domestic
and international arenas, the growing salience of Qadhafi's anti-American stance after 1974
is hardly surprising. Changes in ideological orientation paved the way for some spectacular
tactical reversals. Thus, there are good reasons to assume that his tactical alliance with the
southern Sudanese had more to do with his visceral distaste for Numeiry's pro-American
leanings than with any particular conception of the Libyan national interest. Tripoli's subsequent rapprochement with Khartoum and concomitant severance of its ties with the southern rebellion, in the wake of Saddiq al-Mahdi's accession to power, would seem to confirm
this interpretation. Alliances with the forces of "progressivism," most notably with Marxist
Ethiopia against the Eritrean insurgency (after 1977), must be viewed in much the same light,
and so, also, his exhortations in 1986 to overthrow America's most obedient client state,
Mobutu's Zaire. Not unnaturally, Qadhafi's growing concern about the threat of U.S. imperialism reached obsessive proportions after the U.S. air strike on Tripoli in April 1986. How
else can one explain his monumental gaffe at the September 1986 Non-Aligned Summit in
Harare (Zimbabwe), as he lashed out against some of the more eminent participants for acting
as "puppets of the United States" (*The Herald* September 5, 1986)?

Looking back at the domestic arena, Burgat notes a causal relation between Qadhafi's
"rhetorical liberties" and "his total financial independence"—"a state of affairs that would
last until the collapse of the oil market in 1986" (in this volume). The relationship, of course,
extends far beyond the realm of rhetoric and draws attention to Qadhafi's economic and
military capabilities as a determinant of his foreign policy.

TABLE 2. **Libyan-Sponsored Attempts at Destablization: 1976–1986**

1. *Military training and support of anti-regime elements*

Target	Date	Type of Operation
Burkina Fasso	1982–83	Arms and funding to Colonel Sankara, thus contributing to his successful military take-over (1983)
Chad	1970–86	Arms, funding, and training to *Frolinat*, and subsequently to GUNT factions
Gambia	1981	Arms and funding to instigators of abortive coup
Niger	1976	Abortive Libyan-inspired coup
	1982	Abortive raid against Arlit by Libyan-trained Tamchakent elements (Touaregs) headed by El Hadj Ami
Mali	1982	Abortive raid against Tarara by Libyan-trained commandos presumably headed by key opposition figure Didi Demba Medina Soumbounu
Sudan	1975–85	Military and financial assistance to southern-based rebellion
		Recruitment of Sudanese elements into the Libyan Islamic Legion; training in Libya and subsequent involvement in Chad
		Abortive Libyan-sponsored coups against Numeiri in 1975, 1976, and 1983
		Libyan TU-22 bombs Omdurman (1983)
Tunisia	1980	Raid on Gafsa by Libyan-trained Tunisian "dissidents"
	1982	Raid on Kasserine by Libyan-trained Tunisian "dissidents"
	1984	Libyan-inspired sabotage of pipe-line near Libyan-Tunisian border
Somalia	1978–85	Military and financial support to Somalian Salvation Front
Western Sahara	1976–84	Military and financial support to *Polisario*
Zaire	1976–86	Financial support to National Front for the Liberation of the Congo and Congolese National Movement
		Plot against Mobuto

TABLE 2.—*Continued*

2. *Direct military intervention on behalf of incumbent regimes**

Uganda	1976–79	Approximately 700 Libyan troops sent in as back-up forces to Idi Amin, reinforced by another 300 men plus one Libyan TU-22 supersonic bomber and C-130 transport plane at the time of the Tanzanian invasion (1978–1979); presence of PLO guerrillas fighting on Amin's side attributable to Libya's mediation and funding
Chad	1980–81	Massive intervention of Libya's Islamic Legion on the side of Goukouni Oueddeye's GUNT during the battle of Ndjamena (December 1980) involving Soviet-supplied T-54 and T-55 tanks, multiple rocket launchers and 81 mm mortars; following the fall of Ndjamena (in December 1980) a Libyan occupation force of an estimated 2,000 moved into Chad, but withdrew in November 1983 when asked to do so by the incumbent President Goukouni Oueddeye.

3. *Direct military interventions on behalf of anti-regime factions against incumbent governments*

Egypt	1977	Border war with Egypt
Chad	1973	Libyan troops occupy Aouzou
	1983	Direct intervention of Libyan troops in Faya-Largeau and other localities in support of GUNT "rebels"
	1984–86	Between 3,000 and 5,000 Libyan troops remained on the ground after Libya failed to comply with the terms of the Franco-Libyan mutual withdrawal agreement (1984) intended to serve as back-up for the GUNT rebels; radar installations and Soviet-built Sam-6 anti-aircraft missile sites reported in several localities, including Wadi Doum, approximately 60 miles from Faya

*For a more extensive discussion of the cases of Chad and Uganda, and of the 1977 border war with Egypt, see William Foltz, "Libya's Military Power," in this volume.

Economic and Military Capabilities: Ambition vs. Performance

While there is a clear and straightforward relationship between the sudden expansion of Libya's oil revenues after 1973 and Qadhafi's rising ambitions on the international scene, in recent years the gap between ambition and performance has become equally plain.

The diplomatic successes initially scored by the Jamahiriya through the generous dispensation of its oil wealth are indisputable. The scale, instrumentalities, and distribution of Libyan economic aid between 1973 and 1980 are significantly related to these early victories: "Libya contributed at least $500 million through bilateral and multilateral channels. . . . Zaire and Uganda were the largest recipients of aid, receiving almost half of total Libyan bilateral aid to sub-Saharan Africa from 1973 to 1980. In terms of recorded sums, Libya ranked second to Saudi Arabia as an Arab donor" (Bruce St John in this volume). Primarily funneled through the Libyan-Arab Foreign Bank (LAFB) and the Libyan-Arab Foreign Investment Company (LAFICO), much of this aid took the form of "joint venture companies in a wide variety of economic sectors" (ibid.). Such companies, as St John goes on to note, were established in Benin, Burundi, the Central African Republic, Chad, Gabon, Gambia, Mali, Niger, Sierra Leone, Togo, Uganda, and Upper Volta. Predictably, the majority of the recipients quickly acknowledged their indebtedness to the anti-Zionist rentier-state by severing diplomatic ties with Israel; and not a few, as Pondi notes (in this volume), expressed further gratitude by aligning themselves with Tripoli in the councils of the Organization of African Unity (OAU).

While opening seemingly limitless opportunities to buy friends and influence people, in the end Qadhafi's oil wealth generated more enmities than friendships. His foreign policy tools, as Lilian Craig Harris reminds us, "are basically of the classic carrot-and-sticks variety" (Harris 1986, 84), and with the shift to subversive diplomacy, the threat of military and political sanctions assumed an increasingly high order of priority in the Libyan arsenal. How much of Qadhafi's petrodollars ended up in the treasuries of African opposition movements is impossible to tell. Nor is there any reliable estimate of the amounts spent on buying off the more venal of African statesmen and ministers in anticipation of their support in the OAU. Neither proved particularly wise investments. Whatever political and diplomatic benefits had once accrued from Libyan economic aid were largely nullified by Qadhafi's indiscriminate bankrolling of African opposition groups and personalities. Suspicions of Libyan meddling—even where such interference appeared most improbable, as in Nigeria during the so-called Maitatsine riots of December 1980 (see St John in this volume)—were certainly a key factor behind Libya's growing isolation within and outside the OAU, as Pondi convincingly shows.

Transboundary meddling is one thing; overt military intervention is an entirely different matter, and on this score the Libyan record is only paralleled by South Africa. This is where the case of Chad departs significantly from other instances of political interference. Of all the issues around which African opposition to Libyan intervention has crystallized none has had a more decisive—and divisive—impact on African attitudes than the Chadian crisis.

What makes the case of Chad particularly noteworthy is that it provides a dramatic and conclusive illustration of the gap between Libyan military ambitions and capabilities. For if the scale of the Libyan military build-up is indeed a commentary on the volume of its oil revenues (in 1985 alone between 1.5 and 2 billion dollars was spent on arms purchases [Harris 1986, 116]), the appalling performance of the Jamahiriya's armed forces on the battle fields of Fada and Ouadi Doum raises obvious questions about its ability to make effective use of its huge military arsenal. As Foltz points out, not only have Libya's military expenditures been the highest in Africa for every year since 1978, but the ratio of expenditures to population—showing a per capita annual military expenditure of $1,000, as against $35 for Algeria—is without parallel anywhere in the continent. Ironically, despite this massive arms build-up "dictated ultimately by the improbable scale of Libya's foreign policy ambitions, including the presumption that the Libyan Jamahiriya is merely the center of a much larger [Arab] nation" (Foltz in this volume), the Libyan army suffered its most telling defeat at the hands of a few thousand desert warriors from one of the poorest countries in the continent.

High on the list of explanations advanced by Foltz is the inability of the Libyan army to effectively handle and deploy the kind of highly sophisticated weaponry supplied by the Soviet Union: "The more technologically complex the equipment, the more the mismatch between men and material becomes apparent" (Foltz), a situation that applies not only to ground forces but to Libya's air and naval defense systems. Another crucial factor concerns the inadequacy of the Soviet model of ground warfare—from which Libya draws much of its inspiration—to the conditions of desert *blitzkrieg* imposed upon the Libyans by their Chadian adversaries. The Soviet-inspired combat doctrine "emphasizes tight control over land forces dominated by armor and well-positioned artillery, with ground-based missiles and antiaircraft guns as prime protection against air attack," but as Foltz points out, "in the hands of the Libyans this doctrine is likely to be applied with little imagination"—and, one might add, with little attention paid to the requirements of mobility, tactical flexibility, and individual initiative, all of which were displayed with great skill by the Chadian army. The joining together of traditional methods of warfare with modern weaponry was applied with devastating effect against the Libyan positions during the decisive engagements of January and March 1987, at Fada and Ouadi Doum (see Foltz and Lemarchand in this volume).

Finally, the morale of the Libyan army could only be profoundly affected by its exposure to internal crises and dissentions and by the growing lack of trust displayed by the regime toward the officer corps. That "the regime fears and distrusts the military, and thus imposes conditions on it that limit its effectiveness" (Foltz) is made clear by the number of abortive coups and subsequent purges of the officer corps recorded in recent years. "It has been estimated that there may have been as many coup attempts between 1980 and 1983 as there were in the entire previous decade, and there appears to have been no letup in the following years" (Anderson 1987, 65). More than seventy-five officers were executed in 1985, and twenty-two in 1987, each time on charges of disloyalty; the latest casualty was the commanding officer of the Fada garrison who "escaped by air at the last possible moment—and for his pains was court-martialed and shot when he got home" (Foltz). How far the exposure of the army to the incitements of the revolutionary committees may have further contributed to its flagging morale is impossible to assess; that it has done little to improve its performance and dedication to the regime is a safe assumption.

There is yet another sense in which Libyan involvement in Chad is indicative of a major discrepancy between ambition and performance: In the wake of the Libyan defeat, calls for a generalized *jihad* (holy war) against the forces of imperialism evoked little more than derision through much of Africa, giving Qadhafi's Islamic discourse a conspicuously hollow ring. This is not to deny the significance of Islam as an instrument of Libyan diplomacy (see Joffé in this volume), but only to stress its severe limitations as a mobilizing ideology.

Among other limitations placed upon Qadhafi's hegemonic ambitions, attention has tended to focus on the collapse of petroleum prices and resulting shrinkage in oil revenues. The constraints arising from the sharp contraction in Libya's annual petroleum income—dropping from $22 billion in 1980 to $5 billion in 1986—are undeniable and carry implications that go far beyond the domestic parameters of Qadhafi's revolutionary project. Yet this is hardly a sufficient reason to anticipate a drastic reorientation of his African policies: "With or without its previous levels of wealth, the goals and methods of Libyan diplomacy have remained basically unchanged" (Burgat in this volume). In Libya more than anywhere else in the continent economic penury is a relative concept, and this is also true of other constraints currently facing the regime. As a charismatic patron, Qadhafi is not yet running out of resources; nor has his charisma fully evaporated. Nonetheless, both charisma and patronage are in increasingly short supply. Recourse to naked force, in these conditions, is the most likely alternative to the politics of patronage at the domestic and international levels. Rather than speculate about the ultimate consequences of this situation let us, by way of a conclusion, turn to a brief assessment of Qadhafi's legacy to Africa.

Qadhafi and Africa: An Interim Assessment

In characteristically provocative fashion Ali Mazrui draws the following parallel between Libyan and superpower policies in the continent:

> It is conceivable that Libya is second only to the two superpowers in its record of intervention and interference in other societies. We know that the CIA of the US and the KGB of the Soviet Union have a long record not merely of espionage but also manipulating events in other lands. . . . It looks as if Libya has decided that if a superpower can declare itself unilaterally as the policeman of the world, so can a small country—if the economic resources permit. (Mazrui 1981, 51)

A more pertinent analogy, as our concluding essay suggests, is between Libya and South Africa—not only because their strategies and tactics in dealing with their neighbors have been remarkably similar, but because in each case the record shows just how limited is the leverage available to the superpowers in imposing meaningful sanctions on the hegemonic ambitions of regional actors. Rather than their ability to emulate the interventionist role of the superpowers, the most striking characteristic of Libyan and South African strategies has been their tendency to manipulate superpower ideologies (anticommunism in one case, anti-imperialism in the other) in order to chart their own independent course.

The divisive implications of this "double code"—expressing ideological commitment or moral outrage at one level, a specific calculus of interests at another—are nowhere more evident than in the cleavages brought to light within the OAU during the Western Sahara and Chadian crises. In a scenario strikingly reminiscent of the historic Monrovia-Casablanca rift during the Congo (now Zaire) crisis, on both issues the crystallization of rival superpower sympathies has tended to coincide with pro- and anti-Libyan sympathies. Predictably, on the radical (pro-Libyan) side the line-up included Ethiopia, Congo, Benin, Angola, Mozambique, and Zimbabwe, and on the "moderate" (anti-Libyan) side were Morocco, Senegal, the Ivory Coast, Gabon, Egypt, Tunisia, and the Sudan. While providing Qadhafi with "an international forum for the projection of his doctrine" (Pondi in this volume), the OAU has also served as the setting where inter-African discords over Libyan policies reached their peak, threatening in the process the very survival of the organization.

Whether based on ideological differences or disagreements over specific issues, the legacy of distrust left by Libyan policies is likely to persist within and among African states and, indeed, reinforce pre-existing sources of conflict. This is not the place for an extensive discussion of specific cases. Suffice it to note that African perceptions of Libyan threats—direct or indirect, real or imagined—are bound to have critically important repercussions in domestic and international arenas. Imputations of a Libyan connection to home-grown opposition movements are most likely to intensify internal tensions and greatly complicate the search for a domestic consensus—as the case of Nigeria suggests. When operating at the interstate level, the attribution of pro-Libyan sympathies to neighboring states may have even more serious consequences, leading for example to a sharp rise in military expenditures to meet anticipated Libyan aggression, to security guarantees involving third parties, to growing intolerance toward domestic opponents, and ultimately to a heightening of tension between states. The sudden deterioration of Kenya-Uganda relations following Qadhafi's visit to Kampala, in September 1986, immediately comes to mind as an example. Again, fears of Libyan intervention may so enhance threat perceptions as to pave the way for a drastic reappraisal of diplomatic options—not all of which are likely to promote the cause of African unity. The alacrity with which many of those African states that had broken ties with Israel after the Yom Kippur war proceeded to normalize their diplomatic relations with Tel-Aviv after 1982 is not simply the result of a "bold diplomatic offensive" by Israel (Ogunbadejo 1986, 61). Qadhafi's adventurism also deserves proper credit.

Individual perceptions of Libyan policies, though far more difficult to gauge, reveal mixed reactions—as shown by Chris Dunton's interviews with sub-Saharan students at Gar Younis University (in this volume): "There was nothing but praise for the regime's commitment to welfarism; at the same time there was a general concern . . . that the regime's radical orientation was so delimited by mixed motivations, opportunism, and by its overriding insensitivity to the need to seek a dialogue with sub-Saharan African states rather than to attempt to act as their revolutionary mentor." As Dunton himself concedes, closer attention to the national and ethnic origins of the interviewees would probably reveal major variations on this theme; yet the dominant impression that emerges from his survey is one of considerable skepticism and disillusion over Qadhafi's effort to articulate a leadership role for Libya.

Like students' attitudes about Libya, the costs of Libyan adventurism are anything but evenly distributed—with Chad suffering by far the heaviest costs in terms of casualties, displacement of populations, and economic disruptions. Evaluating these costs is not our intention, but only to note the obvious, that is, that no attempt to assess the Qadhafian legacy can overlook the immense human sufferings and continuing economic hardships that have attended Libya's "imperial temptation."

Looked at from a different perspective, however, the Libyan record may well inspire more positive judgments. Consider again the case of Chad: Despite or because of the costs of his Chadian misadventure Qadhafi has managed to create something approximating unity among Chadian factions, a feat all the more remarkable when one considers the extent of internal chaos since independence (and for which he himself must assume much of the responsibility). Others may point to the economic benefits drawn by recipients of Libyan aid—not just states but individuals, the latter including "economic refugees drawn to Libya during the drought" (Dunton) as well as migrant workers in search of jobs and foreign-exchange earnings. According to Dunton, "hundreds of thousands . . . came into the country from Sudan and West Africa on an informal basis, some trekking into the Fezzan from as far as Ghana." Others still may draw attention to the shock value of his rhetoric, the gadfly element in his discourse, or the attractiveness of his "folk hero" image among the destitute and the oppressed. This last dimension is perhaps best captured by the comments of Zartman and Kluge:

In denouncing imperialism and other evils of the world, in acting like the Jeha or the Asterix or the Popeye of his world, Qadhafi often gets applause as a wily common man folk-hero, doing things people who know better would love to do (if they didn't know better), taking a poke at the big boys and getting away with it. . . . To his admirers Qadhafi is not King Richard the Lion-Hearted or Salah al-Din, but Robin Hood. (Zartman and Kluge 1984, 192)

Asterix, Popeye, Robin Hood—the analogies conjured up by Qadhafi are almost endless, and more often than not incongruous. In some ways this is also true of his policies and motivations. Which of the various stereotypes, parallels, and analogies discussed (or dismissed) in this introduction best fits the Qadhafian mold is for readers to decide. It is hoped that the following chapters will prevent them from making too hasty or final a decision.

REFERENCES

Ajami, Fouad. 1981. *The Arab Predicament*. New York: Cambridge University Press.
Anderson, Lisa. 1982. "The Tripoli Republic, 1918–1922." In *Social and Economic Development of Libya*, edited by E. G. H. Joffé and K. S. McLachlan, 43–66. Wisbech, England: Middle East and North Africa Studies Press Ltd.
———. 1987. "Libya's Qaddafi: Still in Command?" *Current History* 86, no. 517:65–87.
The Economist. 1986. January 11–17.
Georgy, Guy. 1984. "Deux Bergers de l'Islam." *Geopolitique*, no. 7 (Fall):7–78.
Harris, Lillian Craig. 1986. *Libya*. Boulder, CO: Westview Press.
The Herald (Harare). 1986. September 5.
Hersh, Seymour M. 1987. "Target Qaddafi." *The New York Times Magazine*, February 22:16–26.
International Bank for Reconstruction and Development. 1960. *The Economic Development of Libya*. Baltimore: The Johns Hopkins University Press.
Johnson, Paul. 1987. "Apartheid, Disinvestment and the Marxist Assault." *Family Protection Scoreboard* (Special Edition on South Africa):6–7.
Mazrui, Ali. 1981. "Libya: A Superpower in Miniature?" *Africa Now*, (May):51–52.
Ogunbadejo, Oye. 1986. "Qadhafi and Africa's International Relations." *The Journal of Modern African Studies* 24, no. 1:33–68.
Roumani, Jacques. 1983. "From Republic to Jamahiriya: Libya's Search for Political Community." *The Middle East Journal* 37, no. 2 (Spring):151–68.
Schuler, Henry. 1981. Interview with Helena Cobban in *Christian Science Monitor*, December 11.
Al Zahar al-Akhdar. 1983. November 23.
Zartman, William I., and A. G. Kluge. 1984. "Heroic Politics: The Foreign Policy of Libya." In *The Foreign Policies of Arab States*, edited by Bahgat Korany and Ali E. Hillal Dessouki, 175–96. Boulder, CO: Westview Press.

Part One

The Determinants of Libya's African Policies

I.

QADHAFI'S "UNITARY" DOCTRINE
THEORY AND PRACTICE

François Burgat

No attempt to understand Libya's role in the field of inter-Maghrebine relations can overlook the centrality of Qadhafi's doctrine on the subject of regional integration. Qualifying arguments notwithstanding (see Deeb in this volume), the theoretician of the *Jamahiriya* ("The State of the Masses") has been and remains to this day the sole architect of his country's regional policies as well as its all-powerful taskmaster. Our aim in this chapter is to make explicit the "hard core" of the Qadhafian doctrine—the search for Arab unity—before turning to an examination of the various concessions made over the years to the exigencies of contextual realities, including the persistent vitality of state-centered nationalisms. We then move on to an exploration of the several paths through which his inconclusive march toward Arab unity has been charted—the quest for intergovernmental accords, first with the Mashrek, then with the Maghreb, and ultimately the deployment *tous azimuts* of a subversive diplomacy that, through an almost endless flow of petrodollars, sets the parameters for a recurrent theme in Libya's foreign policy orientation.

The Quest For Unity

Contrary to a widespread image that would add to the list of defects attributed to the colonel one that he does not have—inconsistency—Qadhafi's doctrine is far from incoherent. His methods, of course, have changed frequently, joining to the traditional techniques of diplomacy somewhat less conventional ones; the circumstances and tactics may change, the ultimate policy objectives do not.

Puzzling as these tactical shifts may seem to outside observers, the overall strategy of the theoretician of the "Third Way" has preserved, throughout his fifteen years in power, the coherence and intelligibility conferred upon it by certain clearly articulated principles. "Over and above the apparent incoherence of its various manifestations," writes Otayek, "the foreign policy of revolutionary Libya bears the stamp of a remarkable symbolic continuity" (Otayek 1981, 5).

Qadhafi's theory of the "three circles" (borrowed from Nasser), which shapes and structures the hierarchy of his international solidarities, is familiar to the reader; and so, also, the extent to which the most proximate—Arabism—tends to prevail upon the others. Libya's Arabism is not just a "given." Belonging to the Arab nation implies the obligation to bring about its reunification by every possible means. Qadhafi's political practice—domestically and internationally—is profoundly influenced by this imperative; this urge to recover the spirit and substance of Arab unity is the key to an understanding of his foreign policy orientation within and outside the Maghreb: "Everything . . . is inferred from, connected with or subordinated to this version of the future—an independent, unified and socialist Arab nation, for only then can the existence of Israel, expression of US imperialism, be brought to an end" (Bleuchot and Monastiri 1985, 83).

As much as the expression of a calculated objective, the quest for Arab unity is also the pursuit of a dream—the dream of an adolescent growing up under the reign of a complacent Idriss, who took the full measure of the political decadence and economic dependence of his native Libya. Unity provides a magic answer to colonial domination and postcolonial dependence: "It is the historic and decisive response to the challenge of colonialism and Zionism," explains Qadhafi, "not until it is unfurled from the Atlantic Ocean to the Gulf will the standard of Arab unity be really ours; it is not a wish but a necessity" (quoted in Majzoub 1974). For the deracinated Bedouin the myth of unity is also a means by which to exorcise the disillusions of modernity. It cushions the impact of cultural alienation, for only by recovering their lost unity can the Arabs achieve reconciliation with themselves, with their values, including those of their mythical past: "Arab unity is a return to the nature of things" (Majzoub 1974).

No wonder, then, that Article 1 of the constitutional proclamation of September 1, 1969, defines the Libyan people as "part of the Arab nation," and that the latter's unification is seen as a "national priority." Nor is the main thrust of the regime's foreign policy all that surprising. The conquest of greater political and economic autonomy is a first priority, and total national independence is the necessary first step toward the achievement of regional unity.

From 1969 to 1973, however, institution-building at the national level lapsed into suspended animation. During that time "little attention was being paid to domestic political institutions (largely patterned upon the Egyptian model)," notes Otayek, "the assumption being that the new situation about to arise from impending unification will require further institutional adaptions" (Otayek 1980, 30), a situation that Rémi Leveau aptly portrays as "a kind of provisional government fulfilling the functions of a nation-state" (Leveau 1975, 91).

Unification must be achieved on a global scale or not at all; the notion of an intermediate regional stage is only partially admitted by Qadhafi. At best, a link-up with the eastern nucleus of Arabism (of which Egypt is the core) can be no more than a half-way house on the path to global integration. Curiously, a similar rapprochement with the Maghreb was at first seen by Qadhafi as an obstacle on the sacred path to unity.

Nonetheless, there can be little question in Qadhafi's mind that Libya belongs to the Maghreb. Adherence to the notion of a Maghrebine entity is not—initially at least—explicitly rejected. "We belong to the Maghreb," declares the Libyan Minister of Foreign Affairs, echoing Qadhafi, "[but] we turn to the Mashrek in hopes that the Maghreb will follow in our footsteps." Here indeed is the heart of the Qadhafian doctrine: Maghrebine unity is only a tran-

sitional phase in an ongoing process of regional unification, and in this process Libya, by
virtue of its geographical position (a fact repeatedly and graphically thrown into relief by the
regime's official iconography) is destined to play a central role. Shorn of its ultimate goal, the
process of subregional integration has little to commend itself; at times it is even viewed with
suspicion. For Qadhafi "who suspects that the concept of Maghrebine entity has been conceived by Western chanceries to provide a counterweight to total Arab unity" (Majzoub 1974,
82), there are bad unions and good unions. Thus, when his disillusion with Egypt eventually
prompted him to turn to Tunisia, Qadhafi came up with the following distinction: "There
are two ways of conceiving of the partial unification of Arab states: one, encouraged by
imperialism, involves regional regroupings destined to slow down the march towards integral
Arab unity; the other, taking place within the framework of a global strategy, spanning an
area stretching from the Ocean to the Gulf, aims at encouraging transitional piecemeal unions"
(Majzoub, 1974, 82).

Libya's Heart Belongs to the East . . .

Confronted with the challenge of Arabism, yet conscious of the obstacles raised by national
loyalties, Nasser's spiritual heir makes no bones of his geographical, as distinct from national,
preferences. Among Arabs some are more Arab than others. The West (i.e., the Maghreb),
from all evidence, is less attractive than the East (i.e., the Mashrek), cradle of Arabism and
Islam; the East is the more faithful custodian of a language that, in contrast to what happened
in the Maghreb, remains uncontaminated by exposure to French culture. More important
still, it is the battleground in the fight against Zionism, where not too long ago could be heard
the voice of the man who inflicted a quasi-military defeat on the former colonial powers.

For all his awareness of, and respect for, Algeria's historical experience, it is to the East
that Qadhafi, at the outset, turned his attention. Only a few months after the overthrow of
King Idriss, himself a fervent advocate of the Maghrebine cause, and while most outside
observers were at a loss to figure out the orientation of the new regime, the true significance
of Qadhafi's militant Arabism became clear. As Roger Le Tourneau pointed out as early as
1969, "although it is impossible to pass final judgment on the new regime's orientation . . . there can be little doubt that its sympathies are more Arab than Maghrebine" (Le
Tourneau 1970, 23). Subsequent developments soon confirmed this impression. To wit, the
initial declarations and commitments of Nasser's young disciple: "My reason and my heart
lean towards the Orient," he declared in Tripoli in December 1969. Scarcely three months
after he took power, he proceeded to give concrete expression to the dream of his adolescence.
The result was the Tripoli Charter, intended to link Libya's destiny with Naser's Egypt and
Numeiri's Sudan—the first in a long series of now defunct unification agreements.

Granted that the first stage on the path to Arab unity was only intended to be a "partial
and transitional union," it was not a matter of coincidence that it happened to signal an
opening to the East. To his neighbors in the Maghreb Qadhafi appeared to deny even the
option of entering into "good" or "bad" regional unions. "The agreement we just signed,"
he declared in Tripoli on the day the Federation of Arab Republics was born, "is a first step
in the direction of unity with the Arab world. By seeking to create a separate Maghrebine

union, Algeria, Tunisia and Morocco may end up retarding this fusion and remain dependent upon Europe. More serious still, this idea of a Greater Maghreb could bring about a psychological demobilization of the people of North Africa at a time when we should all rally around a single objective—the liberation of Palestine."

In fact, by March 1970, Qadhafi did not hesitate to match his words with action—first by refusing to take part in the Conference of the Ministers of the Maghreb, held in Rabat, and then, six months later, by taking Libya out of the Maghreb Permanent Consultative Committee (MPCC). The latter, created in October 1964 in Rabat, then stood as the sole and fragile institutional expression of the region's unitary aspirations. As his Petroleum Minister, Ezzedine Al-Mabrouk, explained: "We do not want the Maghreb to become an autonomous entity, thereby drawing a wedge between Maghreb and Mashrek."

And yet, in spite of all this, Libya's diplomacy would soon seek an overture toward the Maghreb. The sequence of events following the Tripoli Charter offered few other alternatives. By 1973, at a time when the fusion announced in the Tripoli Charter was about to materialize, the vectors of nationalism emerged far stronger than Qadhafi had anticipated. Their presence at the Tripoli rendez-vous did not go unnoticed, any more than their subsequent impact on the so-called "unity march," loudly advertised throughout Libya as a means of breathing new life into the unification process. After penetrating a few kilometers into Egypt the march dissolved into the sands, leaving most participants unmoved by this eloquent fiasco, except for its promoter.

. . . And Its Reason to the Maghreb

On September 1, 1973, while attending the celebration of the fourth anniversary of Libya's revolution on the very day the Tripoli Charter was supposed to come into effect, Habib Bourguiba evidently had little trouble convincing Qadhafi of the futility of his unification efforts with the East. The "Supreme Combattant" did not mince his words: "There are too many differences between the Maghreb and the Mashrek,"said Bourguiba, reminding his host of his Libyan origins."The union with Egypt is a piece of fluff. . . . I give you until December to make up your mind and then you will come and see me. . . . And we shall talk again about the Maghreb, which is ready to welcome you." Significantly, a few days later Bourguiba took advantage of the Non-Aligned Summit in Algiers to suggest the creation of "a confederation of Algeria, Tunisia and Libya, later to include Morocco."

More than the beckoning of the West, the "treason" of the East was what paved the way for the return of Libya to the fold of the Maghreb. On October 8, 1973, the Yom Kippur war erupted over the Suez canal. Of the impending hostilities the vibrant defender of the Arab cause had not even been informed, and, to add insult to injury, his participation in the war had not even been solicited. "This war is not mine," said Qadhafi at the time. "I am in profound disagreement with Presidents Sadat and Assad." It is from this fateful day that one can trace the origins of the endless Libyan-Egyptian discord, soon to reach its highest level of acrimony with the signature of the Camp David accords. Fifteen years later the conflict remained unresolved.

The conditions for an opening to the Maghreb were henceforth met: thwarted in the East by Egypt's obduracy, Qadhafi's activism sought new outlets in the southern Sahara (in Chad), in black Africa, but also in the Maghreb. On two different occasions, in Constantine and in Hassi Messaoud, on February 17 and March 31, 1973 respectively, Algeria's Boumedienne allowed himself to make some timid moves toward regional unity—resulting in the setting up of a mixed Libyan-Algerian commission. Two years later, Algeria's prudent rapprochement still held, but at a much heavier price. In return for the illusory promise of "abolishing Algerian-Libyan borders in case Egypt formally recognized the Zionist entity" (*Al Zahf al Akhdar*, March 1, 1984), Qadhafi agreed, prudently at first and more explicitly after February 1979, to keep supporting Boumedienne politically and financially in the nascent Western Sahara conflict he himself had—as early as 1972—helped create. For the next eight years Libya found itself bogged down in the service of a cause that to this day raises one of the most insuperable obstacles on the road to Maghrebine unity.

With Tunisia, the result of Qadhafi's negotiations seemed at long last consonant with the magnitude of his efforts. On January 12, the Djerba Treaty laid the foundation for nothing less than the complete fusion of Tunisia and Libya—"from now on constituting one single Republic, to be named Islamic Arab Republic, endowed with a single constitution, a single President, a single army, and the same legislative, executive and judicial powers." History will some day unravel the motivations that led the pragmatic Bourguiba to endorse a document of such momentous significance. Besides ushering in a major crisis in Libyan-Tunisian relations, one of the lesser casualties of the Djerba Treaty was Bourguiba's Minister of Foreign Affairs, dismissed for charting a course fraught with obvious dangers. As a bizarre follow-up to the abortive merger, a series of delicate negotiations were conducted with Libya to recover the text of the treaty, which Qadhafi never ceased to regard as binding; only in 1982 was the document returned to Bourguiba, as a token of Libyan good will and "moderation."

Access to the Maghreb was thereafter denied to Qadhafi for years to come, a state of affairs that mirrored the growing mood of suspicion surrounding his brand of diplomacy. His repeated calls to unity met with little more than polite reticence among his Maghrebine "brothers," now unanimous in stressing the need for a long preparatory phase, stretching from a few months to a few centuries (as in the case of Bourguiba). Undaunted, in May 1978, speaking in Algiers, Qadhafi renewed his plea for a Maghreb Federation; a year later he insisted on the implementation of the Hassi Messaoud Charter, aimed at a fusion with Algeria; three years later his strategy shifted to a "step-by-step union" before threatening, on March 2, 1983, to "resort to force to achieve the unity of the Maghreb." By then what little trust he enjoyed among his Algerian and Tunisian "friends" had all but evaporated.

Paradoxically, the last chapter in Qadhafi's unification saga was written in Morocco, on enemy soil. It began, unexpectedly, with the Oujda Treaty of August 1984, and ended in July 1986 after the closing of a two-year parenthesis in the long history of Moroccan-Libyan incompatibilities. With the benefit of hindsight one can better appreciate the misgivings inspired by the Oujda Treaty (see Mark Tessler in this volume). More than anything else the short-lived Arab-African Union is a tribute to Hassan's consummate skill at knocking the Libyan props from under the *Popular Front for the Liberation of Saguia el-Hamra and Rio de Oro (Polisario)*. Equally noteworthy, at the beginning of 1984 Qadhafi's isolation on the international scene was such that he could be expected to make significant concessions for the sake of regional unity, up to and including a drastic reconsideration of his options on the Western Sahara issue. It is not unreasonable to assume that he welcomed this opportunity to bring to an end his costly commitment to the birth of a new state in the Sahara. Promoting political fragmentation, after all, is hardly the best way to serve the cause of regional unity.

The Shift to Subversive Diplomacy

Betrayed in the East by Sadat, deceived in the West by Bourguiba, by 1973–74 Qadhafi's reading of the behavior of Arab states gave him ample justification for a shift of tactics. Having failed to achieve unification through interstate negotiations, his conviction was that the time had come to bypass government and state institutions and appeal directly to the masses. Rightly or wrongly, only among the masses did he detect a genuine potential of aspirations toward unity waiting to be tapped.

Subversive diplomacy thus emerged as the prime vector of Libyan interventionism: behind this change of tactics lay a basic postulate, that is, that the overthrow of incumbent neighboring Arab regimes was the necessary first step for making any headway on the road toward unification. From this postulate Qadhafi did not hesitate to draw the necessary conclusions. Except for some occasional steps in the direction of institutional contacts in the mid-1980s, as a mode of political action, subversion became a permanent feature of Libyan diplomacy, or, perhaps more accurately, a substitute for diplomacy.

Nineteen seventy-three was not only the year of unfulfilled unitary hopes; it was also the year of the Zuwara speech, the year of the "masses." On May 16, in an effort to break away from the traditional elites and eliminate competing centers of authority, the colonel formally announced his decision to take Libya into the adventure of direct democracy. From now on people's committees and congresses were to replace administrative and party structures—a move paralleled by the shortcuts Libyan diplomacy was about to take vis-à-vis the more conventional modes of interstate relations. Qadhafi, in a word, proceeded to rid himself of all institutional constraints.

Out of this experiment emerged a new and thoroughly unconventional diplomatic style. Tunisian officials became increasingly apprehensive of a sudden announcement that the colonel's plane was about to land on their national territory. Arab heads of state evinced a growing concern over Qadhafi's increasingly outspoken tone, along with his habit of addressing the masses directly, over the heads of their leaders. In Algiers and Tunis, for example, the colonel did not hesitate to express his criticisms of the official position of the Maghreb states on the unification issue before youthful and sympathetic audiences, to the consternation of his hosts. As he subsequently admitted, "Regimes don't interest me anymore; I address myself to the Arab masses" (*Le Monde* February 11, 1976).

His lack of oratorical self-restraint was even more evident in his dealings with the West, being, after all, under no obligation to render accounts to anyone, least of all to western governments. Nineteen seventy-three was also the year of the oil crisis and of the economic and diplomatic victories scored by the Organization of Petroleum Exporting Countries (OPEC) against the West, with Libya all along "acting as a prod to generalized price increases for all producers" (First 1974, 204). Qadhafi could now confidently move beyond the phase of "conference diplomacy" and make full use of "dollar diplomacy" to give wider scope, if not greater efficiency, to his foreign policy.

The Power of Money

If one considers that Libya's main source of foreign exchange once came from the sale of scrap metal left behind by alien belligerents during World War II, one can readily appreciate the implications of its sudden access to prodigious wealth. In the wake of the nationalizations that swept the oil industry from 1969 to 1973 the price of Libyan crude reached the unprecedented level of $3.47 a barrel (an increase of 35 percent over the 1971 price-fixing agreement with the Majors). The degree of autonomy thereby conferred upon the Libyan state opened up a whole new range of policy initiatives.

Internally sheltered from all serious opposition by its inexhaustible resources, the Libyan regime could also afford the luxury of purchasing the political consensus necessary for its revolutionary breakthroughs. Despite the initial setbacks that followed certain unfortunate economic and institutional moves, Qadhafi's generous welfare policies, along with the tangible success of his first development plans, quickly restored his bases of support. Equally noteworthy were the mobilizing impact of his populist discourse and undeniable charismatic appeal, both of which also contributed to his rising popularity.

The ease with which the regime managed to free itself of the contingencies of classical diplomacy bears testimony to what must be seen as the most valuable by-product of its petroleum wealth: Qadhafi's rhetorical liberties are in a sense the expression of his total financial independence, a state of affairs that would last until the collapse of the oil market in 1986. In other words, he could now state loud and clear what many in the Third World thought but never dared to articulate for fear of paying a price far in excess of what they could afford. Rendering accounts to the West, or anyone else, is clearly the least of his worries.

Appearing at the podium on certain formal occasions, at home or abroad, was no longer enough; by now radio Tripoli beamed far and wide the extreme outspokenness of his discourse, the latter evoking even greater sympathies from his international audience than among the "Libyan sons of the September revolution."

Now as then his rhetorical exuberance allows no room for the self-imposed limitations of the reason of state; these limitations he has long jettisoned; his is the language of the Arab heart. Anti-Western diatribes, denunciations of the "valets" of American imperialism (with pride of place given to Saudi Arabia), hymns to unity—all of this and more is openly ventilated and endorsed by the Libyan state. As in Khomeini's Iran, Qadhafi's Libya articulates the aspirations of the downtrodden, and gives them the kind of recognition, if only verbally, that other regimes are unwilling to proffer, mindful as they are of the verbal prudence imposed upon them by their external alliances.

Exporting the language of refusal is one thing; doing away with national solidarities and cleavages is a very different matter, a fact that became painfully evident as Qadhafi tried—and failed—to capitalize upon the initial fund of good will produced by his anti-Western rhetoric. After the patent failure of the so-called Gafsa coup, in 1980, the turning of the tide had become clear. As will be remembered, his efforts to use a few dozen Tunisian *emigrés*, armed and trained in Libya, to trigger a popular uprising ended in dismal failure. Once again the fragility of his "unitarian" brand of diplomacy came into full view. His decision, five years later, to expel thirty-two thousand Tunisian workers in hopes that it would hasten the fall of the aging Bourguiba proved equally mistaken. If anything, the result has been to give a new lease on life to Tunisia's vacillating regime.

And yet, once all is said and done, the psychological impact of Qadhafi's role in the Maghreb stands in sharp contrast with his unbroken record of failure on unification. The Libyan "gadfly" makes it difficult, if not impossible, for the heads of state of the region to turn their backs to the issue of regional unity; and it provides them with a moral conscience to resist the temptation of sacrificing the credo of Arabism to the constraints of the economic conjuncture.

Subversion, furthermore, does not exclude the use of financial arguments that smack of a more conventional view of diplomacy; sticks and carrots are not mutually exclusive, and the latter have often taken the form of generous credit facilities. Libya's economic and financial presence is by no means solely reducible to the tons of armaments shipped, from 1975 to 1983, to the battlefields of the Saharawi Arab Democratic Republic (SADR), whose creation owes a great deal to Tripoli's efforts to thwart Moroccan interests. In Tunisia this presence has taken the form of joint-ventures involving transport, banking and publishing houses, as well as a few direct loans. Until their relations turned sour, Libyan tourism also brought Tunisia a significant volume of foreign exchange. More significant, however, is Tripoli's influence in Mauretania. Following Mokhtar Ould Dadah's visit to Tripoli in September 1972, Mauretania became the first country in the region to receive substantial loans for infrastructural developments, ranging from road building, irrigation projects, and the construction of an Institute for Islamic Studies and a mosque, to a majority share in the Arab Libyan-Mauretanian Bank for External Trade and Development. Mauretania's privileged status among recipients of Libyan aid is not too surprising if one considers that the political climate in Nouakchott at the time was far more congenial to Libyan designs than that of other countries in the region (Otayek 1980; Mattes 1987).

More revealing is Qadhafi's track record in dealing with migrant workers. Libya acts as host country for a few thousand Mauretanian workers, yet it also claims as large a Tunisian labor force as France does. It is easy to appreciate the risks facing Tunisia should massive expulsions of its nationals add to the social tensions currently experienced by Tunisian society. Nonetheless, if the events of the summer of 1985 leave few doubts as to Qadhafi's ability to use such extreme measures, they also demonstrate their limitations as a foreign policy weapon. Tunis, as may be recalled, used the pretext of "foreign aggression" to clamp down on the trade-unions; wielding this highly unpopular weapon proved just as dangerous for Qadhafi as it did for Boumedienne in 1976, when Algeria felt the boomerang effect of a move directed against Morocco. Short of ordering a massive exodus of migrant workers, Tripoli may, by way of an alternative, seek to endoctrinate this labor force, already subject to a relentless propaganda campaign. Though not negligible, the scale of such endoctrination does not exceed Tunisian capacities to deal with it effectively, even at the price of a few police measures against returnees, as happened in 1985 and after the Gafsa affair.

The funding of opposition movements abroad constitutes yet another form of intervention that is clearly linked to the financial circumstances of the Libyan regime. But if the reality of the phenomenon is undeniable, its exact scale is hard to tell—harder still its effectiveness and significance. That certain oppositional fringes in Morocco and Tunisia did receive Libyan money—at least until 1983—is quite probable, but these do not include the *Union Générale des Travailleurs Tunisiens* (UGTT) as has been falsely claimed by Tunisian authorities in order to cast discredit upon its leader, H. Achour. Even less open to question is the case of the *Mouvement pour la Démocratie en Algérie* (MDA), which also figures among recipients of Libyan "subsidies," and through which former Algerian President Ahmed Ben Bella hopes to recapture power.

Reference must also be made in this connection to the Islamic Call Society (*Dawa al-Islamiya*) created in 1972 in Tripoli, which seeks to spread a militant brand of Islam that bears the stamp of the Qadhafian vision (Mattes 1986). Its official mouthpiece, *Jihad*, published in four languages, is the main vehicle of its message, but presumably not the only one. In fact, since the revision of its statutes in 1981, the society is no longer obligated to rely exclusively on peaceful means to propagate its creed. The revised version of Article 2 now reads: "The Society has as its main objective to spread Islam throughout the world by any means." Yet it is dubious that anything like an organic link exists between *Dawa al-Islamiya* and the Maghreb's Islamic movements. The numerous executions of "Muslim Brothers" (to use the regime's own designation) that have taken place in Libya since 1980 give them ample grounds for caution.

Over the last five years a new parameter has been added to Qadhafi's Maghrebine policies as a result of its declining oil wealth (down to $10 billion in 1985, or half of its total oil revenue for 1980). Few observers, however, would go so far as to suggest a direct relationship between the current economic squeeze and his recent policy pronouncements. With or without its previous levels of wealth, the goals and methods of Libyan diplomacy have remained basically unchanged. To be sure, the dominant tone of its Arab thrust is one of moderation. Illustrative of this new mood is Qadhafi's "reconciliation" with a variety of more or less moderate elements in the regional landscape, along with his apparent willingness to forego the rigidity of his principles for the sake of accommodation: with Saudi Arabia, for example, from 1983 onward (even though the Saud dynasty had been consistently branded in the past as representing "the renegades of Islam," therefore to be vigorously combatted); with the Palestinian Liberation Organization (PLO), whose "legalism" was once viewed with profound distaste; and, more spectacularly still, with Morocco, through the unexpected and short-lived Arab-African Union, following the Oujda treaty.

And yet, only in a very limited sense can one speak of a "mellowing" of the Libyan regime that would reflect its internal difficulties. Relations with Tunisia (no less execrated than Hasan's Morocco prior to the Oujda treaty) deteriorated sharply after 1984. The break came in May of that year, when, following the infiltration of a hit squad into Libya, Qadhafi could no longer avoid the suspicion that Bourguiba was actively involved in a plot to assassinate him. Relations with Algeria, a long-time ally, underwent a similar deterioration. Having once threatened to use force to bring about unity among Libya, Tunisia, and Algeria, in 1984 Qadhafi saw the latter two sign a treaty of "fraternity and concord" from which Libya was deliberately excluded. The impression one gets is that the regime's militant diplomatic stance is intended to serve as a safety valve against its internal enemies, enabling it to maintain a relatively high level of political mobilization in hopes that it might take the wind out of the sails of a sharply rising domestic opposition.

If nothing else, the U.S. strike of April 1986 showed just how lukewarm were the sympathies of the Maghreb states for their victimized brother. With his image irreparably tarnished, and his regional bases of support dangerously eroded, it is hard to see how the bellwether of Arab unity can recoup its losses, especially at a time when, throughout the Maghreb, the dominant trend is clearly in the direction of *Realpolitik*. Ironically, forced into a corner by his Maghrebine brothers, Qadhafi finds himself further ostracized by the ideologues of Islam: Neither the devotees of the modern nation-state nor the zealots of Islamic Fundamentalism are willing to admit the colonel into their midst, his Arab credentials notwithstanding. After its meteoric rise on the North African scene, the conclusion that Qadhafi's star is rapidly reaching its nadir is difficult to avoid.

REFERENCES

Barouhi, Abdelaziz. 1980. "Comment l'armée a repris le dessus." *Jeune Afrique*, no. 998 (February 20):45–49.

Bleuchot, Hervé, and Taoufik Monastiri. 1985. "La Logique Unitaire Libyenne et les mobiles du Colonel Qadhafi." *Hérodote* (March): 81–89.

First, Ruth. 1974. *Libya: The Elusive Revolution*. Baltimore: Penguin Books.

Le Tourneau, Roger. 1970. "Chronique Libye: 1969." In *Annuaire de l'Afrique du Nord*, 20–24. Paris: Centre National de la Recherche Scientifique.

Leveau, Rémi. 1970. "Le Système Politique Libyen." In *La Libye Nouvelle: Rupture et Continuité*, 83–100. Paris: Centre Nationale de la Recherche Scientifique.

Majzoub, Mohamed Said. 1974. *La Libye et l'Unité Maghrébine*. Aix-en-Provence: Mémoire pour le Diplôme d'Etudes Supérieures, Faculté de Droit.

Mattes, Hanspeter. 1986. *Die innere und äussere islamische Mission Libyens*. Hamburg: Kaiser Grunewald.

———. 1987. "A Survey of Libya's Economic Relations as an Instrument of Foreign Policy." In *The Economic Development of Libya*, edited by Bichara Khader and Bashir El-Wifati, 81–86. London: Croom Helm.

Le Monde. 1976. February 11.

Otayek, René. 1980. *La Politique Africaine de la Libye*. Thèse de Troisième Cycle. Bordeaux: Université de Bordeaux.

———. 1981. "La Libye Révolutionnaire au Sud du Sahara." Unpublished manuscript.

Al Zahf al Akhdar. 1984. March 1.

II.

THE PRIMACY OF LIBYA'S NATIONAL INTEREST

Mary-Jane Deeb

Libya's foreign policy has been analyzed quite extensively by a number of academicians, policymakers, and journalists who fall by and large into two schools of thought. The first group approaches Libya's foreign policy from the point of view of the psychological determinants of Colonel Muammar al Qadhafi's personality. They see him as an irrational, bloodthirsty, megalomaniac tyrant, whose hegemonic ambitions are limitless and who lacks all sense of perspective and reality (Haley 1984; Tripp 1984, 317–29). The second school of thought approaches the subject from the angle of Qadhafi's ideological preferences and sees him as a more rational man, dedicated to the pursuit of the ideals of Arab nationalism, Islamic reformism, and a form of utopian socialism that he has labeled his Third Universal Theory (St John 1983, 481–90; Otayek 1981, 5–35; Ogunbadejo 1983, 154–78).

The psychological school of thought has had little to offer to our understanding of Libya's foreign policy under Qadhafi. To try to find the explanation for what appears to be irrational policy in the presumed irrational or megalomaniac personality of the Libyan leader is almost tautological. If Qadhafi were so out of touch with reality and his perceptions and expectations so irrational and distorted, it is unlikely that he would have remained in power for so long or played such an active role in Arab and African affairs over the past sixteen years.

The ideological school of thought, on the other hand, has contributed much to our understanding of many of Qadhafi's foreign policy goals in the world in general, but it has been unable to explain specific goals and policies in the regional context of North Africa. One is forced to raise certain questions to proponents of the ideological school of thought, such as: Why did Qadhafi, an Arab nationalist, support Ethiopia, an African, primarily Christian country, against the Sudan (under Numeiry), an Arab country with a Muslim majority? Why did he, a major Muslim reformist, support animists and Christians in southern Sudan against Arab Muslim northerners in the first half of the 1980s? How could a self-styled revolutionary and socialist support and set up unity agreements in 1984 with a traditional, pro-Western monarch in Morocco, whom Qadhafi had previously described as corrupt? The list is long, and to dismiss those facts by saying they are just exceptions to the rule is to miss the whole point of Qadhafi's foreign policy in the region.

Libyan National Interests: Levels and Contexts

Thus another approach is needed to complement the ideological approach and to analyze those aspects of Libya's foreign policy that cannot be otherwise understood, especially on the regional level. This chapter attempts to set up a general model for Libya's foreign policy, and then view Libya's foreign policy toward Egypt and the Sudan from what we shall refer to here as the "national interest" approach. This is based on Morgenthau's concept of the primary national interest as the protection of a nation's "physical, political and cultural identity against encroachments by other nations" (Morgenthau 1958, 66). Thus, if we are to understand Qadhafi's foreign policy in North Africa, we should take into account, as we would with any other country or state in the region, (1) the country's primary national interest; (2) its strategic geographic location on the Mediterranean, bordered by six different nations, among which is Egypt, the most powerful and populous of all North African nations; (3) its size, population, level of development, and economic potential; (4) its historical, cultural, religious, and ideological structures; and (5) its leader, the major source of foreign-policy decisions in Libya.

From that angle Qadhafi's foreign policy can be viewed as a pyramid made up of five overlapping levels. Each level includes a number of countries and certain policy orientations. As one moves from the top of the pyramid downward, a larger number of countries are included, and the content of his foreign policy becomes more diffuse, although paradoxically also more revolutionary.

At the very top of the pyramid stands North Africa, namely, Egypt and the Sudan on Libya's eastern flank, and Tunisia, Algeria, and Morocco on its western flank. Libya's foreign policy orientation toward those countries frequently involves other countries in the region as well, primarily Chad, but also the Western Sahara (at least until 1983), Niger, Mauritania, Mali, Ethiopia, and Somalia. Libya's policy at the top of the pyramid is primarily determined by its national interest, or at the very least by Qadhafi's perception of Libya's national interest. At the top of the pyramid ideological considerations, whether Arab, Islamic, or revolutionary, play a secondary role.

The second level, which overlaps to some degree the first, includes the Arab world in general but focuses primarily on those countries east of Egypt, in the Mashriq. Arab nationalist ideology is a prime determinant of Libya's foreign policy at this level. Rhetoric directed against Israel, support for the Palestinians, support for Arab unity and Arab revolutions are the basic themes with respect to that region. The only exception here is Libya's support of Iran, a non-Arab, Shiite Muslim state, in its war against Iraq, an Arab state with a socialist regime.

The third level of the pyramid is the Islamic world. This includes the countries in the above two levels as well as many states in Africa and Asia (such as Pakistan, Indonesia, the Philippines) that are not Arab and to whose Islamic populations Libya has long been active in giving economic, military, and political support. At this level Islamic ideology does play a very important role in determining Libya's foreign policy.

The fourth level is that of the Third World in general. It includes many of the states and groups at the previous levels, but also others that are neither Arab nor Muslim, in Latin America, Africa, and Asia. Qadhafi's "revolutionary socialism" determines, at least in part, his foreign policy toward those countries, from Nicaragua to New Caledonia to Zaire (Woodward 1985, A19).

And finally, the fifth level is composed of the industrialized countries of the North, including those of the West and the East blocs. Contrary to prevailing beliefs, Libya, especially in the early 1970s, had a similar orientation toward both sides: a combination of pragmatism and ideological fervor. It traded with all those countries, irrespective of ideology, and was critical of both capitalism and communism. Qadhafi offered his Third Universal Theory, itself a brand of utopian socialism, as an alternative to capitalism and communism. However, especially in the past eight years, after the signing of the Egyptian-Israeli peace treaty, Libya has moved closer to the Soviet Union, as it perceived U.S. military aid to Egypt as a threat to its security.

This chapter will deal only with the first level of the pyramid, where Qadhafi perceives Libya's national interest to be at stake. His foreign policy in that region can be viewed as being primarily determined by Libya's geographical location between the Maghreb, on its western border, and Egypt and the Sudan on its eastern border. The question therefore arises, if the strategic location has been such an important determinant of Libya's foreign policy, how could two modern rulers of Libya, namely, King Idriss and Colonel Qadhafi, adopt such different foreign policies in the region?

Morgenthau puts the problem succinctly: "Small nations have always owed their independence either to the balance of power . . . or to the preponderance of one protecting power . . . or to their lack of attractiveness for imperialistic aspirations" (Morgenthau 1985, 196). Looking at Libya from that angle, the reason for the difference in foreign policy between King Idriss and Qadhafi becomes clear. King Idriss was able to protect Libya's borders by having Western military bases (British and American), which were symbolic reminders to any would-be invader of the Western protection Libya enjoyed. Furthermore, Libya's poverty, lack of natural resources, and the vastness of its desert territory were powerful deterrents to any neighboring power with "imperialistic aspirations."

With the coming to power of Qadhafi in 1969, however, the situation changed radically. In order to legitimize the military coup and the overthrowing of a traditional Sanussi monarch, Qadhafi had to oust the "imperialist forces," that is, remove the foreign military bases from Libya, and nationalize, or "Libyanize," the economy. In other words, he had to give the Libyans something they wanted—economic and political control of their country—in return for being accepted as their new leader. Yet by removing the U.S. and British bases, he exposed the country to the danger of outside intervention. And this time the danger was real: oil had been discovered (and was beginning to be exported in the early 1960s). Libya was on its way to becoming a very wealthy country indeed, and consequently a most attractive prey for any strong neighbor.

Qadhafi's dilemma was that if he chose to have the foreign bases returned to Libya in order to protect it from external intervention, he would lose the legitimacy he had acquired domestically; but without the bases, Libya was so vulnerable that it could easily be invaded by its neighbors, primarily Egypt. His options were few. One that was open to him but not really to his predecessor (except, perhaps, in the last few years of his reign) was to build up a Libyan army and an arsenal of weapons that could deter intervention by making any invasion by Libya's neighbors a costly affair. This was made possible by the tremendous oil wealth that accrued to Libya, especially after the nationalization of the oil companies, and increasing ever more rapidly after the 1973 oil embargo. The second option open to him was to play an active role in North Africa, to ensure that a balance of power existed in the region, so that the countries on Libya's eastern and western flanks did not form alliances or blocs that could threaten Libya's borders or undermine his regime.

Egypt and the Sudan

Libya felt most threatened by Egypt and the Sudan. Time and again Qadhafi warned Libyans that Egyptians or Sudanese, or both together, or with U.S. support, would invade Libya because of its oil wealth. "The true conflict . . . now taking place in the world is the conflict over oil," Qadhafi pointed out (FBIS MEA 1980, 12). Even at the very earliest stage Qadhafi was very much aware of the need to protect his boundaries and protect his regime from external intervention, while at the same time consolidating his power at home. It is this fear that was the driving force behind many of his policies in the region. Libya's effort to safeguard its national interest is revealed most clearly in its behavior toward Egypt and the Sudan and its attempts at Arab unity, its reaction to U.S. military aid to Egypt and the Sudan, its pursuit of the Libyan opposition in Cairo and Khartoum, its policies in Chad, and its support for the southern Sudanese rebellion.

On December 27, 1969, Qadhafi signed the "Tripoli Charter" with President Ja'far al-Numeiry of Sudan and President Gamal Abdel Nasser of Egypt, with the goal of creating a federation between Libya and her two strong neighbors, Egypt and the Sudan. This attempt, although viewed as a prime example of Libya's ideological fervor for Arab nationalism and Arab unity, could also be viewed from another, more pragmatic angle. Peter K. Bechtold, a close observer of the evolution of this attempt at federation, noted shrewdly that both Qadhafi and Numeiry needed this alliance with Egypt to boost "their questionable legitimacy at home by being associated with Abd al-Nasir" (Bechtold 1973, 153). Furthermore, it is very likely that Qadhafi needed more than just legitimacy—he may have needed protection as well from military coups within Libya and attempts at his ouster from outside the country. In fact, two such attempts had taken place, the first in December 1969, when some of the fringe members of the Revolutionary Command Council plotted to overthrow him; and the second in February 1970, when Prince Abdallah al-Abid al-Sanussi, the "Black Prince" related to the deposed King Idriss, attempted a coup by moving into the Fezzan, the southern province of Libya, from Chad, with the support of sympathetic local tribes such as the Seif al-Nasr clan (Cooley 1982, 98, 99). Thus, even at the earliest stage Qadhafi was aware of the need for powerful allies in the region, and the highest priority on his agenda was the development of an alliance with Egypt, primarily, as well as with the Sudan, that would ensure the security of Libya's borders and new regime.

The Federation of Arab Republics, promulgated in September 1971, was a continued attempt to cement Libya's alliance with Egypt, especially after Nasser's death. Although the Sudan was not part of this new federation for domestic reasons of its own, Syria's new regime under President Hafiz al-Assad had now joined Egypt and Libya. Although somewhat weakened by Nasser's death, Qadhafi acquired more legitimacy at home because of his new role as the " 'ideologue' and driving force behind unitary movements in the Arab world in general" (Bechtold 1973, 159).

Security problems remained of uppermost concern for both Qadhafi and Numeiry during the early 1970s. When, in 1971, a coup against president Numeiry of Sudan was quelled with Egyptian and Libyan assistance, president Sadat justified such external assistance by referring to the Tripoli Charter. In other words, the federation between the three states had been understood by all parties concerned as ensuring the protection of the regimes and the boundaries of each state. Thus, although Arab nationalism did have a role to play, the "national interest" of Libya may have also been a primary consideration in those early attempts at unity with Egypt.

The issue of borders and security vis-à-vis Egypt and the Sudan is at the heart of Libya's tumultuous relationship with Chad. Throughout his years in power, one of Qadhafi's basic preoccupations has been to "prevent the encircling of Libya by forces hostile to him," (Neuberger 1982, 60). One of the major factors for this involvement has been strategic. "The Libyan presence in Chad had . . . a double function—one offensive and one defensive. Chad is an ideal stepping stone for infiltrating and destabilizing Sudan and Egypt, and at the same time a Libyan presence in Chad prevents it from becoming a base for operations for the enemies of Qadhafi's regime" (Neuberger 1982,60; see also Zartman 1983, 4). In other words, although both Islamic and Arab ideological factors may have played a role in the Libyan involvement and occupation of Chad, other major strategic factors were very much a basis for Qadhafi's policies in that country.

Qadhafi's fear of encirclement appeared to be justified, at least after 1977. It is a fact that at the time of the border war between Egypt and Libya in the summer of 1977, Egyptian and Sudanese interest in Chad intensified markedly. Hosni Mubarak, then Egyptian vice-president, visited Chad as head of an Egyptian-Sudanese delegation and declared Egypt's and Sudan's support for the Chadian government of General Felix Malloum, which was vehemently opposed to Libyan involvement in Chad. Furthermore, they backed Malloum's demand to initiate discussions and negotiations on the issue of the Aouzou Strip, the 150 kilometer strip of land on the northern border of Chad with Libya, a direct blow to Libya's claim over the area.

It is interesting to note here that by getting into the Chadian conflict, Egypt was able to deflect the Libyan-Egyptian confrontation of 1977 to Chad, that is, to a more neutral territory, where the conflict could continue without the consequences of direct military confrontation. Since then, Egypt and the Sudan have continued to support Qadhafi's enemies in Chad: Malloum, between 1975 and 1978; the Malloum-Habre coalition of August 1978 to February 1979; the *Gouvernement d'Union Nationale Transitoire* (GUNT), based on a coalition of Goukouni Weddeye and Hissene Habre, between March 1979 and March 1980; and when that coalition broke up, Habre's FAN (*Forces Armées du Nord*).

The implication of the above is that Chad has sometimes been used by Libya as well as by Egypt and the Sudan to fight out their own differences. Thus, a war by proxy, parallel to the more than twenty-year-old Chadian civil war between the North and the South, has been taking place in Chad at least since 1977. Pan-Arab, Islamic, and socialist ideologies have had very little to do with that dimension of the Chadian conflict.

Libya's complex relation to Egypt and the Sudan can also be viewed in light of U.S. military aid to those countries. As shown earlier, until 1973 Libya had friendly relations with Cairo and Khartoum. However, after the 1973 war with Israel, Libya's relations with Egypt and also with the Sudan began deteriorating. There were several reasons for this. First, by not having been informed that Egypt was launching a war against Israel, Libya had been slighted and ignored by the countries it felt should have been its natural allies. That was not only humiliating to Qadhafi personally but also detracted from his legitimacy at home as a major Arab leader.

Second, and most important, Egypt took up friendly relations with the United States. This was seen as changing the balance of power in the region and threatening Libyan security. Qadhafi viewed the U.S. role in the region with much suspicion. The Libyan Jamahiriya News

Agency (JANA) was to comment later that Kissinger's step-by-step diplomacy during the
mid-1970s was an attempt by the United States to link "the domination of oil resources to
the strength of the Zionists" (FBIS MEA 1980, 11). Qadhafi has believed all along that the
United States, for its own security reasons, wished to control directly or indirectly those
countries in the Middle East that had major oil reserves. He saw the peace process as one
that enhanced Israel's power in the region, brought Egypt under U.S. influence, and rendered
Libya much more vulnerable to external intervention and domination. Instead of being the
protector, as in the early 1970s, Egypt had become an ally to those forces, the United States
and Israel, whose aim was to dominate the region as a means to control its oil resources.
Again and again Qadhafi would insist: "The United States intends to attack Libya and subject
it to its domination" (FBIS MEA 1981, 148–56, 183). However, he also qualified the statement
by saying that the United States need not occupy Libya directly. It could supply the arms to
Egypt and the Sudan to assist them in undermining the Libyan regime. "Preparations are
now underway for the implementation of an Egyptian-Sudanese-American attack against the
Jamahiriya's people," (FBIS MEA 1981, 192) JANA would warn the Libyans in 1981. The
rationale behind the argument was that since Egypt had made peace with Israel, the military
hardware that it had been receiving from the United States since 1978 could have no other
purpose than to overthrow the Libyan government. Furthermore, one could even argue that
one of the reasons for Qadhafi's rejection of the Camp David agreement may have been the
fear that Egypt could now shift its military forces from its eastern borders with Israel to its
western border with Libya.

Operation Bright Star, under which more than four thousand U.S. troops were deployed
in Egypt in November 1981 for joint military maneuvers with Egypt, the Sudan, Oman, and
Somalia, was perceived by Qadhafi as having been launched to topple his regime. JANA
reported on October 14, 1981, "State Department officials told journalists that a decision has
been made to expand these maneuvers to make them an exercise for the invasion of Libya"
(FBIS MEA 1981, 199). In the face of this perceived threat to Libya's security and primary
national interest, Qadhafi's response was to withdraw Libya's forces from Chad in late 1981.
This withdrawal was a conciliatory gesture, a tactical move to prevent a major attack on Libya.
As Zartman and Kluge point out, "It appears that Libyan foreign policy is a policy of opportunity conducted on the basis of rather constant principles. . . . When an opportunity
presents itself, Libya acts. When opposition is too strong, Libya affects a strategic withdrawal,
but not a change in goals" (Zartman and Kluge 1984, 175–95).

It would appear, therefore, that Libya's relations to both Sudan and Egypt have been
affected by the latter's ties to the United States. Qadhafi has perceived those ties as dangerous
to Libya's security and to the survival of his own regime, and this has led him to move closer
to the Soviet Union in an effort to deter any aggression on his eastern borders. Nor was his
withdrawal from Chad the product of any ideological consideration, but rather the result of
a pragmatic assessment of the politico-military balance in the region at the time.

The Play of Libyan Opposition Forces

Libya's foreign policy toward Egypt and the Sudan has also been affected by the fact that
since Qadhafi's military coup of 1969, Egypt, and later Sudan, harbored Libyan opposition

members and groups in their capitals. King Idriss, the deposed Libyan monarch, settled in Cairo in 1969; 'Umar al-Muhayshi, a colleague of Qadhafi who attempted to overthrow him in 1975, also sought refuge in the Egyptian capital for a while. Abd al-Hamid Bakkush, a former prime minister under the Libyan monarchy and a major opposition figure, was to follow later, and by the late 1970s Cairo had become a major center for the Libyan opposition. In 1980 it was the turn of Muhammad Youssef Magharif, a former United Nations ambassador, to defect, followed by another diplomat, Ahmad Ahwas. In 1981, they set up an opposition organization in Khartoum called the National Front for the Salvation of Libya. This group was perhaps the best organized of all the opposition groups. Its political wing published regular newsletters in French, English, and Arabic, and its military wing was responsible for the attack on Qadhafi's military headquarters at Bab al-Aziziya in May 1984 (Deeb and Deeb 1985, 138–40). Since 1982 it has been broadcasting programs from the Sudan against the Libyan regime.

It may be possible to interpret a number of terrorist acts by Libya against the Sudan and Egypt either as aimed directly at the Libyan opposition in those countries, or as a means of pressuring the Sudanese and Egyptian governments to turn members of the Libyan opposition over to Qadhafi, or at least to expel them. A case in point is the March 1984 bombing of the national radio station in Omdurman in the Sudan, where the Libyan opposition (among others) broadcast programs against Qadhafi's regime. The crisis of the mining of the Suez canal, which the Egyptians traced to a Libyan cargo ship, the Ghat, occurred in July 1984. Although Libya vehemently denied any involvement in the incident, it offered Egypt $5 million during the crisis to return a Libyan pilot who had defected in April of that year, as well as to expel all the Libyan opposition groups from Egypt (*Al-Inqadh* 1984, 45).

It is interesting to note that former Sudanese president Numeiry claimed in an interview with *The Washington Post* that Qadhafi had made him a similar offer (*The Washington Post* 1985). Although both cases are to some degree conjectural, Qadhafi has used both the carrot (political support, economic aid, outright gifts of large sums of money, and withdrawal of support for opposition groups) and the stick (subversion, sabotage, support for opposition groups, bombings) to obtain what he wants. He clearly perceives the Libyan opposition, especially that which is to be found in the various countries of North Africa, as a very grave threat to his regime. Consequently, he will let nothing stand in the way of destroying that opposition (least of all ideological considerations).

It is finally through Libya's support of the southern Sudanese rebellion that one can view most clearly Qadhafi's pragmatic approach to foreign policy in the region. From 1980 the situation in southern Sudan began to deteriorate rapidly. The reasons were many: major economic problems which were given little attention by the Numeiry regime, a pipeline that was being built to carry oil found in the southern part of Sudan to a terminal in the north at Port Sudan, the rotation of military troops from north to south, the application of the Islamic Shari'a law in Sudan, including the south, which is mainly Christian and animist, and so forth (*Maghreb-Machrek* 1985, 102). In early 1983 southern soldiers from the Bor and Pibor garrisons in the Upper Nile area of Jonglei mutinied, and northern troops were sent to crush the rebellion. By mid-1983 a large number of southern troops had deserted, among whom was Colonel John Garang de Mabior, who then emerged in July 1983 heading a new southern opposition front to the Numeiry regime called the Sudan People's Liberation Movement (SPLM) (Lesch 1985a, 10–11).

Qadhafi found a new opportunity to destabilize a government that he considered a threat to his own regime. He did not hesitate to back a movement composed of Christians and animists who do not consider themselves Arab against a Muslim Arab regime (Wells 1984, 60–61). Neither Islamic nor Arab nationalist considerations prevented him from backing the movement. Furthermore, Qadhafi was swift to cut off aid to the SPLM when the transitional Sudanese government of Suwar al-Dhahab showed signs of changing its foreign policy and accommodating some of Qadhafi's demands. The Sudanese regime began distancing itself from Washington and Cairo by canceling joint U.S.-Sudanese maneuvers, in mid-1985 (Lesch 1985b, 9). It also made the integration agreement between Egypt and the Sudan, the *Takamul*, a dead letter, after arresting the secretary-general for integration on charges of corruption. In April 1985, less than a month after his coup in the Sudan, Suwar al-Dhahab went to Libya, and in July 1985, the Sudanese defense minister signed a military protocol with Tripoli.

In short, Libya's support for the southern Sudanese rebellion had been purely tactical, to put pressure on Khartoum to meet some of Qadhafi's demands. Once Khartoum was ready to improve its relations with Libya and to distance itself somewhat from Cairo and Washington, Libya became amenable to stopping its aid to the SPLM. As in the other cases, Libya's policy toward the Sudan was based on its national interest and not on any ideological consideration. Qadhafi may yet resume his assistance to Garang if he becomes displeased with Khartoum, for whatever reason.

From this analysis of Libya's relationship to Egypt and the Sudan, it becomes apparent that it is futile to try to explain Libya's foreign policy only in terms of the psychological determinants of Qadhafi's personality or his ideological preferences. A third approach, such as the one discussed in this chapter may be necessary. However, it is important to understand Qadhafi's perception of the world, his *weltanschauung*, as well as to realize the role his ideology does play in some of his relations with countries around the world. On the other hand, those considerations should not obscure the fact that Qadhafi has been a very shrewd observer of the North African political scene and is highly aware of the vulnerability of the Libyan state and of his own regime.

His policy in the region has been focused on preventing any state—whether Egypt, the United States, or the Soviet Union, for that matter—from having even limited influence on Libya's domestic politics or its foreign policy. Qadhafi has attempted to ensure a balance of power in the region that would keep his neighbors tied up with their own domestic problems and regional rivalries, and consequently uninvolved in Libyan affairs. As we have shown with Sudan and Egypt, Qadhafi's policy aimed at driving a wedge between the two countries to prevent a bloc from being formed on his eastern border that might threaten Libya's sovereignty. When that failed, he supported opposition movements in southern Sudan to destabilize the Numeiry regime. In fact, with the new Sudanese government in power, Libya's policy toward the Sudan has changed completely. Qadhafi supported Sadiq al-Mahdi, the new Sudanese prime minister, when he was in exile because of his opposition to the Numeiry regime. And although al-Mahdi is by no means a follower or an admirer of Qadhafi, he has always believed in distancing the Sudan from Egypt's sometimes overwhelming influence on Sudanese politics, a stand that Qadhafi whole-heartedly supports.

In the wake of the U.S. air raid on Libya on April 14, 1986, it is likely that Libya will take advantage of the limited support it has gained from Arab and African states to build bridges and enter into new alliances. With respect to Egypt it is very probable that Qadhafi will once again seek its protection, appealing to common ideals of Arab nationalism and Arab unity. He may be less successful with Egypt than he has been with the Sudan, but he still retains certain options to improve relations. One of those options might be to withdraw Libyan troops from Chad, as in 1981, in order to pacify its neighbors and preempt another U.S. raid on Tripoli and Benghazi. The options are limited and time may not be on his side, but Qadhafi may yet find ways of remaining in power and continuing to play an active role in the region.

REFERENCES

Bechtold, Peter K. 1973. "New Attempts at Arab Cooperation: The Federation of Arab Republics, 1971-?" *Middle East Journal* 27,no. 2 (Spring):153, 159.
Cooley, John K. 1982. *Libyan Sandstorm: The Complete Account of Qaddafi's Revolution*. New York: Holt, Rinehart and Winston. 98–99.
Deeb, Marius, and Mary-Jane Deeb. 1985. "Libya: Internal Developments and Regional Politics." In *The Middle East Annual: Issues and Events*, vol. 4, 1984, edited by David H. Partington, 13–40. Boston: G. K. Hall.
Foreign Broadcast Information Service Daily Report. Middle East and Africa (FBIS MEA). 1980. 5, no. 226 (November 20).
———. 1980. 5, no. 251 (December 29).
———. 1981. 5, no. 183 (September 22).
Haley, Edward. 1984. *Qaddafi and the United States since 1969*. New York: Praeger.
Al-Inqadh. 1984. 3,11 (November):45.
JANA. 1981. Quoted in FBIS MEA 5, no. 192 (October 5).
———. 1981. Quoted in FBIS MEA 5, 199 (October 15).
Lesch, Ann Mosely. 1985a. "Rebellion in the Southern Sudan." UFSI Reports, Africa no. 8:10–11.
———. 1985b. "Transition in the Sudan: Aspirations and Constraints." UFSI Reports, Africa, no. 20:9.
Maghreb-Machrek. 1985. No. 107, (January–March): 102.
Morgenthau, Hans J. 1958. *Dilemmas of Politics*. Chicago: University of Chicago Press.
———. 1985. *Politics Among Nations: The Struggle for Power and Peace*. 6th ed. New York: Alfred A. Knopf.
Neuberger, Benyamin. 1982. *Involvement, Invasion, and Withdrawal: Qadhafi's Libya and Chad 1969–1981*. Tel Aviv: Tel Aviv University.
Ogunbadejo, Oye. 1983. "Qaddafi's North African Design." *International Security* 8, no. 1 (Summer):154–78.
Otayek, René. 1981. "La Libye révolutionnaire au sud du Sahara." *Maghreb-Machrek*, no. 94 (October–December):5–35.
St John, Bruce. 1983. "The Ideology of Mu'ammar al-Qadhdhafi: Theory and Practice." *International Journal of Middle East Studies* 15, 4(November):471–90.
Tripp, Charles. 1984. "La Libye et L'Afrique." *Politique Etrangère*, 2(Summer):317–29.
The Washington Post. 1985. April 3.
Wells, Rick. 1984. "Nimiery under Siege." *Africa Report*, (May–June):60–61.
Woodward, Bob. 1985. "CIA Anti-Qaddafi Plan Backed." *The Washington Post*, November 3.
Zartman, William. 1983. "What's at Stake in Chad." *World View* 16, 11(November):4.
Zartman, William, and A.C. Kluge. 1984. "Heroic Politics: The Foreign Policy of Libya." In *The Foreign Policies of Arab States*, edited by Bahgat Korany and Ali E. Hillal Dessouki, 175–95. Boulder, CO: Westview Press.

III.

THE ROLE OF ISLAM

E. G. H. Joffé

In the words of a leading authority on contemporary Libya, "the Libyan revolution is not to be viewed as anti-Islamic but, to the contrary, as a force that derives its impetus from the concepts of a regenerated Islam, Freedom, Socialism and Unity" (Mattes 1986, 193). This is a fair, if somewhat overly idealistic assessment of the ideological underpinnings of the Libyan Jamahiriya. But if we are to make sense of Libyan policies in the continent the argument needs to be carried a few steps further. Clearly, the convoluted ups and downs that have accompanied Libyan policies in Chad are scarcely reducible to a modernized Islamic vision of freedom, unity and socialism. Nor can one seriously contend that Islam is the surest guide to an understanding of the contradictions that underlie Tripoli's attitudes towards its neighbors in the Maghreb. In brief, a host of other factors have contributed to the formulation of Libyan policies in the continent, a point nicely captured in Scarcia Amoretti's statement: "Libya pursues policies which in some respects can be described as 'Islamic', but this element is only one pillar, which, along with Arabism, Africanism, and a pragmatic assessment of Libya's political and strategic interests, motivates and constrains the conduct of its foreign policy" (Scarcia Amoretti 1983, 66).

If so, the question arises as to what kinds of relationships exist among these various factors, and whether Islam is merely an influence on policymakers—an intellectual or political environment, as it were, within which concrete decisions are made—or whether specifically Islamic values play an active role in determining policy choices (Dawisha 1983, 5). Whether or not Islam plays an active role in policy formulation and execution, there is yet another dimension that needs to be clarified—the specific effect of the doctrinal content of Libyan Islam, as it relates to the political thought of Colonel Qadhafi—the Third Universal Theory and the *Green Book* (Ayoub 1987, 75).

Any attempt to evaluate the role of Islam within the formulation and practice of Libyan foreign policy must therefore take into account the role of Islam within the structure of the Libyan state itself. The modern state—the Jamahiriya or "state of the masses," to give the term its conventional, if somewhat inaccurate formulation in English—claims a revolutionary pedigree, however. Indeed, a key feature of the revolutionary process has been the so-called "Islamic revolution" of 1978, which had the twofold objective of destroying the entrenched power of Islamic tradition and reformulating Islamic values in "modern, progressive and revolutionary" terms (Mattes 1986, 60–61). That the Islamic revolution occurred is tangible proof that Islam in Libya is a multifaceted experience which has been evolving through a continuing conflict between tradition and modernity.

This conflict finds an echo in Libya's African policies for, long before the September 1, 1969, coup, militant Islamic movements based in Cyrenaica had penetrated into the Sahel, while mercantile groups in Tripolitania and the Fezzan had traditionally based their wealth on trans-Saharan trade. Even Fascist Italy saw Libya as a potential base for a new Islamic African order in which Rome, as in classical times, would exercise a hegemonic overrule (Wright 1985, 52). In legitimizing its policies toward African states in Islamic terms, modern "revolutionary" Libya is merely capitalizing on this precolonial and colonial tradition.

The tension between traditionalism and modernity also manifests itself in the foreign policy arena; efforts to eradicate African memories of Libya's Islamic past (Mattes 1986, 187–88) do not rule out the use of Islamic symbols as a technique to address different African publics. Modernist and revolutionary Islamic values are used to address informal and popular institutions, while the more formal and traditional Islamic values are used to amplify secular diplomatic discourse with the institutions of foreign states (Otayek 1986, 80). However, insofar as this duality is an expression of the contradictions within the Libyan Jamahiriya, it too can only be adequately explained by first investigating the development and role of Islam within revolutionary Libya itself.

Islam and the Libyan Revolution

Independent Libya was formed in a crucible of Islamic tradition and foreign domination that stretched back to the beginning of the second Ottoman occupation in 1835. Libyan awareness of these external threats to the survival of the Qaramanli dynasty really began with the growth of trade with Malta after 1806, when Britain began to exert pressure on the Regency of Tripoli to honor its commercial debts (Joffé 1985, 32). By 1832, the weakness of the Qaramanlis paved the way for a rebellion that broke out in the Manshiya, the orchard and market garden area to the southeast of Tripoli and which ultimately resulted in the Ottoman intervention in 1835. The rebellion, although in part stimulated by British ambitions to counter French influence in Tripoli, was also a statement of indigenous resentment at the terms of a treaty imposed on the Pasha by France (El-Horeir 1981, 31–32). Even more significant was the fact that its supporters—mainly members of the Tripoli-based commercial elite, together with major tribal leaders from the Jefara plain—used a specifically Islamic idiom to justify rebellion against their nominal overlord, the Ottoman sultan in Istanbul.

The Senussiya

This alignment of Islam with popular resistance (Anderson 1986, 13) is a phenomenon of considerable importance in the Libyan context; during the next 150 years, it served as the anvil on which the modern Libyan state was forged out of its component parts of Tripolitania, Cyrenaica, and the Fezzan under the pressure of colonial occupation. Its most striking manifestation was the growth of Sanusi influence in Cyrenaica in the mid-nineteenth century. The Sanusi Order, a missionary Islamic Sufi order founded by the Algerian scholar and reformer, Sayyid Muhammad bin Ali al-Sanusi, created its first *zawiya* (lodges) in Cyrenaica at Al-Bayda in 1843 in response to the European threat he considered European occupation posed to Muslim North Africa, in the wake of France's occupation of Algeria thirteen years earlier.

To some extent, Cyrenaica was the only option open to the Sanusi Order, for both Mecca (where the order had originated) and Cairo were closed to it by the local authorities who believed that it threatened their own prestige and control (Evans-Pritchard 1947, 14). Once in Cyrenaica, however, the Sanusi Order rapidly expanded its activities by developing a symbiotic pattern of political and religious interaction with the local tribes. It thus became a major unifying factor within the normatively anarchic system of tribal egalitarianism through-out Cyrenaica and parts of eastern and central Tripolitania and the Fezzan. Sanusi reformism was flexible enough to encompass tribal traditions of maraboutism and to recruit tribal energies into a more efficient organization of trans-Saharan commerce while, at the same time, leading the *jihad* (holy war) against alien occupation (Morsy 1984, 276–77).

Despite its hold on the indigenous populations of Cyrenaica and Tripolitania, the Sanusi Order still had to deal with the Ottoman authorities that controlled the coastal towns. Inter-estingly enough, despite its reformist traditions, missionary zeal, and militant opposition, the order and the Ottomans struck a distant and uneasy *modus vivendi*, in which Sanusi political control of the Libyan hinterland—except in the Jefara Plain and the Jabal where its influence was, in any case, weak—was not disturbed. However, the center of Sanusi influence moved away from the Cyrenaican coast, southward to Jaghbub (1856) and then to Kufra (1895), while Sanusi influence moved southward into Borku (1899) and westward into southern Tunisia and eastern Algeria to confront French penetration into North and Central Africa (Morsy 1984, 279–82). The expansion of the order into what was to become the modern state of Chad foreshadowed independent Libya's own future interest in the Sahel region, while confirming the longstanding commercial traditions linking Tripoli and Benghazi with Central Africa. Its greatest challenge, however, was to come with the Italian invasion of Libya in 1911.

The Italo-Sanusi wars eventually led to a transformation in the nature of the Sanusi Order in Libya. Although individuals such as Sayyid Ahmad al-Sharif or Sidi Umar al-Mukhtar were recognized as authoritative figures (i.e., *marabat*s and *mujahid*s), the Sanusi family as a whole—which by now dominated the order almost as if it were a personal fief—"played an incon-spicuous and inglorious part in the resistance" (Evans-Pritchard 1947, 167). The end result was that tribal Libya lay prostrate under Italian occupation after sixteen years of warfare while the Sanusi family found itself in Egypt living as pensioners of Great Britain. Although the Sanusi put up a stiff resistance to Italy during the Second World War, and while the order's popularity was still strong in Cyrenaica its image was inevitably tainted by its collaboration with Britain (Wright 1969, 198). There were many other areas of disagreement among the myriad political groupings and parties that made up the nationalist mosaic of postwar Libya, but the UN decision to impose independence on the country by 1951 brought them together in a collective effort to create an effective set of political institutions under the leadership of the head of the Sanusi Order, Sayyid Idris (Wright 1969, 220). Nonetheless, the birth of the new state barely concealed the continuing discords over federalism and the role of the Sanusi, and these were to poison the first two decades of independence.

The September Revolution

The overthrow of the Sanusi monarchy by members of the Union of Free Officers on September 1, 1969 was first and foremost an attempt by a new generation to substitute the ideology of Nasirist Arab nationalism for what it saw as an obscurantist and traditionalist, pro-Western monarchical government, which had betrayed the true interests of Libya and the Arab world. As the new constitution, prepared by the Revolutionary Command Council and published on December 11, 1969 makes clear, its primary concerns were freedom through opposition to imperialism (Preambule), unity within the Arab nation (Article 1) and development through socialist economic principles (Articles 7 and 8), in which private property and inheritance were respected and the state was to provide coherence through its control of development planning (Ansell and Al-Arif 1972, 108–13). Islam was only mentioned in Article 2, as the religion of the state, alongside Arabic as the official language and guarantees of freedom of religious expression. It is difficult, therefore, to argue that the September revolution was inherently and primarily Islamic in content and intent (Ayoub 1987, 17).

Yet there can be little question that Islam provided the intellectual and moral environment in which these ideas were articulated. The first communique issued by the new Revolutionary Command Council made this clear when it stated, "By socialism, we mean above all an Islamic socialism. We are a Muslim nation. We shall therefore respect, as commanded in the Qur'an, the principle of private property, even of hereditary property" (Ayoub 1987, 23). It is also true that Colonel Qadhafi, in his early speeches after the revolution, laid great emphasis on the role of Islam in explaining his success. Yet, at the Libyan Intellectual Seminar, held in May 1970, Islam was not a topic for active discussion although considerable attention was paid to future political and social organization (Ansell and Al-Arif 1972, 253–300). The role of Islam was assumed by the participants as part of the cultural mosaic against which specific measures would be taken and, in consequence, was rarely mentioned. Only on one occasion was there a call for specifically Islamic measures to be put into practice with respect to Quranic education.

At the same time, however, the new leaders, particularly Colonel Qadhafi whose tribal background and upbringing clearly show the conditioning influence of Islam, despite the growing importance of Nasirism as he grew older (Craig Harris, 1986, 45), were well aware that the new regime would only be legitimized for the majority of Libyans by a demonstration of its adherence to Islamic precept. Furthermore, it would only survive if it could also destroy the prestige of the existing religious elites, particularly those connected with the Sanusi in Cyrenaica (El Fathaly and Palmer 1980, 58). Rural Libyans, for example, considered religious piety the most important attribute of the traditional elites, twice as important, indeed, as tribal affiliation (El Fathaly, Palmer, and Chackerian 1977, 80). In other words, the conscious adoption of Islamic principles by the new regime was a response to the political problem of ensuring its domestic stability and legitimacy, as much as a deliberate expression of personal commitment by its leadership under the dominating personality of Colonel Qadhafi. Furthermore, insofar as the colonel's personal preference for explicitly Islamic justification for specific political decisions was a dominant element, this was in large measure because of its usefulness in attacking the corruption and lack of Islamic fervor of the previous government and the society it had fostered. Islam became a vehicle for the colonel's articulation of populist rejection of the old order and its replacement by new ideological constructs.

Indeed, from 1970 onward the development of the domestic role of Islam has been one of an antiphonal interaction between its use as a factor to legitimize established political institutions, whatever their own specific ideological content might be, and its use as a source of inspiration and innovation for the political ideology which Colonel Qadhafi has enunciated with increasing openness since his speech at Zuwara in April 1973. The balance between these two functions has increasingly swung toward the use of Islam to justify the radical populist ideology articulated in the Third Universal Theory and has, in consequence, brought the Libyan regime into conflict with most aspects of established Islam in Libya and elsewhere (El-Khawas 1986, 98).

Up to 1973, however, Islam's predominant role was to legitimize the regime. An austere morality was introduced with new laws to ban alcoholic consumption, prostitution, and nightclubs, laws on *halal* slaughtering of imported meat, the conversion of churches into mosques, and the introduction of an official Islamic calendar. More positive stimulation of an Islamic character followed with the revision of the legal code to conform with the *sharia*. Regime control of the political process was enhanced by the reform of *waqf* properties so that they fell directly under state control, while the state also made the *hajj* more accessible to the population. The numbers of pilgrims traveling to Mecca began to rise rapidly, virtually doubling between 1970 and 1973 (Mattes 1986, 27). Although the religious establishment was brought into the picture, particularly over the question of legal reform, it also had to face considerable loss of autonomy. Furthermore, as the state now controlled the *waqf* revenues, it also disbursed funds for religious purposes. Although there was a heavy subsidy (LD4.85 mn out of total *awqaf* of LD5.51 mn in 1974, when total expenditure ran at LD6.08 mn, and LD5.2 mn out of total receipts of LD6.05 mn in 1978 [Mattes 1986, 40–43]), the traditional religious elite effectively became state employees, a situation that can hardly have been eased even by the fact that 324 new mosques were built between 1973 and 1982, bringing the total up to 2,565 (Mattes 1986, 36).

The Zuwara Speech

The crucial change between the use of Islam as a source of legitimization for the regime and as an input into Colonel Qadhafi's own political vision occured in April 1973. The colonel had frequently spoken of his interpretation of the political implications of Islam in the modern world before this date, making it clear that, unlike many Arab nationalists in the Mashreq, he found no contradiction between Islamic unity and Arab nationalism—not least because, unlike the Middle East, the Eastern Maghreb is virtually culturally uniform so that Islam and Arabism *do* coincide. Equally, Islam was frequently described as a revolutionary and progressive force, whose universality and egalitarianism justified its adoption as a more powerful political ideology than either capitalism or communism (Bleuchot 1982, 141–46). Finally, in an implicit reference to his own origins within the *murabit* Qadhadhfa tribe (Anderson 1986, 51, 261) and the egalitarian vision of *bedouin* life, the colonel began to argue that Islam required no professional mediator between God and man (Mattes 1986, 63).

The Zuwara speech was to mark the beginning of a process by which Colonel Qadhafi tried not only to impose a new political order on Libya but sought to resolve the dichotomy between *din* and *dawla*, i.e., between religion and the state. Such a dichotomy should not be allowed to exist, since it was popularly believed to have been artificially imposed on the Muslim world. The Zuwara speech called for an Islamic legal code, the elimination of dissident ideologies and ideas that threatened Libya's Islamic and Arab heritage, the evolution of concepts of popular freedom and the extension of the revolutionary process to the administration of the state (Ayoub 1987, 32).

In addition to its explicit appeal to Islamic precept, the Zuwara speech articulated the role to be played by the Third Universal Theory in creating a political system based on Arab unity, Islamic socialism, and direct popular democracy. As Hanspeter Mattes points out (Mattes 1986, 50) each of these elements in the theory can be justified by reference to the Quran (sura 3, verse 98 or 110; sura 17, verses 21 and 32; sura 42, verse 36 respectively), thus allowing the colonel to claim the coincidence of *din* and *dawla* inherent in it. Furthermore, Colonel Qadhafi is known to have been strongly influenced in his ideological development by a group of south Tunisian Islamists led by Ibn Malik. It was through this influence, rather than through the much vaunted familiarity with Rousseau, that Qadhafi came to endorse the notion of direct popular democracy. Even so, it is difficult to escape the conclusion that many of the sources for these ideas derive from the colonel's own early experiences in the narrow confines of tribal egalitarianism dominated by an Islamic climate in which Islam is also a vehicle of social and political protest (Bleuchot 1982, 140–41, 143, 148–49).

Shortly after the speech, Qadhafi called for the formation of popular committees to take over the media. During the next four years, Libyan society and polity were gradually radicalized, with the popular committee system being extended in 1975 and the famous *Green Book* beginning to appear in 1976. Finally, in March 1977, the jamahiriya was established. Popular sovereignty was formally intended to replace the old Nasirist vision of the Revolutionary Command Council; the Nasirist Arab Socialist Union congress was henceforth transformed into the General People's Congress, whose members were drawn from the basic popular congresses; from the People's Congress would be appointed the General People's Committee, in charge of handling the affairs of government on a day-to-day basis.

Although the jamahiri system has been given religious sanction by the assimilation of *din* and *dawla* as described above, in reality the imposition of direct popular democracy was a radical attempt to sweep away continuing opposition to the Qadhafi regime. Even though the remnants of the monarchy had long been removed, traditionalist patterns of thought and political behavior still persisted and the structures originally designed to eliminate them had failed to serve this purpose (El Fathaly and Palmer 1980, 135). Hence, more radical techniques were required, and the Third Universal Theory provided them. Furthermore, insofar as opposition to the regime persisted among social groups with specific economic interests, the further transformation of the state by their elimination was inevitable. This was accomplished in 1978 when the private sector gave way to cooperative management of the economy.

Islamic Revolution

The economic reforms spelled the final break between Libya's religious establishment and the Qadhafi regime. The nationalization of the economy meant that *waqf* was nationalized as well. Although the state had taken over management of all *awqaf* at the start of the 1970s so that the religious establishment could not control it in any case, the *ulama* in Tripoli attacked the move on religious grounds as an attack on the sanctioned right to private property. The attack brought the *ulama* into direct conflict with Colonel Qadhafi—even though he had abandoned his formal political position within the Libyan state—for their statements were seen as a direct contravention of a decree in 1975 that they should not publicly discuss political questions (Mattes 1986, 63).

He riposted, typically, that there was little need for the *ulama* since the Quran was written in Arabic, which all Arabs could understand. He went on to warn them to comply and proclaimed an Islamic revolution in May 1978 (Bearman 1986, 163). In July 1978, he widened his attack, arguing that the traditional corpus of Quran, *sunna* and *hadith*, which together with the intellectual practice of *qiyas* (reasoning by analogy) and *ijma* (consensus) form the basis of the four major schools of Islamic law, constituted *shirk* (error) since the Quran, the sole respository of the word of God had been thereby placed at the same level as manmade criteria (*sunna, hadith, qiyas* and *ijma*) (Mattes 1986, 65). *Sharia* law, in the colonel's view, is no different from any other system of manmade law. Only when it derives specifically from the Quran can it claim full religious sanction. The argument was Qadhafi's response to the objections raised by the *ulama* that the *Green Book* was at variance with the *sunna* and thus incompatible with Islam.

Having declared the *ulama* unnecessary and the Quran the sole source of Islamic law, Qadhafi then went on to argue that every Muslim had the right to have recourse to independent reasoning (*ijtihad*) in order to adapt Islam to modern conditions. Rather than to consult qualified experts in religious law (the *fuqaha*) independent judgment was encouraged as a means of by-passing the arbitration of the *fuqaha*. In his reformist zeal the colonel went even further, arguing that the Islamic calendar should be revamped so as to begin with the Prophet's death rather than with the *hijra* to Mecca; that the traditional *hadd* punishments were merely symbolic, that *hajj* to Mecca was no longer a pillar of Islamic belief; and that *zakat* (Islamic taxation) could vary in nature and amount. He thus provided himself with a doctrinal weapon that could be used to ensure the coincidence of his political vision with Islamic legitimization, while rendering Islam itself infinitely more flexible in dealing with the world as it is. And in so doing, he has placed himself and his ideology beyond the pale of orthodoxy. In fact, Qadhafi's concept of *ijtihad* and his rejection of the *sunna* and the *hadith* are seen by most Muslims as little short of heretical.

The attack on the *ulama*, in part provoked by their resistance to the economic reforms initiated in 1978, was also motivated by Qadhafi's anxiety over the popular support that certain elements of the *ulama* received from the population at large as a result of their attacks on the regime. This situation was particularly troublesome since support for the *ulama* came from youth—precisely the group from which the regime had expected the most enthusiasm for its policies. Even after Colonel Qadhafi's threats in 1978, certain *alims* continued to criticize his policies, chief among them Shaikh Al-Beshti in Tripoli, who was seen as a modernist theologian in the *salafi* tradition, which had dominated reformist Islam in North Africa. He was far removed from the *Ikhwan Muslimin* and the *Hizb al-Tahrir al-Islami*, two fundamentalist movements which the colonel has always condemned out of hand. Nonetheless, the Shaikh's criticisms were unacceptable to the regime, although it could not attack him directly. He disappeared in 1980, a victim of the growing intolerance that had come to characterize revolutionary Islam in Libya.

The Role of Islam within Libya

The Al-Beshti incident underlines a crucial aspect of Islam's role in Libya today—its use as a tool of political conformity and coercion. Within the context of the *jamahiriya* Islam has acquired a unique set of functions that serve both to legitimize the regime and to provide it with a highly flexible ideological tool. The fact that Islam provides the basic cultural environment, even after seventeen years of political radicalism, forces the regime to ensure that its policies coincide with Islamic precept. At the same time, Islam has been summoned to justify the modernizing ideology introduced after 1975, thus transforming Libya into a large-scale replica of the consensual, egalitarian, and collective values that typify traditional life. Islam also serves as a weapon to uproot established institutions that stand in the way of the regime. Through Colonel Qadhafi's innovative use of *ijtihad*, Islam has now become an infinitely flexible technique through which future policies can be said to conform with an established cultural tradition. This unique interaction between a radical political ideology and its religious and cultural environment is mirrored in Libya's foreign policy insofar as genuine Islamic and radical commitment has repeatedly come into conflict with the Libyan national interest.

Islam and Libya's Foreign Policy

The significance of Africa to Libya was clear from the very start of the revolution in 1969. Article 1 of the 1969 constitution makes it clear that, while Libya is part of the "Arab Nation," its territory, "is part of Africa" (Ansell and Al-Arif 1972, 108). However, until 1973–74, Africa was by no means at the forefront of Libyan foreign policy concerns. Instead, the new regime devoted itself to its relations with the Middle East and to the problems of relations with the West and with the international oil industry. Insofar as Africa was an element within the overall foreign policy picture, this was largely a reflection of Libya's Middle Eastern concerns—the concerted campaign to destroy Israeli influence in sub-Saharan Africa in 1971–72 being one example, and the intermittent attempts up to 1973 to prosecute moves toward unity arrangements with Egypt, Sudan, Algeria, and Tunisia being another. The other major strand in Libya's African policies—support for Frolinat against the Tombalbaye regime in Chad and moves to assert claims to the Aouzou strip in northern Chad after 1972—was, in some sense, atavistic, reflecting as it did precolonial links, as well as a legalistic preoccupation with the principle of *uti possidetis* in justifying its support for Italian colonial claims to Aouzou (Joffé 1987, 57).

It is difficult to identify the foreign policies of the early years of revolutionary Libya as being specifically or even predominantly Islamic in nature. They were, indeed, far closer to the conventional Nasirist vision of the three circles of influence—Arab, African, and Islamic (Mortimer 1982, 282). Primarily concerned with Arab unity—whether in the Middle East or North Africa (Ajami 1981, 125)—Islam was, as in domestic politics, merely the context within which policies were articulated. Growing attention was paid, it is true, to Islamic proselytism, with the creation of the *Jamiyat ad-Dawa al-Islamiya* (the Islamic Call Society) in December 1970 (Mattes 1986, 116). But this was generally consonant with the cultural environment that Islam provided in Libya itself and differed little from similar activities carried out by other Arab states in Africa.

It was only in the wake of the Zuwara speech, in April 1973, and the cultural revolution that Libya began to place greater importance on its policies toward Africa. Although this transformation was triggered by Sadat's rejection of Libya as an active ally in the 1973 October war and the consequent hostility between Libya and Egypt, it was also a consequence of the ideological changes that were taking place in Libya itself. Qadhafi made a conscious effort to manipulate Islam in order to generate a coherent ideology appropriate to domestic reform and activism abroad. Islam now began to take a more specific and prominent place inside policy formulation, as a specific element within a revolutionary corpus. Islam, furthermore, was to be mobilized as justification for the extension of the Libyan experience into a wider world—one that was not necessarily Muslim. Nonetheless, the more traditional aspect of Islamic foreign policy continued to play an important role in facilitating Libyan access to the Muslim regions of sub-Saharan Africa.

As Otayek and Mattes suggest, the Islamic factor in Libyan policy toward Africa involves a double code, one revolutionary for popular consumption and the other formal as part of the diplomatic discourse with other states (Otayek 1986, 80). The balance between them is a function of political structure of the target state.

The Geographic Arena

Islam in Africa has penetrated far beyond the Sahara and is the dominant religion in most areas of West, Central, and East Africa. However, North Africa—the Maghreb together with Mauritania, Egypt, and northern Sudan—is distingushed not only by the fact that Islam is the universal and dominant culture but also by the fact that Arabic has become the dominant linguistic mode. Arabic is spoken elsewhere, of course, but in the Sahel, for instance, it must compete with other local languages. Islamic culture may thus differ from the Maghribi norm, which still underpins Islam in Libya.

Libyan foreign policy has taken full account of these discontinuities. According to Otayek three geopolitical arenas can be distingushed (Otayek 1980, 195). The first consists of the Maghreb states, together with Mauritania and the Western Sahara. The second involves the Sahel states—Mali, Burkina Faso, Niger, and Chad—while the third stretches across an outer ring of states such as Guinea, the Central African Republic, Kenya, Benin, Ghana, Nigeria, the Congo, Ethiopia, and Uganda. This classification, while useful, has been overtaken by events, and it is difficult to subsume Libyan policies toward Benin and Ghana, on the one hand, or Burkino Faso on the other, under the general rubrics singled out by Otayek.

Nonetheless, this modified classification does provide a rough guide to the complex patterns of Libyan policy initiatives in Africa. In the Maghreb, Libyan concerns have differed little from the predominant Arab nationalism of the pre-1974 period, although the radicalism inherent in the Third World theory has also occasionally been called into play, particularly with Tunisia. In the Sahel, Libya's Islamic thrust has played a major role, both at the popular and at the state level—a duality that has done much to harm Libya's political aspirations. In the wider ring of states, Islamic proselytism has been confined to the activities of the Islamic Call Society, while other policy objectives have been couched in far more secular terms. With radicals, such as Ghana, Benin, and Burkina Faso, Libyan political radicalism has been emphasized, at the expense of Islamic legitimization. The same is true of Ethiopia.

In the case of Sudan and Chad, far older, historic considerations have come into play, coupled with an attempt to impose radical political solutions on regimes that are perceived as inherently conservative. The Numeiry regime in Sudan, after all, was predominantly Islamic in complexion, particularly after 1983. Nonetheless, Libya was prepared to support the southern rebels, many of whom are nominally Christian, because of the overt antagonism of Khartoum toward Libyan policy objectives, particularly in the Sahel. Chad, too, represents a complex issue for Libyan foreign policy. While Colonel Qadhafi may call for a *jihad* against the French presence there and seek unity as he did in 1980, the truth is that Libyan national interests eventually dominate all other considerations. As Colonel Qadhafi made clear in an address to Libyan students at Tripoli University in May 1980, Libyan intervention in Chad aims only at reclaiming territory that was rightfully Libyan—the Aouzou strip (Joffé 1981, 95). That aim has less to do with Islam than with Libya's territorial claims inherited from the colonial and precolonial past.

Islam and Policy

Despite these correctives to assumptions of an unbroken Islamic thread woven into Libya's foreign policy, Islam has played an important part in its formulation. Particularly since 1974, certain common strands can be identified which stem directly from the domestic role played by Islam in Libya. Libyan foreign policy is anti-Zionist, anti-imperialist, supportive of radicalism in the African world, and integrative in its efforts to obliterate colonial boundaries. Practically all these objectives combine a Nasirist legacy with Islamic legitimization and are often buttressed by specific Islamic objectives involving the extension of Islamic values. They derive from the three basic principles of the September revolution—freedom, unity, and socialism—reinterpreted to accommodate the post-1973 Islamization of ideology through the *Green Book* and the Third Universal Theory (Mattes 1986, 86).

Freedom

Freedom, in terms of foreign policy, means the removal of oppressive political structures, as was attempted in Morocco in 1971 and in Tunisia in 1980. In the Tunisian case, Libyan support went to a movement that was specifically Islamic in its orientation. While this may have been incidental to Tripoli's ultimate goals, its decision to throw its weight behind the Polisario Front (until 1984) reflects a different set of motives. Its aim was to confront a regime seen as corrupt and support a movement that it considered progressive. Indeed, Libyan support for the Polisario Front was tempered by Qadhafi's awareness that victory by the Polisario could only result in further fragmentation of the Arab nation. Characteristically, Tripoli has yet to recognize the Polisario Front's constitutional counterpart, the Arab Sahara Democractic Republic.

Elsewhere in Africa, "freedom" may be used to justify support to the Sudan's Southern People's Liberation Army SPLA—a predominantly Christian grouping, although Libyan aid was directed primarily toward a Muslim affiliate resistance group. It may also be used to justify links with radical or progressive regimes that are not Muslim at all, such as Ethiopia, Ghana, or Benin. As one observer has suggested, this is perhaps best seen as an example of "Islamic pragmatism" (Scarcia Amoretti 1983, 65). There is, in short, a continuity of practice in Libyan support for movements of national liberation.

The principle of freedom also implies support for activity designed to remove the remnants of Western neocolonial influence. Insofar as these are seen as a by-product of Israel's diplomatic thrust into the sub-Saharan Africa, anti-Zionism is but the flip side of anti-imperialism. This led to a sustained anti-Zionist offensive at the start of the 1970s which, in conjunction with pressure from other Arab states in the post-1973 era, virtually eliminated Israeli influence from the region until the mid-1980s.

Political developments in the more recent period have fueled Libyan distrust of Christianity and the West. Colonel Qadhafi considers that the recent wave of Western activism toward the developing world, particularly in the Middle East and Africa, is merely a reenactment of the Crusades (Mattes 1986, 94). As such, it must be confronted by *jihad*, traditionally the struggle to preserve the Muslim world from physical and moral danger, but in modern Libyan parlance an extension of the need to confront imperialism and neocolonialism (Mattes 1986, 94). *Jihad*, however, does not necessarily mean physical warfare in this context but rather a "hearts and minds" operation, in which the Islamic Call Society finds its true role as propagator of Islamic values and culture, as well as source of development in a struggle against poverty and exploitation.

In the African context, however, Christianity has always been considered by revolutionary Libya a vehicle of colonial oppression. Christian creeds are rejected as interpretations of Holy Writ and thus inferior to Islam *a priori*. Furthermore, as was made clear in 1976, during the Muslim-Christian dialogue held in Tripoli, the colonel believes that a proper reading of Christian scripture would lead to conclusions little different from Islam and that Islam is, therefore, the appropriate religious vision for the developing world (Mattes 1986, 110). Indeed, true freedom can only be obtained through the articulation of Islam within the secular political sphere, through the Third Universal Theory.

Unity

The issue of unity in Libyan foreign policy is complex. In North Africa itself, it has followed the more conventional patterns of Libyan policy typical of the pre-1974 period and in conformity with the Arab nationalist vision. Although it has been suggested that Colonel Qadhafi has recast Nasirism in Islamic terms (Scarcia Amoretti 1983, 59), this does not really apply to North Africa in the wake of the October 1973 war—except, perhaps, in the case of Tunisia in 1974. The principles of the Third Universal Theory, after all, could hardly be used to justify the ephemeral Arab-African Union signed between Libya and Morocco in August 1984. Nor could the unseemly squabble over border delimitation between Algeria and Libya (which prevented Tripoli from becoming a member of the Algerian-Tunisian-Mauritanian Treaty of Concord and Fraternity) be easily explained away by the Third Universal Theory or by Arab unity.

By a simple extension of the principle of Islamic unity to its goals, Libya proceeded to set up the Islamic Legion, which has been directly involved in military interventions in Uganda and Chad—albeit with little success. Nonetheless, insofar as it offers Libya regional status in African eyes, it has fostered the illusion that Libya also embodies progressive African aspirations through its reinterpretation of the revolutionary potential of Islam (Otayek 1986, 88).

Qadhafi thus feels entirely free to articulate his belief in the value of African and Islamic unity without considering himself guilty of hegemonism. This was essentially the logic behind his call for unity between Libya and Chad in 1981. Since the transitional government in Ndjamena was allied to Libya, it was appropriate that as a fellow progressive regime it should unify with Libya, adopting the same political structures and ideology. The offer was promptly declined. Although it may be argued that its major purpose was to ensure Libyan control of the Aouzou strip, other motives can be detected—a vague longing for the precolonial Sanusi role in northern Chad, a desire to resuscitate the social links between Tibesti and Murzuq, and keep alive the trans-Saharan commercial contacts within the frame of a progressive Islamic vision.

The cultural aspect of unity has been far more pervasive. Racial, social, and economic equality is brought into a vision of universal brotherhood (Mattes 1986, 96) designed to counter African memories of its unhappy precolonial contact with the Arab world. The kind of *jihad* that is required to achieve development and combat Western neocolonialism is the practical expression of this policy. It is also seen as an attempt to restore the unity of the Islamic world (Scarcia Amoretti 1983, 60). Similarly, since Arabic is the language of the Quran and, in Colonel Qadhafi's eyes, *ijtihad* is a right and duty incumbent on all Muslims, the teaching of Arabic is an integral part of the Libyan-inspired "New Muslim Cultural Revolution"—although, surprisingly, Colonel Qadhafi is also prepared to accept translation of the Quran in an attempt to spread its message (Mattes 1986, 99).

Socialism

To a large extent, the original objective of socialism expressed in the 1969 September revolution has been subsumed into the search for freedom and unity. It is inherent in the objectives of the New Muslim Cultural Revolution and is also an element in Libya's extensive aid programs in Africa. Significantly, seven of Libya's twenty-four foreign bank participations are located in Africa, and thirty-four of Libya's ninety-three joint stock companies worldwide are located in sub-Saharan Africa (Mattes 1987, 102–3).

The Cultural Dimension

The major vehicle for the dissemination of Islam is the Islamic Call Society. It was first proposed in 1970 and funded by the Libyan government for the first time in 1972. It is active world-wide, and yet, ironically enough, its major area of activity is Europe, which receives 49 percent of its funding, followed by the Middle East with 38 percent. However, eighteen African countries in the Sahel and sub-Saharan Africa claim 4 percent of such funds (Mattes 1986, 149). More important, perhaps, is the fact that Libyan economic aid is often tied to agreement to allow the society to operate freely within a state's national boundaries (Otayek 1986, 85). Indeed, the society often operates as the cultural arm of the Libyan government abroad.

The society's functions involve the sending of missionaries, the organization of Islamic cultural centers and the management of mosques financed by the Libyan government. It also provides emergency relief aid, organizes conferences and delegations, is involved in radio broadcasts about Islam, prints and distributes Islamic literature both in hard copy and on cassette, and even supports foreign publishing houses in this type of work. Its most important function, however, is the provision of Arabic teaching abroad.

Associated with the society and also created by the Islamic Missionary Conference in Tripoli in 1970 is the *Kulliyat ad-Dawa al-Islamiya* (the Faculty of the Islamic Call), based in the universities of Benghazi and Tripoli. The faculty is specifically designed to cater to the needs of foreign students of Islam in Libya, particularly those intended to be employed in the Islamic centers created by the Islamic Call Society. It also specializes in the teaching of Arabic and involves around 150 students annually. Both these institutions formally come under the control of *Majlis al-Alami lid-Dawa al-Islamiya* (the World Council of the Islamic Call), based in Tripoli, which also administers the *Sunduq al-Jihad* (the Jihad Fund), the main source of finance for their activities. Although other organizations also exist, they have little to do with Africa, being concerned mainly with Eastern and Western Europe.

The Role of Islam in Libya's Foreign Policy

There is little doubt that Libya's cultural offensive in parts of Africa where Islam already has a strong presence has often elicited a positive response. In large measure this corresponds to the radicalism of the message that it can offer. Islamic Africa is, like much of the Middle East, anxious for a radical Islamic message of change and renewal. However, in terms of achieving one of its major goals—the conversion of Africans to Islam, it is difficult to claim that it has enjoyed a major success. Although detailed statistics are not available, it appears that annual conversion rates are in the low hundreds. Even the occasional conversion of politicians usually seems to have more to do with tactical objectives than with religious conviction. Furthermore, Libya faces competition in the cultural sphere. Several other Arab states have initiated similar policies, particularly Saudi Arabia. Here the very radicalism of the Libyan message, particularly those elements that are conventionally defined as heretical, minimize its effect (Otayek 1986, 91).

The role of Islam in Libyan foreign policy is far more closely linked to the dissemination of the Third Universal Theory and the replication of Libya's domestic political, and economic experience abroad than it is to specific foreign policy objectives. It has done little to popularize Libyan policies toward unity, either in the Arab world or in Africa. Nor has it persuaded other progressive regimes in Africa to adopt its principles. In fact, it has provided support to those states fearful of Libyan interventionism in Africa, for, in addition to the threat of Libyan radicalism, there is now the added danger of heretical interpretations of Islam for other Muslim states or of an Islamic cultural invasion for non-Muslim African states. In short, Colonel Qadhafi's attempt to legitimize political radicalism by Islamic exegesis and to modernize Islam through interaction with secular political ideology and social tradition seems to have done little, in itself, to alter Libya's position in Africa. Instead, the pressures of Libya's national interests, as a nation-state in a continent of nation-states, have continued to constrain and define its relations with the rest of Africa.

REFERENCES

Ajami, F. 1981. *The Arab Predicament: Arab Political Thought and Practice since 1967*. Cambridge: Cambridge University Press.
Anderson, L. 1986. *The State and Social Transformation in Tunisia and Libya, 1830–1980*. Princeton: Princeton University Press.
Ansell, M. O., and I. M. Al-Arif. 1972. *The Libyan Revolution: A Sourcebook of Legal and Historical Documents*. Harrow: Oleander Press.

Ayoub, M. M. 1987. *Islam and the Third Universal Theory: The Religious Thought of Mu^cammar al-Qadhdhafi.* London: KPI.

Bearman, J. 1986. *Qadhafi's Libya.* London: Zed Books.

Bleuchot, H. 1982. "The Green Book: Its Context and Meaning." In *Libya since Independence*, edited by J. A. Allan. London: Croom Helm.

———. 1983. *Chroniques et documents libyens, 1969–1980.* Paris: Editions du CNRS.

Dawisha, A. 1983. "Islam in Foreign Policy, Some Methodological Issues." In *Islam in Foreign Policy*, edited by A. Dawisha. Cambridge: Cambridge University Press.

Evans-Pritchard, E. E. 1947. *The Sanusi of Cyrenaica.* Oxford: Clarendon Press.

El Fathaly, O. I., and M. Palmer. 1980. *Political Development and Social Change in Libya.* Lexington, KY: Lexington Books.

El Fathaly, O. I., M. Palmer, and R. Chackerian. 1977. *Political Development and Bureaucracy in Libya.* Lexington, KY: Lexington Books.

Harris, L. C. 1985. *Libya: Qadhafi's Revolution and the Modern State.* London: Croom Helm.

El-Horeir, A. S. 1981. *Social and Economic Transformations in the Libyan Hinterland during the Second Half of the Nineteenth Century: The Role of Sayyid Ahmad al-Sharif al-Sanussi.* Ph.D. diss. University of California at Los Angeles.

Joffé, E. G. H. 1981. "Libya and Chad," *Review of African Political Economy* 21 (May–Sept.).

———. 1985. "British Malta and the Qaramanli Dynasty (1800–1835)," *Revue d'Histoire Maghrebine* 37–38 (June).

———. 1987. "Frontiers in North Africa." In *Boundaries and State Territory in the Middle East and North Africa*, edited by G. H. Blake and R. N. Schofield. Wisbech, UK: Middle East and North Africa Studies Press.

El-Khawas, M. A. 1986. *Qaddafi: His Ideology in Theory and Practice.* Brattleboro, VT: Amana Books.

Mattes, H. 1986. *Die innere und äussere islamische Mission Libyens.* Munich: Kaiser Verlag.

———. 1987. "Libya's Economic Relations as an Instrument of Foreign Policy." In *The Economic Development of Libya*, edited by B. Khader and B. El-Wifati. London: Croom Helm.

Morsy, M. 1984. *North Africa 1800–1900: A Survey from the Nile Valley to the Atlantic.* London: Longman.

Mortimer, E. 1982. *Faith and Power: The Politics of Islam.* London: Faber and Faber.

Otayek, R. 1980. *La politique africaine de la Libye. Thèse de 3ème Cycle.* Bordeaux: CEAN.

———. 1986. *La politique africaine de la Libye (1969–1985).* Paris: Editions Karthala.

Scarcia Amoretti, B. 1983. "Libyan Loneliness in Facing the World: The Challenge of Islam?" In *Islam in Foreign Policy*, edited by A. Dawisha. Cambridge: Cambridge University Press.

Wright, J. 1969. *Libya.* London: Benn.

———. 1985. "Italian Fascism and Libyan Human Resources." In *Planning and Development in Modern Libya*, edited by M. M. Buru, S. M. Ghanem, and K. S. McLachlan. Wisbech, UK: Middle East and North African Studies Press.

IV.

LIBYA'S MILITARY POWER

William J. Foltz

The Great Socialist People's Libyan Arab Jamahiriya has been built on a presumption of military power. From the entry on stage of Qadhafi and the Free Unionist Officers, the political and the military realms have been intimately intertwined. It has been presumed that military force would constitute an essential tool of foreign policy. As the goals of policy have expanded to encompass the restructuring of the Arab world and much of Africa north of the equator, the destruction of Israel, and a world-wide fight against "imperialism," the need to acquire and deploy military force has expanded apace. The vast scale of Libya's military buildup and the absence of firm boundaries between the domestic and foreign policy realms have had repercussions on internal political order.

As Libya has acquired the physical trappings of military power, however, the professional military have been moved further and further away from control over political decisions, and the control of political groups over military decisions has greatly increased. At the same time, the combat performance of the Libyan military has ranged from the inadequate to the downright humiliating. This chapter analyzes the organization and performance of the Libyan military in an attempt to understand the causes of its limited successes and dramatic failures, and the possible repercussions of these on Libya's international and domestic affairs.

Restructuring the military and expanding its resources were among the first orders of business on the Revolutionary Command Council's agenda following the September 1, 1969 coup. The National Security Force and the Cyrenaican Defence Force were incorporated into the army, nearly tripling its size to twenty thousand men. The entire senior officer ranks were pensioned off and suspect junior officers purged (Dyer 1983, 368). Within months of seizing power, Qadhafi dispatched his right-hand man, Major Abdul Salam Jalloud, to China in an attempt to buy an atomic bomb (ibid., 373-74). When that naive attempt at instant great-power status failed, the new regime began negotiating internationally to purchase advanced conventional arms.

Thanks to growing oil revenues, the monarchy had already laid the groundwork for military expansion. The 1968 five-year plan projected military expenditures of over one billion dollars. The monarchy had, furthermore, started to break its traditional dependence on British and American equipment by negotiating a major purchase, including two hundred tanks, from the Soviet Union in 1967. These were to be delivered only in July and August 1970 (Bessis 1986, 90). For the new radical regime, however, France was to be the arms provider of choice.

Economically, France represented a major and rapidly growing market for Libyan oil. Politically, under President Pompidou, France maintained a haughty Gaullist independence from *les Anglo-Saxons*, Britain and the United States, whose use of Libyan military facilities had been considered one of the prime humiliations of the Idriss regime. Certainly, France seemed preferable to the Soviet Union, whose Marxism-Leninism was anathema to the young officers' Islamic nationalism, and whose record of military cooperation had evidently received poor reviews from Egypt's Nasser, patron saint of the new order. Above all, France was heavily committed to modernizing its own forces and enthusiastic about selling similar arms to attain the cost advantages of longer production runs. Within four months after the coup, Guy Georgy, the particularly influential French ambassador, had concluded a deal for 200 AMX tanks and 110 Mirage jets, both top-of-the-line models, along with much ancillary equipment. French technicians were hired for operational roles at the former British and American military installations (Otayek 1986, 110–11).

During the first four years of the new regime, Libyan arms purchases from France and a variety of other suppliers were broadly consistent with the goal of modernizing and expanding the military forces of a small but wealthy country so that it could defend itself against any likely attack and project modest military force across its own borders, should the need arise. A succession of foreign policy set-backs in the early 1970s, culminating in what Qadhafi took to be Egypt's double betrayal—launching war against Israel without consulting Libya, and intending that war to be a limited one leading to a brokered peace settlement—set the stage for a radical expansion of Libyan military ambition. The France of Valéry Giscard d'Estaing quite possibly found it impolitic to meet Qadhafi's heightened aspirations for arms; almost certainly it lacked the production capacity to fulfill them quickly. In the event, an alternative was ready and waiting in the Soviet Union, whose leaders were no happier than Libya's with the turn of events in the Middle East. Jalloud had already paid a visit to Moscow in 1972 and signed a modest agreement for economic and technical cooperation. In May 1974, he returned from a lavish reception by the Soviet authorities having signed a major protocol making the Soviet Union Libya's principal supplier of arms, a position that it continues to occupy to its considerable financial advantage.

No completely satisfactory figures are available to measure the cost of Libya's arms purchases. United States Arms Control and Disarmament Agency (ACDA) figures put them at $17,260 million (in current dollars) between 1973 and 1983 (ACDA 1985). Between 1979 and 1983, Libyan imports of military hardware amounted to $12,095 million, or 36 percent of all arms imported into Africa (43 percent if Egypt is excluded). The unusually well-informed Lillian Craig Harris estimates Libya's 1970 to 1985 total expenditures on overseas purchases of military goods and services at some $29 billion, of which less than 30 percent represents purchases from the West (Harris 1986, 123).

As for total military expenditures, domestic as well as foreign, ACDA figures reveal Libya's to have been the highest in Africa for every year since 1978, with only Egypt and South Africa spending more in the preceding five years. It is when Libya's military buildup is considered in relation to population that the disproportion becomes stark. Libya's military expenditures are approximately twice those of Algeria, a country with six times Libya's population. On a continent where per capita military expenditure averages $35 a year, Libya's figure regularly exceeds $1,000. (The only other countries in the world whose per capita military expenditures regularly exceed $1,000 are Oman, Qatar, Saudi Arabia . . . and Israel.)

TABLE 1. **Major Weapons Systems, 1986**

	Libya	Algeria	Egypt
Population (millions)	3.6	21.2	50.0
Army—Personnel	80,000	120,700	327,000
Armor			
Tanks	3,050	954	1,639
Reconnaissance Vehicles	1,010	412	740
Armored Personnel Carriers	>1,590	>611	>3,529
Surface-to-Surface Armament			
Towed Artillery	>830	>460	>1,300
Self-Propelled Artillery	>464	180	295
Multiple Rocket Launchers	556	92	300
S-S Missile Launchers	92	18	64
Antitank Guns	>200	12	2,000
Antitank Missile Firing Sta.	>3,990	NA	1,621
Surface-to-Air Armament			
Artillery	490	400	>1,460
S-A Missile Launchers	>495	124	817
Air Force—Personnel	15,000	14,000	30,000
Aircraft			
Interceptors	277	116	175
Multirole/Tactical Support	246	90	378
Reconnaissance	16	4	32
Bombers	8	13	14
Heavy/Med. Transports	100	24	45
Training	515	173	416
Helicopters			
Attack	50	37	38
Multirole	71	68	>61
Transport & Liaison	124	8	98
Navy—Personnel	6,000	8,000	37,000
Submarines	6	2	16
Frigates	2	3	8
Corvettes	9	3	2
Missile Patrol Boats	24	17	30
Other Patrol Boats	15	6	72
ASW Helicopters	35	—	23

Source: Military Powers, The League of Arab States, vol. 1. 1987, pp. 57–58.

So, what has Libya got for its money? There can be no doubt that Libya has acquired at least the *physical* means to become a major regional military power. In plain hardware terms, the buildup is impressive, and is made all the more so by comparison with Libya's much larger neighbors, Algeria and Egypt, as indicated in table 1.

The numbers in table 1 attest amply to the quantitative scale of Libya's arsenal. It should be added that most of this equipment is good-quality material in current production. In those cases in which the material acquired is not the latest or the fanciest, there appear to be good reasons. Such equipment may be inappropriate to Libyan conditions (e.g., a main battle tank designed for Central Europe), or so new as to be in limited supply or filled with sensitive technology (and thus confined to the Warsaw Pact), or simply too sophisticated for Libyans to operate, even with outside help (probably the case with MiG-27s, supplied to Algeria). Many of Libya's acquisitions are first-line systems, for example the MI-24 Hind helicopter and the latest version of the SA-6 air defense missile system. The backbone of the Libyan arsenal, however, is made up of more prosaic—if thoroughly serviceable—systems like the T-55 and T-62 medium tanks, BTR and BMP armored personnel carriers, and BM-21 (Stalin Organ) rocket launchers on the ground, and MiG-23 fighters, TU-22 bombers, and IL-76 cargo planes in the air.

As with military expenditures, the scale of Libya's arsenal appears startling when its population base is taken into account. Algeria has one tank for every seventeen thousand Algerians, Egypt one tank for every twenty-seven thousand Egyptians. Libya has one tank for every eleven hundred of its inhabitants—men, women, children, and guest workers included. By any measure that includes the ability of its society to use its weaponry, Libya is vastly over-armed.

Why, then, this extraordinary and costly stockpile of seemingly unusable weapons? Two common explanations can be set aside. First, evidence does not support the hypothesis that the excessive armament represents a planned Soviet arsenal strategically placed for Soviet use in a complaisant North African country. Libya paid hard currency for this material, which even Qadhafi would not likely do on behalf of the Soviets. Until recently, the stockpiled material has not been stored under anything like the conditions the Soviet army requires. (Reports abound of rockets, whose guidance mechanisms are sensitive to heat, being stored in the open in desert areas.) Because of inferior conditions, much of the material may not be immediately operational; indeed, some of it may now be well past any use.

Neither does evidence support the hypothesis that the Soviets have intentionally sold the Libyans shoddy equipment without spare parts, thus requiring multiple units for eventual cannibalization of needed parts. The scale of the buildup surpasses even what would be required for a full-scale repair-through-cannibalization program. Furthermore, interviews with knowledgeable persons who inspected the Libyan arsenal captured by the Chadians at Ouadi Doum in March 1987, confirm that the warehouses held full complements of spares, repair tools, and manuals. In short, while no doubt willing to sell the maximum to a naively enthusiastic buyer with ready cash, the Soviets appear to have played fair with what they have sold.

Rather, the scale of hardware purchases would appear to be dictated ultimately by the improbable scale of Libya's foreign policy ambitions, including the presumption that the Libyan Jamahiriya is merely the center of a much larger nation. At the most ambitious level, the armory is scaled for the whole *umma*, to be used in its worldwide battle against Zionism, imperialism, and their agents. At a level only slightly more realistic, the armory would be used in conjunction with the "revolutionary program of total mobilization" called for in the People's Congress of 1983 that would ultimately lead to abolishing the army and replacing it with a totally militarized society (*Military Powers* 1987, 60). Meanwhile, and much closer to reality, the huge stockpile can be used to ship supplies to friendly movements and revolutions in need. Indeed, the ability to provide such arms is a useful adjunct to standard Libyan foreign policy. Such transfers are not without costs, however. Neighbors object, and one such un-authorized transfer of Soviet equipment to Iran is reported to have seriously upset Moscow (Harris 1986, 98). Finally, one must take into account the possibility that when petrodollars seemed unlimited, buying and storing more and more arms may have seemed the easiest and least politically disruptive action the government could take on behalf of the elusive revolution. In this sense, stockpiling arms may be a substitute for more meaningful action.

The Libyan military claims something on the order of one hundred thousand troops, in-cluding auxiliary units and reserves on active service at any one time.[1] As a primarily conscript army, in most ways it reflects the larger society from which it stems. Most of its members will have urban or peri-urban backgrounds. Very few will be from the Saharan oases, or descended from groups having a recent military tradition. More than 80 percent of Libyans live in the coastal or highland areas; the more fractious Saharan tribes and other groups associated with the Senussi are considered untrustworthy (Harris 1986, 33). Though well-schooled by Third World standards, few of the soldiers will have technical training or much mechanical experience. As Dyer notes, "Libya still has difficulty in finding an adequate num-ber of recruits with suitable backgrounds for mastering complex weapons systems" (1983, 370).

The more technologically complex the equipment, the more the mismatch between men and material becomes apparent. The central air defense system provides a good example. The Libyan Arab Air Defense Command (LAADC) has the task of providing air defense for the principal Libyan cities and coastal economic installations. It is well-equipped with standard Soviet missile systems, including the long-range SA-5 and the SA-9, of which Libya was only the second country outside the Warsaw Pact (after Syria) to take delivery (Bermudez 1986, 880-81). It has been estimated that adequate operation of the LAADC systems would require between fifteen thousand and eighteen thousand persons, of which a maximum of two thou-sand could reasonably be expected to be foreigners. The number of Libyans actually available for service in the LAADC seems only to lie in the six to nine thousand range, however, with the result that the air defense system remains seriously understaffed and operating below 60 percent of its equipment potential. This has apparently resulted in a situation whereby the LAADC has opted to deploy a large number of SAM brigades that are understaffed and at a marginal level of operational readiness, rather than a small number of fully-operationally ready SAM brigades (ibid., 881).

Similar difficulties arise with the other technologically complex branches of the military, the air force and the navy. The Libyan air force has some 700 aircraft and 245 helicopters, not counting those used for training, but only about 100 trained Libyan pilots. (Algeria, by comparison, has a pilot/aircraft ratio of 1/1.5.) Libya's solution has been to hire foreign pilots, perhaps 350 of them, principally Soviets, Poles, East Germans, Syrians, and Palestinians. Indeed, no Libyans are thought to be capable as yet of flying some of the more advanced equipment, like the 60 MiG-25s (*Military Powers* 1987, 67).

Libya's principal naval weapons—for use, in theory, to enforce the "line of death" that Qadhafi in his imagination has stretched across the Gulf of Sirte—are its six Soviet-built "Foxtrot" class diesel-electric-powered attack submarines. "The Libyan 'Foxtrots,' however, apparently rarely go to sea. It is extremely doubtful that all six boats are operational" (Isby 1986, 882). The principal problem, once again, is that of trained manpower, both for maintenance and operations. Submarine expertise is hard to come by on the international labor market, and it is not at all clear that the Soviet Union would care to have its own citizens directly involved in confrontations with the Sixth Fleet in international waters.

As with the Libyan civilian economy, the military can go into the international marketplace to hire needed skills to compensate for domestic lacks and the brain-drain in the form of Libyans sent abroad for study who never come back. There are particular problems associated with hiring skilled military personnel, however. Hired hands are not as likely to be as reliable as comparably-skilled nationals in front-line situations of actual combat. Unless sent as part of a regular expeditionary force under their own national command, which is not the case in Libya, foreigners may be understandably reluctant to take an aggressive approach to their craft when danger looms. Aside from what their own common sense may tell them, skilled foreigners from politically-significant countries are likely to be under stern injunction to avoid being captured or killed and identified. This should limit their combat effectiveness, particularly for service outside Libyan territory, narrowly construed.

Such political constraints do not apply to the rank-and-file end of military recruiting. Indeed, more than just a necessity to alleviate manpower shortages, recruitment of foreign nationals into Libya's Islamic Legion has been presented as a political demonstration of the Jamahiriya's international vocation and revolutionary appeal. Originally slated to be a well-armed elite force, seven thousand strong, recruited throughout the *umma* and commanded by Libyan and Palestinian officers, its present reality falls far short of that ideal. Rather than being made up of dedicated volunteers drawn by the spirit of adventure and inspired by the ideals of the Green Book, most members of the Islamic Legion appear to be among life's losers, poor boys from Saharan and Sahelian populations who had hoped to find remunerative civilian employ at Libyan farms or factories. Brought by recruiters along the "Qadhafi Trail" across southern Algeria, or simply seized on the streets of Tripoli, they are threatened with imprisonment and expulsion without papers if they do not accept military service. In effect, they are press-ganged in pure eighteenth-century style.[2] Given the most summary military instruction—and evidently no political indoctrination—the foreign contingents are then sent into the most exposed positions. In contrast to the case of senior military technicians from significant countries, the death or capture of these poor unknowns is likely to disturb Tripoli less than the equivalent loss of Libyans. For all that, the Islamic Legion can hardly be counted as a significant addition to Libya's military capacities.

Whatever the utility of foreign specialists in defensive and support roles, the basic ability of the Libyan army to put its hardware to effective use will be determined by the fighting qualities of the Libyans themselves. The Libyan manpower pool could potentially provide satisfactory raw material for an effective army, assuming that it were well-trained and well-commanded, that military doctrine were adapted to the task at hand, and that its morale received support from within the army and from society at large. None of these conditions is adequately met.

The fundamental problem appears to be a political one. The regime fears and distrusts the military, and thus imposes conditions on it that limit its effectiveness. Whereas at the time of the Free Officers' coup the military was seen in Nasserian terms as the repository of martial and civic virtue, it is now perceived as the prime source of danger to the regime—and with reason. Harris counts "fifteen serious assassination attempts . . . on Qadhafi since 1976, almost all conducted by the military" (Harris 1986, 76). The top military positions are all in the hands of Qadhafi loyalists, relatives, and the faithful remnant of the original RCC. Below these central positions, the military—like other parts of Libyan society—is characterized by "overlapping lines of authority and shadowy chains of command" (ibid., 72). The Popular Resistance Forces, the Security and Military Intelligence Services, Revolutionary Committees, and the special Deterrent Battalion all attempt to oversee the regular military and one another. As documents captured from the Libyan garrison at Fada (Chad) reveal, these structures are operative right down to field unit level (Soudan 1987b, 13). In at least some circumstances, the rule seems to be that those controlling the weapons will not also control access to the ammunition. At the time of the April 1986 U.S. air strike, outraged military personnel attacked revolutionary committee leaders who controlled anti-aircraft ammunition and were unavailable to release their supplies in time (Harris 1986, 81).

Security concerns affect training as well. Regular units are sent only on very limited field training exercises, and there are virtually no full-scale maneuvers with weapons and ammunition. Troops thus get little preparation for the shock and noisy confusion of actual battle. Militia units receive little more than the most basic training with personal weapons, and reservists are given little continuing training, but both are likely to be posted alongside regular troops in combat units for reasons of political security. In such circumstances, rotation of reserves and militia into front-line units will serve less to raise the level of the part-timers than to lower further the combat readiness of regular troops.

Standard Libyan military doctrine—choice of weapons mix, tactics, and command procedures—is derived from the Soviet. Combat doctrine is ground-warfare oriented. It emphasizes tight control over land forces dominated by armor and well-positioned artillery, with ground-based missiles and anti-aircraft guns as prime protection against air attack. The emphasis is on careful preparation, centralized command, with little initiative given to local and small-unit commanders. In the hands of the Libyans, this doctrine is likely to be applied with little imagination, as even senior field commanders will fear being reported for unorthodox behavior that might appear threatening. At lower ranks such lack of innovation is likely to be reinforced by the generally quiescent patience of the larger Libyan society aware that "lack of incentive is rewarded and initiative . . . can mean trouble" (ibid., 40). Such stolid schoolbook preparation is likely to be most effective against an opponent who also goes by the book, or against an inexperienced rabble that cracks under battle conditions.

Morale factors, as always, are difficult to judge. On the material level, the Libyan military appears to make a serious effort to provide its troops in the field with the basic comforts of home. Interviews with Chadians who lived through the Libyan occupation of Abeche, 1980–81, report on the (by local standards) luxurious self-sufficiency of the occupying army. "Rather like the Americans in Vietnam, but the Libyans didn't share their chewing gum," reported one informant. The principal Libyan base in northern Chad, Ouadi Doum, provided air conditioning (at least for the officers), piped-in music, sports facilities, an extensive sick-bay, an irrigated wheat field, and even a Jersey cow for the commander's milk.

Such material comforts are not enough to assure good morale, much less victory in battle. There must, additionally, be some sense of compelling loyalty to the military, whether as a whole or, more probably, as the individual unit, and also some sense of dedication to the military's mission. Evidence on the former, most of it quite negative, comes from defectors and prisoners of war seized by the Chadians. Such evidence must be taken with a fistful of salt; those with high morale do not defect, and prisoners of war—particularly those held by the Chadians—have little to gain by proclaiming their enthusiasm for service in Qadhafi's army. Still, there is no evidence to support a claim that Libyan expeditionary forces are a particularly happy band. Other evidence suggests, logically enough, that morale varies greatly with the nature of the mission. Attacks on the Libyan homeland, whether that of the Egyptians in 1977 or that of the Americans in 1986, produce a rally-around-the-green-flag response, though not necessarily superb military performance (Dyer 1983, 371; Anderson 1987, 86-87). Dangerous missions abroad in pursuit of Qadhafi's exalted visions, on the other hand, seem to inspire little societal support, and such attitudes appear to be reflected within the military. A telling measure of disillusionment is contained in the thirty-three "Resolutions on Chad" formulated by the People's Committees of Libya and broadcast over Radio Tripoli on February 26, 1987. Eight of these resolutions indicated serious morale problems in the army and in society at large. They included such injunctions as: "Set up committees composed of police and militia elements to bring back armed forces deserters to their posts"; "Forbid listening to enemy radio stations"; and "Give one last chance to reservists who have not answered the call, and make available to them the necessary transportation." The picture is not one of a society or a military establishment aching for battle.

Performance

The ultimate test of the military, of course, is how it performs on the battlefield. Measuring performance, however, is not as straightforward as it might seem. One must take into account not just whether an engagement was won or lost, but the conditions of winning or losing— whether the outcome of the conflict served larger policy goals, whether even a clear loss obliged an opponent to take such extreme and costly measures as to have paid an unacceptable price not obvious from the immediate results. Even more difficult to judge is how successful is the passive use of the military: as a deterrent force keeping the opposition from doing something it might otherwise have done against your interests; or as an intimidating force, posing enough of a threat that the opponent yields to your wishes without a fight. We shall briefly examine four principal engagements of the Libyan military: defense against Egyptian attack in 1977; defense against United States attack in 1986; the Uganda expedition to bolster Idi Amin in 1979; and the long attempt to control Chad, from 1973 to 1987.

Egypt

On July 21, 1977, following an extended period of tension, which featured Libya's increasingly blatant denunciations of Sadat and attempts to destabilize the Numeiry regime in Sudan, Egyptian forces attacked Libya. More of a punitive raid than a full-scale invasion, Egyptian armored forces came across the border along the coastal road, penetrating some fifteen miles, while paratroopers struck further inland. At the same time aircraft attacked the main Libyan interceptor base at El Adem, near Tobruk. This attack did little damage except, evidently, to radar installations, but the airstrike was renewed on the twenty-third and this time caught the Libyan Mirages on the ground. The next day both sides accepted a cease-fire hastily worked out by the Palestine Liberation Organization's Yassir Arafat. Against negligible Egyptian losses, Libya lost between ten and twenty Mirages and thirty to forty tanks. Its Ninth Armored Battalion was put out of action (Dyer 1983, 371).

Libya's military performance was thoroughly unimpressive. Despite clear warnings from the Soviets that the Egyptians were likely to attack, the Libyans were caught napping and clearly got the worst of the fighting. It should be noted, however, that the Libyan response was sufficient to deny Egypt a larger political victory. However unimpressively, the army stood and fought and became a rallying point for popular sentiment. Buoyed by a surge of popular patriotic feeling, the regime mobilized the Militia, distributed arms and uniforms profligately, and emerged politically strengthened from the whole episode. The Egyptians noted the countereffect of their actions. In subsequent periods of tension between the two countries, such as the one sparked off by an Egyptian sting operation in November 1984 that tricked Qadhafi into bragging about an assassination plot in Cairo that he mistakenly thought had succeeded, Egyptian troops have rattled their armor near the Libyan border, but have gone no further when Libyans have mobilized. Nor did Egypt respond to more recent United States urgings that it seize any one of a number of available pretexts to launch another punitive attack that might give the United States reason to intervene.

With the greater part of the Libyan army concentrated in the eastern half of the country, from Tobruk and Benghazi to Kufra and Ma'aten es Sarra in the south, the Libyans have succeeded, however inefficiently and inelegantly, in deterring subsequent Egyptian military expeditions. One may guess that such deterrence will hold up to the point at which Egypt would have truly compelling reasons of its own state security to attack, coupled with a willingness to accept the costs of sustaining action long enough to force political changes. Such a level of deterrence, while hardly glorious, does effectively serve the regime's purposes.

United States

The United States has provoked three direct military confrontations with Libya and inflicted superior punishment in all three cases. In August 1981, U.S. naval maneuvers, which featured air attack runs toward Libyan targets with the airplanes veering off just short of national airspace, enticed Libyan jets to fire a missile in the direction of the incoming planes. The Americans returned fire and destroyed two SU-22 interceptors.

On March 24–25, 1986, American naval maneuvers inside the Gulf of Sirte drew Libyan fire. Surface ships and airplanes attacked four Libyan attack vessels, sinking two of them, and seriously damaged ground-based radar and missile sites. "The LAADC is known to have fired at least five SA-5 and one SA-2 missiles, none of which hit their targets" (Bermudez 1986, 881). There were no American losses, and Libya declined American enticements to renew the engagements.

On April 15, 1986, the United States launched a carefully-planned and coordinated air strike on Libyan coastal areas. Altogether thirty naval attack and support planes were launched from two carriers in the Mediterranean, and twenty-nine F-111 Air Force bombers took off from their base in Britain. The raid did serious damage to military targets and narrowly missed killing Qadhafi, whose death was apparently the principal aim of the raid (Hersh 1987). The bombs also did substantial collateral damage to a residential neighborhood of Tripoli, including to the French embassy. Following the fighting of March 24–25, the LAADC had redeployed a number of its mobile units to plug gaps that had become apparent. While initially slow in responding on April 15, the LAADC managed to put up a high volume of anti-aircraft artillery fire and launched large numbers of SA-2/3/6/8 and French-made Crotale missiles. The Americans lost one F-111. As Anderson notes, "Libyan defenses proved embarrassingly porous, particularly in view of their enormous cost" (1987, 86).

"Unimpressive" would seem to be a mild epithet for these examples of Libyan military performance. Such a summary judgement may miss, however, some important if less obvious ways in which Libyan military power has served to deter hostile action and permitted the regime to turn what should be an embarrassment to its own advantage.

Porous defenses are not the same as no defenses, particularly in the minds of those who must plan and participate in an attack. The Reagan administration had wanted to use military confrontation as a pretext for a bombing raid in January 1986, following terrorist airport bombings in Vienna and Rome on December 27 that the administration preferred to blame on Libyan agents. As Hersh recounts the event, however, the Joint Chiefs of Staff were concerned about the threat to the attacking airplanes from "500 Libyan fighters." They argued that an attack would require at least three carrier task forces, while even with leaves cancelled and fleet deployment schedules disrupted, not all of that number could be on station off Libya before late March (Hersh 1987). In effect, the deterrent effect of the Libyan arsenal alone was enough to convince the American Joint Chiefs that they had to delay attacking until they could deploy one of the greatest concentrations of naval power since the Battle of Midway, at least $45 billion of floating and flying hardware, not excluding attack-submarine escorts to deal with any of the Libyan Foxtrots that might try for a lucky shot. A signals intelligence satellite was redeployed from its normal station over Poland and the Ukraine to monitor Libyan communications. (It remained over Libya long enough to miss the communications emanating from the Chernobyl disaster.) No wonder that when Qadhafi did not rise to the bait offered in March, the third carrier was sent home and the provocative exercises in the Gulf of Sirte ended early.

Concern over taking losses contributed to the complex design of the April 15 raid, and determined the decision to fly F-111s twenty-eight hundred nautical miles from their bases in Britain. Concern over missile defenses meant that the raid would have to be conducted at very low level (75 meters) and high speed (450 knots). Only the F-111 had the equipment to assure reasonable accuracy under those conditions. The one F-111 that did not return to its base was lost either to anti-aircraft artillery fire or as a result of pilot disorientation or systems failure, the likelihood of which would be reinforced by the length and complexity of the mission. However substandard and inefficient the defensive performance of the Libyans turned out to be, its equipment was sufficient to deter anything but the most determined, complex, and expensive attack from a major power.[3]

Once again the political effect of the American attacks was to produce a patriotic upsurge of domestic support for the Qadhafi regime, and a year later to allow Qadhafi to distract his people's attention from his forces' debacle in Chad by a vast celebration of the first anniversary of the "great victory of the Jamahiriya over imperialism" (Anderson 1987; see also, Frachon 1987).

Uganda

In January 1972, a year after seizing power from Milton Obote, one of Israel's staunchest supporters in Africa, Idi Amin Dada made a combined religio-political pilgrimage to Mecca, to Nasser's tomb, and to Tripoli. His formal break with Israel two months later was viewed in Tripoli as a major triumph for the new revolutionary diplomacy, and Libya contributed oil, arms, and occasional pay for the Ugandan army to encourage Idi Amin in his path. In September 1972, Qadhafi sent four hundred Libyan troops to help quiet a brief period of unrest, and in March 1977, proudly proclaimed "Whoever declares war on President Amin declares it on Libya" (Otayek 1986). As Idi Amin's regime grew more and more disorganized, Libyan support became more and more essential, and it was maintained even after other opportunistic supporters like the Soviet Union quietly withdrew.

Libya's armed intervention came in response to an open invasion of Uganda by Tanzanian People's Defense Forces and Ugandan oppositionists in the opening days of 1979. The invasion was itself a riposte to Amin's imprudent and ramshackle attempt to seize the Kagera salient in northern Tanzania. Libya's first reaction was an attempt to mediate the dispute, but when this was rejected by Tanzanian President Nyerere, Qadhafi seems to have found himself obliged to make good on his earlier boasts. With minimal consultation and preparation, a force of two thousand men was sent off to save Idi Amin's regime. The expeditionary force was well equipped with T-54 tanks, armored personnel carriers, multiple rocket launchers, supported by MIGs and at least one TU-22 bomber.

The Libyans' first major engagement came at Lukaya in southern Uganda. An initial rocket barrage panicked the Tanzanians, who fled into the swamps. If at this moment the Libyans and their Ugandan allies had pursued aggressively, they might have pushed the main Tanzanian force out of Uganda. Instead, they halted their advance and the next day at dawn were routed by a Tanzanian counterattack. The Tanzanians counted some four hundred enemy dead, half of them Libyans.[4] The Libyan-Ugandan forces never recovered the initiative, and the Libyans shared fully in the organizational collapse of Amin's army. Speaking no Swahili and very little English, the Libyan soldiers easily lost their way and were picked off by civilians as well as the invading forces. Most of the sophisticated equipment sent to Uganda quickly fell into Tanzanian hands. The one serious attempt to use Libyan air power, a bombing raid on the Tanzanian city of Mwanza, missed its target, but did serious damage to the gazelles in a nearby game park. Libyan losses were estimated by the Tanzanians at six hundred killed; fifty-nine prisoners survived the war, eventually to be sent home via Algerian good offices.[5] Libyan losses would have been much higher, had not Nyerere ordered his troops to leave an escape corridor so that the Libyans could fall back to Jinja and then informed Qadhafi where to send the transports to pick them up.

Considering that the Tanzanian People's Defense Force was something less than a military juggernaut and was operating far from its home base, eating off the land like a seventeenth-century army, the Libyan performance was disastrous. The reasons seem fairly straightforward. First, it must be recognized that the task was a difficult one. Facing what eventually grew to a forty-five-thousand-man invasion force, two thousand Libyans could have usefully stiffened a well-organized Ugandan army or done rear-guard duty to free local troops for fighting on their home ground. Idi Amin's disorganized forces would have required much more than that, however, to withstand the Tanzanians. With a rabble like Amin's men as allies, a two-thousand-man intervention force would have had to consist of elite troops capable of rallying and leading the Ugandans, while efficiently exploiting their own superior equipment. The Libyans were far from an elite force. As prisoner interviews indicated, they were a mixture of regulars, militia, and hapless Islamic Legionnaires low in skills and motivation. Some claimed they had never been told they were being sent to a combat area. With poor communications and no intelligence system of their own, the Libyans were quite literally lost once their Ugandan allies abandoned them. The only bright spot in the record is the performance of the logistics system, which with reasonable effectiveness delivered the men and equipment at considerable distance from Libya itself.

The biggest failure was the decision to intervene under such unpromising circumstances. Qadhafi appears to have taken the decision rashly out of desperation to avert the collapse of his most promising African ally (Otayek 1986, 162–63).[6] The intervention was hastily prepared, and once the troops were committed little was done to back them up. Once the mistake was made of not following up the initial success at Lukaya, the Libyans would have had to mount a much larger effort, in effect virtually to replace the Ugandans, not just support them. Without firm local allies, a two-thousand-man force could not prevail, and most of their fancy equipment ended up in the hands of the enemy.

Chad

If Uganda represented a far-flung venture, lightly undertaken and just as easily regretted, Chad represents a major, long-term commitment in a contiguous area with which Libya has many historic and ethnic links. As Qadhafi likes to describe it, Chad is Libya's natural hinterland. The confusions over the unratified Laval-Mussolini treaty of 1935 additionally gave the Libyans some tenuous claim on a slice of land within Chad, the Aouzou strip, which even King Idriss attempted to press. Finally, Chad is, even by African standards, exceptionally poor and from 1965 on has been prey to such rampant factionalism that there has been no dearth of ardent solicitations from ambitious and opportunistic Chadians for the Libyans to get involved. Unlike the Ugandan intervention, haste and ignorance of local conditions do not explain poor performance.

Libya's intervention in Chad has had its elements of success. The occupation of the Aouzou strip in 1973 was essentially uncontested, if never publicly accepted by the Chadian government of Tombalbaye. With the strip under direct administration as an integral part of Libya, the Libyans constructed, in 1977, a major military base that straddles the internationally recognized border between the two countries. South of the Aouzou strip, and prior to 1987, Libya's military engagement on behalf of one or another faction has usually been decisive unless directly opposed by major deployment of French combat forces. Throughout most of this period, the Libyan military presence has been sufficient to raise the costs high enough that the French have been deterred from doing more than protecting the sub-Saharan part of the country, in effect leaving the northern two-fifths under Libyan suzerainty (Spartacus 1985). Indeed, until 1987, Chad could be said to represent the closest thing to a "success" for Libya's African policy (Otayek 1986, 177). Most of the fruits of this success have been jeopardized by Qadhafi's erratic policies, however, and quite possibly definitively lost on the battlefield during 1987.

Before turning to the humiliating defeats of 1987, it is worth looking at some of the earlier Libyan military successes. The first major commitment of Libyan force in central Chad came in the fight for the capital, Ndjamena, in 1980. Libyan forces intervened to support so-called Transitional National Unity Government (GUNT), or more precisely the allied factional armies of Goukouni Oueddeye and Abdel Kader Kamougué, against the *Forces Armées du Nord* (FAN) of Hissene Habré, a staunch opponent of Libyan aims in Chad. France, which officially recognized the GUNT although some of its military sympathized with Habré, stayed on the sidelines. The Libyan commitment was a major one, and its logistics were impressive. Setting up a base and airstrip sixty kilometers north of the capital, the Libyans brought in two to three thousand men, armored personnel carriers, heavy artillery, and at least one helicopter by air, and sent T-54/55 tanks overland from Aouzou, a three-week journey (*Jeune Afrique* Dec. 24, 1980; *Le Monde* Dec. 17, 1980; *L'Express* Dec. 27, 1980). The weight of equipment and firepower, which Habré's forces could not match, was decisive. The many foreign observers watching the battle from the Cameroonian side of the river estimated the number of artillery shells fired in the culminating three days of the battle at ten thousand, the great majority of them by the Libyans and their allies. Habré's forces had no armor (though one ingenious engineer constructed a "tank" by attaching metal plates to a bulldozer and mounting a mortar on it) and only a scattering of anti-tank grenade launchers captured from their opponents. They finally recognized the inevitable and, under the cover of darkness, withdrew what was left of their forces.

Despite contemporary press reports that credited Libyan troops with the victory, subsequent interviews suggest that in fact most of the actual fighting was done by Libya's Chadian allies, experienced and determined combatants used to battle conditions. The decisive Libyan contribution was the delivery of hardware. Nonetheless, the collective Libyan-GUNT forces looked impressive. A French military observer of the battle calculated that if France were to try to chase the Libyans out of Ndjamena, it would require "two weeks, the use of Cameroonian territory to support the attack, good cooperation from key Chadians, and 5,000 men" (Dumoulin 1980). The Libyans and their allies made one serious mistake: They did not seriously pursue the remnants of Habré's forces, which succeeded in making the long march across the breadth of Chad to safety in Numeiry's Sudan.

What they had won on the battlefield, the Libyans and their allies proceeded to lose in the pursuit of international glory and factional advantage. To considerable international surprise, Qadhafi acceded to a request from the Organization of African Unity (OAU) that Libya withdraw its forces from Chad, to be replaced by the OAU peace-keeping force. At the time, Qadhafi was ardently seeking the OAU presidency and the distinction that goes with it of being Africa's spokesman for a year. His willingness to withdraw the troops may well have been abetted by French assurances that they had no intention of intervening against the government the Libyans had helped install in Ndjamena and by the cost of maintaining the expeditionary force, reckoned at $2 million a day (Otayek 1986, 197). The withdrawal was accomplished within three weeks and with great logistic efficiency. The Libyans left behind an administration in shambles, however, in part the result of Libyan playing one Chadian faction against another to maximize their own power (Buijtenhuijs 1984). Meanwhile Habré's FAN had received enough clandestine arms and money from the United States, Egypt, and, quite likely, Saudi Arabia, to begin the reconquest of power from its base in the Sudan. The FAN simply walked around the installations manned by the OAU force and with surprising ease chased the GUNT from Ndjamena. They declared Chad's Third Republic on June 7, 1982, and occupied the principal centers south of the Tibesti mountains, where the GUNT took refuge.

Qadhafi's efforts at becoming OAU president having come to nothing, Libya reengaged in Chad with another major logistic effort to support the GUNT. The key encounter took place in the northern oasis of Faya-Largeau, Habré's hometown, in August 1983. With reequipped GUNT forces attacking on the ground, Libya kept up steady aerial bombing and strafing attacks launched from their base at Aouzou. As Habré's troops had neither their own air support nor effective anti-aircraft weapons, they were eventually forced to retreat.[7] Again, the Libyans and their allies failed to pursue and destroy the retreating enemy forces.

The renewed Libyan support for the GUNT was decisive and would no doubt have allowed them to install their protégés once more in Ndjamena, had not France intervened with a major military effort of its own. Under considerable pressure from its African allies, and a public injunction from Ronald Reagan that "France assume its historic responsibilities" in Chad, the government of François Mitterrand mounted Operation Manta (Stingray).[8] This force of thirty-five hundred professional soldiers backed with airpower, was deployed along first the fifteenth and then the sixteenth parallel, rough dividing lines between Saharan Chad and what the French have historically called *le Tchad utile*. The French government clearly had no intention of doing more than protecting the southern portion of the country.[9] Using French forces to chase the Libyans out of Chad was presumed to have required a massive effort, well beyond anything that would have been economically or politically supportable.

Under these circumstances, Mitterrand was only too pleased on September 17, 1984, to strike a deal with Qadhafi providing for the "total and simultaneous" withdrawal of French and Libyan forces from Chad. In the event, only the French left; the Libyans stayed, constructed a major airbase at Ouadi Doum in northeastern Chad, occupied the principal Saharan oases south of the Aouzou strip, and prepared their allies for further adventures. When in February 1986, the GUNT forces attempted on their own to push south against Habré's forces, with little success, French forces returned to Chad. This time they came in the form of Operation Epervier (Sparrowhawk), to reestablish air cover up to the sixteenth parallel, in effect to keep the Libyans from using south of that line the airpower that had provided their decisive military edge heretofore. The ground fighting was left to Habré's men, now re-equipped and reorganized as the Forces de l'Armée Nationale Tchadienne (FANT), who on their own repulsed the GUNT attacks and in March chased one column 150 kilometers north of the 16th parallel—to the great distress of the French.

Before the year was out, Libya's Chad venture began to fall apart. The collapse began with the aggravation of the GUNT's endemic factionalism by frustration at the previous offensive's failure and by Libyan manipulation of differences. In June, Kamougué publicly quit the GUNT, where he was already a spent force. More seriously, open fighting broke out between the largely Arab *Conseil Démocratique Révolutionnaire* (CDR) faction and Goukouni's largely Toubou group. Libya threw its support to the CDR, and as things further degenerated, put Goukouni under house arrest in Tripoli, where he was wounded in an armed scuffle with Libyan guards. Faced with this, on October 22, Goukouni's field commanders agreed to a ceasefire with the FANT and joint action against the Libyans. This deprived the Libyans of two to three thousand experienced desert fighters, but even more important, of men who knew the difficult terrain and the even more difficult local populations in the Chadian north.

At the same time, Hissene Habré had with great skill conducted a national reconciliation campaign that by mid-1986 had induced or intimidated most active internal opponents into the governmental fold. In response to the February attacks, French and American military aid to the FANT had increased substantially; American aid in 1986 totalled some $25 million, and French aid was easily twice that, exclusive of the cost of Epervier. Its principal goal was to equip the FANT to use more effectively, and over greater distances, a basic modus operandi they themselves had earlier used to great success (Spartacus 1985, 74–76). In this, the core weapon system is a four-wheel drive Toyota pickup truck, or jeep equivalent, with a recoilless rifle, multiple grenade launcher, or anti-tank missile mounted or carried by footsoldiers crowded in the back, and driven at eighty to one hundred kilometers an hour across the desert. Able to go over virtually any terrain, the Toyotas attack in swarms, moving faster than armor can traverse their weapons and closing so quickly and tightly with the enemy as to make aerial and artillery bombardment impracticable. Light, shoulder-fired anti-aircraft missiles are carried as the principal means of fending off air attack or keeping it at such a high altitude that bombing is inaccurate.[10]

In December, encouraged quietly by the Americans and not discouraged by French misgivings, the FANT began moving north across the sixteenth parallel. At four in the morning of January 2, 1987, the Chadians attacked a major Libyan garrison at Fada, the principal town in the Ennedi region, and by noon had overwhelmed the command post. The Libyan commander escaped by air at the last possible moment (and for his pains was court-martialed and condemned to death when he got home). Few others made it out. Of the 1,222-man garrison, 784 were killed and 81 captured. The FANT counted about 50 killed (18 officially) and 100 wounded.[11] Over the next three months the FANT continued their march north, climaxed by a major battle for the heavily defended airbase at Ouadi Doum on March 22–23. By June, the Libyans had abandoned or been chased out of all but isolated pockets in the Tibesti, south of the Aouzou strip.

Total Libyan losses out of the 15–20,000 deployed in Chad were 4,069 killed and 890 captured, in just three months of operations. The Libyans lost vast amounts of equipment, much of it abandoned untouched. The FANT added a total of 257 Toyotas to its inventory and huge quantities of arms, whether directly useful or not. Among the latter—in addition to the tracked armored personnel carriers and T-55 tanks that the Chadians disdain as clumsy iron coffins— are such technically complex items as mobile radar systems, SAM-6 and -13 air defense systems, and an intact MI-24 helicopter, over whose custody Chad's French and American allies carried on an indecorous wrangle.

Three factors explain Libya's military debacle in Chad. Pride of place must be given to the extraordinary fighting abilities of the FANT and their Goukounist allies. The FANT commander, Hassane Djamouss, certainly deserves to be counted among history's geniuses of desert warfare, for making the most recent application of the classic lessons taught by Rommel and Leclerc—move fast and concentrate firepower quickly. The credit must be spread through all ranks. The FANT are an extremely motivated and individually courageous group, with individual units able to take appropriate action on their own—as was demonstrated at Ouadi Doum, where the four senior commanders were all knocked out of action before the end of the battle. It should be noted also that while northerners play a particularly important role because of their local knowledge, the FANT is in every sense a national army in its makeup. However limited their military repertoires may be, the Chadians' mastery of rapid attacks in the desert is unmatched.

A second factor is the help that Chadians got from their friends, especially the French and Americans. The supplies and equipment for long-range transport, destroying tanks, and fending off air attack were absolutely essential. Without them, Habré's forces would have suffered the fate they met in Ndjamena in 1980 and Faya in 1983. French and American weapons in Chadian hands tipped the balance against Soviet hardware in Libyan hands.[12]

The third factor has to be Libyan military incompetence, plain and simple. This has been demonstrated at all levels. At the base of the military hierarchy, the ordinary soldiers appear as poorly motivated as they are badly trained. In battle after battle equipment is abandoned by troops in flight at the first shock of attack. "Key in the ignition and motor running is the way we find the tanks," said one FANT officer. A significant percentage of Libyan casualties at Ouadi Doum appear to have been caused by soldiers fleeing across the minefields set to protect them from attack. At higher levels, basic tactics are stereotyped, sluggish, and invariant. Tanks are dug in or deployed in regular columns, which the Chadians attack broadside by roaring Toyotas. Infantry is shut up in APCs, which are easily destroyed (fifty-four at Ouadi Doum), instead of being deployed on foot to protect the tanks. Static defenses are laid out according to classic principles, but basic life-preserving discipline, like keeping alert watch, seems deficient. (At Fada, the Chadians broke through five defensive perimeters in succession and still caught headquarters staff asleep.) On those occasions on which the Libyans meet with some success, they quit when they are safe and fail to follow and destroy the enemy. This pattern at Lukaya in 1979, Ndjamena in 1980, and Faya in 1983 was repeated at Yarda in March 1987, when Libyan tanks and airplanes had a large FANT force trapped in open ground. The Chadians had taken heavy casualties and had virtually run out of ammunition. As their fire slackened, the Libyans broke off the engagement well before dusk, allowing the Chadians to escape.

The logistic services—largely staffed by foreigners?—are the one bright spot in the record. They do deliver enormous stocks of weapons and supplies to the men in the field. But the very abundance of equipment seems counterproductive. It is as if it induces in the military a blind faith in hardware and deep allegiance to an invariant doctrine on how it is to be used, as if equipment and doctrine sufficed to win battles without the intervention of human thought and activity.

Ultimate responsibility for Libya's military failures belongs at the top—and in more than a legal or moral sense. The failures in battle stem from unrealistic policy and inept political performance. The former sets impossible tasks and the latter denies adequate support to the army. The Ugandan expedition was a failure from first conception. Morale—and therefore performance—among troops in Chad has been disastrous, because the regime has no popular support for the endeavor. Most of the problems can be traced to a single political choice: the army is organized to assure one thing before all else, its inability to overthrow the regime. As a result of its overlapping chains of authority, insufficient training, and rotation of command, it is incapable of being an effective fighting force. So long as Qadhafi remains in power, this choice seems unlikely to be changed. To be an effective fighting force, the Libyan military must be reconciled to the government and the government reconciled with its people. Qadhafi's announced solution for this, abolition of the professional army and turning defense over to a *levée en masse* of the citizenry—a modern version of the classic Arab *mehallah*—would hardly accomplish that goal.

In reviewing Libya's military performance, one pleasant irony stands out. The most effective use of the Libyan military is in the passive role of deterring direct attack by the world's great powers, the United States and, in Chad, France. For sound political reasons, these countries are unwilling to risk even a small chance of taking significant losses to counter Libyan actions that, in the final analysis, are no more than annoyances for them. Libyan military power has suffered its greatest humiliation at the hands of one of the weakest and poorest states in the world. For the Chadians, the Libyans represent far more than an annoyance, and to free themselves they have had the courage to attack directly, to risk all—and to puncture the myth of Libya's military power.

NOTES

1. This figure is taken from *Military Powers, The League of Arab States, vol. 1*. (Paris: Société I³C, 1986). The number is greater than other published figures, but seems overall more reliable. It should be treated only as an order of magnitude.

2. A particularly telling account of a group of Mauretanians eventually killed or captured in Chad is by François Soudan (1987a).

3. It should be noted that this was something of an all-Libyan defensive performance. Soviet ships that had been serving as Libya's air defense pickets had withdrawn from their positions near the coast before the raids (*Jane's Defence Weekly*, 739).

4. In what is the best account of the war, Tony Avirgan and Martha Honey point out that at Lukaya only one Libyan prisoner was taken. "More could have been captured instead of shot, but Tanzanian soldiers were in no state of mind to take Libyan prisoners. For days before the battle their political education instructors had been psyching them up by telling them that Arabs were coming back to try to reintroduce slavery" (1982, 91).

5. Contrary to rumor, the prisoners were not held for ransom. Indeed, Qadhafi seemingly evinced little interest in their fate (Avirgan and Honey, 122–23).

6. The Libyan leader subsequently said publicly that he regretted the decision to intervene and that he had been fooled into believing Amin was a "true progressive" (Harris 1986, 105).

7. The FAN had a few shoulder-fired SA-7 missiles they had captured from the GUNT, but according to interviews these had a "nine-out-of-ten misfire rate," perhaps because the Chadians were not properly trained in their use. In addition, the FAN were assisted by a small group of French mercenaries who had American-made Redeye missiles. According to Chadians at the battle, however, the mercenaries were so concerned about their own safety that they were useless.

8. On Manta, see the book by a participant, the pseudonymous Colonel Spartacus (1985). On the French politics of intervention, see Jean François Bayart (1984, esp. 71–84, 99–102, and 110–21).

9. As Colonel Spartacus puts it, "Manta n'est définitivement pas une force offensive destinée à 'casser du Libyen', mais plutôt une espèce de contingent 'casques bleus' fait pour empêcher les deux factions tchadiennes de se battre" (Spartacus 1985, 79).

10. Key equipment added to the FANT arsenal included 106 mm. recoilless rifles, Mk-19 multiple grenade launchers, Milan and LAW anti-tank missiles, as well as American jeeps, French AML armored cars and ACMAT long-distance transport and reconnaissance vehicles, and Redeye anti-aircraft missiles. The Chadians were miffed at not being given the top of the line TOW anti-tank and Stinger anti-aircraft missiles by the Americans in time for their offensives in early 1987, particularly when the former were sold to the Iranians and the latter given to Jonas Savimbi's UNITA. The FANT has ostentatiously preferred the Milan to the LAW and captured Soviet SAM-7-2s to the Redeye. In August, 1987, the United States prepared to ship both TOWs and Stingers to the FANT.

11. The battle at Fada has been well reported by François Soudan (1987b) and Pierre Devoluy (1987).

12. Much has been written about more direct French and American participation in the Chadian victories. Careful inquiries have convinced this writer that such stories are vastly exaggerated. A prime participant is supposedly the French 11th battalion "Choc." The 11th Choc is an intelligence-gathering detachment, which the FANT view with disdain as spies sent to report on their activities. No doubt the French, like the Americans, do share significant intelligence, particularly electronic intercepts, with the Chadians. A rumor repeated in *Jeune Afrique*'s otherwise reliable reporting, to the effect that fifty American staff officers were quartered in Ndjamena, is an absurdity that quite possibly had its origins in Admiral Poindexter's ill-fated campaign of disinformation directed against Qadhafi.

REFERENCES

Anderson, Lisa. 1987. "Libya's Qaddafi: Still in Command?" *Current History* 86, no. 517 (February):65–86.
Avirgan, Tony, and Martha Honey. 1982. *War in Uganda: The Legacy of Idi Amin*. Westport, CT: Lawrence Hill.
Bayart, Jean-François. 1984. *La Politique Africaine de François Mitterrand*. Paris: Karthala.
Bermudez, Joseph S., Jr. 1986. "Libyan SAMs and Air Defences." *Jane's Defence Weekly*, 17 (May):882.
Bessis, Juliette. 1986. *La Libye Contemporaine*. Paris: Karthala.
Buijtenhuijs, Robert. 1984. "Le Frolinat à l'épreuve du pouvoir." *Politique Africaine* 16 (December):19–29.
Devoluy, Pierre. 1987. "Stratégie et tactique des forces armées nationales." *Géopolitique Africaine* 5 (April):33–44.
Dumoulin, Jérôme. 1980. "La Victoire de Kadhafi." *L'Express*, December 27.
Dyer, Gwynne. 1983. "Libya." In *World Armies*, 2d ed., edited by John Keegan, 362–70. Detroit: Gale Research Company.
Frachon, Alain. 1987. "De l'art d'escamoter les réalités gênantes . . . " *Le Monde*, April 21.
Harris, Lillian Craig. 1986. *Libya: Qadhafi's Revolution and the Modern State*. Boulder, CO: Westview Press.
Hersh, Seymour M. 1987. "Target Qaddafi." *The New York Times Magazine*, February 22.
Isby, David C. 1986. "Libyan Submarine Force Poses Limited Threat to Sixth Fleet." *Jane's Defence Weekly*, 17 (May):882.
Jane's Defence Weekly. 1986. 26 (April):739.
Jeune Afrique. 1980. No. 1042, 24 (December).
Military Powers, The League of Arab States. 1987. Vol. 1, 60, 67. Paris: Société I³C.
Otayek, René. 1986. *La Politique africaine de la Libye*. Paris: Karthala.
Soudan, François. 1987a. "La Stupéfiante confession d'un 'mercenaire' de Kaddafi." *Jeune Afrique Magazine*, no. 35 (March):34–39.
———. 1987b. "Les Documents de l'état-major libyen de Fada." *Jeune Afrique*, no. 1366 (March 11):13.
Spartacus, Colonel. 1985. *Opération Manta: Les Documents Secrets*. Paris: Plon.
United States Arms Control and Disarmament Agency. 1985. *World Military Expenditure and Arms Transfers*. Washington, D.C.: Government Printing Office.

Part Two
Contextual Arenas

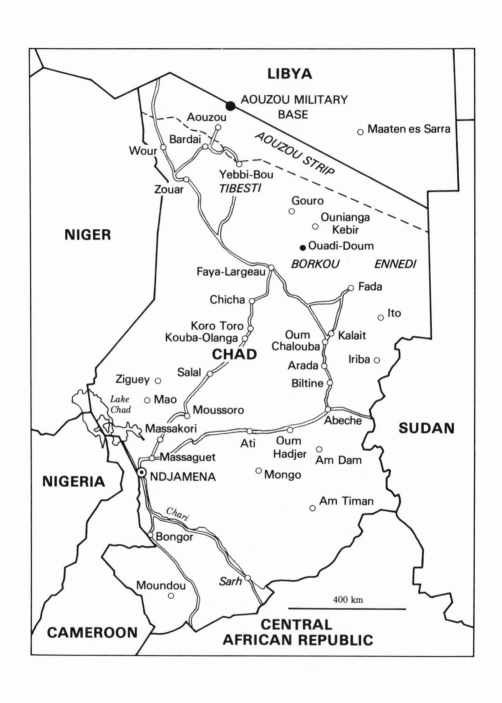

V.

LIBYA IN THE MAGHREB
THE UNION WITH MOROCCO AND
RELATED DEVELOPMENTS

Mark Tessler

The alliance formed between Libya and Morocco in the summer of 1984 constitutes a brief but fascinating chapter in the recent history of North Africa. It also offers an excellent opportunity to assess the relative importance of ideology and political interest in the determination of Libyan foreign policy. The Arab-African Union established between the two countries was in certain respects compatible with ideological positions staked out by the regime in Tripoli. In particular, it furthered the cause of Arab unity to which Muammar Qadhafi had consistently claimed commitment. Indeed, in contrast to other unity schemes in which Libya had been involved, the Arab-African Union was not limited to symbolic pronouncements professing an intention to work for unity in the future. It was marked by the actual creation of federal political institutions, some of which had begun to function by the end of 1984.

More complicated is the possibility that Qadhafi may have seen the union as an opportunity to penetrate Morocco and, thereby, to undermine the Rabat regime from within. Qadhafi and King Hassan of Morocco are political and ideological adversaries of long duration, and the Libyan leader has traditionally regarded Hassan as a reactionary who, along with others, seeks to block the advance of progressive and revolutionary forces in the Arab world. Mindful of growing opposition to Hassan within Morocco itself, Qadhafi may accordingly have entered into a union with Rabat in the hope that he could exploit the king's weaknesses and, in so doing, advance the cause of revolution in the Arab world.

While these considerations may have contributed to Qadhafi's thinking, suggesting that ideological considerations were among the stimuli to which the union was a response, the analysis to follow supports the argument that considerations of national and personal interest provided the principal motivation for the formation of the Arab-African Union. This is particularly clear in the case of Morocco, with Hassan seeking both to contain domestic political and economic pressures and, also, to neutralize challenges in the broader North African political arena. In the Libyan case as well, however, domestic uncertainties and regional challenges occupied a prominent place in Qadhafi's calculations and contributed directly to his interest in a union with Morocco. Indeed, given that the Libyan leader was associating himself with a monarch and a regime he had repeatedly denounced, it may plausibly be argued that the alliance was formed in spite of, rather than in response to, ideological considerations.

The major role played by ideology in the Arab-African Union was its manipulation for political purposes by both Qadhafi and Hassan. Along with direct political and economic benefits, each leader saw the union as providing an opportunity for the manipulation of normative symbols in order to project a particular image. Qadhafi sought to enhance his legitimacy and to reduce his international isolation by showing himself to be an acceptable ally of the more conservative king of Morocco. Hassan, by contrast, sought to present himself as an independent-minded political actor and, through his ties to Qadhafi, to counter the charge that he was in league with the United States and other imperialist powers. Both men sought to project these images for reasons of self-interest, however, and not in response to genuine ideological commitments.

These themes, pursued in the analysis to follow, support the proposition that ideology has been at best a secondary factor in the regional behavior of Qadhafi (and Hassan) and that calculations of personal and national interest are the key to an understanding of the Arab-African Union. The role of ideology should not be dismissed entirely. It is in part for ideological reasons that Qadhafi opposed the overtures toward Israel made by Hassan in 1985 and 1986. Ideological considerations also contributed to the continuation of Qadhafi's international adventurism even after the formation of the Arab-African Union. On balance, however, as argued by Mary-Jane Deeb in chapter 2 of this volume, explanations of Libyan behavior that emphasize the defense and pursuit of political interests are much more compelling than those based on ideology.

Morocco and Libya

On August 13, 1984, King Hassan II of Morocco and Colonel Muammar Qadhafi of Libya announced their intention to form a union between their two countries. This announcement caught many observers by surprise, and Washington in particular was disturbed that Hassan, its faithful North African ally, would accept a union with the unpredictable and militantly anti-Western Qadhafi. Equally astonishing, at least from the U.S. viewpoint, the initiative for the union had in large measure come from the Moroccan king.

The two North African leaders, long bitter rivals, met in Oujda in Western Morocco and decided to form the Arab-African Union. The arrangement they envisioned was a loose confederation rather than a unified state to which participants would surrender sovereignty. Nevertheless, the agreement called for a presidency that would rotate between the two heads of state, an executive committee to carry out presidential directives, a permanent secretariat with offices in each capital, and mutual defense. It was the latter provision that was probably most disturbing to Rabat's Western allies. Not only did it raise questions about possible Moroccan support for Libya's foreign adventures, it also caused concern, especially in Washington, that some of the U.S. arms supplied to Morocco might find their way to Libya.

Implementation of the Oujda agreement involved the establishment of both new political institutions and new economic ties, with cooperation between Morocco and Libya expanding at a slow but steady pace for the next eighteen to twenty months. In December 1984, a delegation of Moroccan parliamentarians, led by speaker Ahmed Osman, spent two days in Tripoli making plans for the federal legislative assembly envisioned in the Oujda accord. These plans had been translated into reality by summer 1985, and Morocco and Libya held the inaugural session of their joint sixty-man legislature in Rabat from July 9 to 12. Hassan himself presided over the session, which, among other things, endorsed Moroccan claims to Ceuta and Melilla, two Spanish enclaves along the Mediterranean coast. Other federal institutions were also established during this period. By the time the union celebrated its first anniversary, a secretariat was functioning in both Rabat and Tripoli, each with its own resident minister and the beginnings of a permanent staff.

Other political institutions proposed for the union developed much more slowly, or in some cases not at all. For example, the Oujda agreement envisioned a unified court of justice and specialized executive councils devoted to defense, political affairs, and economic cooperation, but none of these had come into existence by the fall of 1985. Also, although the countries had agreed on a budget of $60 million to support the work of the union's secretariat, to be shared equally by the two partners, the actual provision of these funds was repeatedly delayed and the full amount was never made available. On the other hand, institution building and cooperation continued, albeit at a modest pace, and to many observers this was at least as significant as the work that lagged or remained undone. The union's assembly set up a number of working committees, which were functioning by the latter part of 1985 or early 1986.

In February 1986, for example, the Committee for Cultural and Technical Action concluded its deliberations and presented its report in Rabat. Among other things, the document envisioned cooperative ventures relating to education, scientific research, information, youth, and sports. It presented detailed proposals in each of these areas and stated that such activities would contribute to the realization of its overall objective, which was the transformation of the Mediterranean into a zone of "peace and cultural communication." The report also called for the creation of common cultural centers in a number of African countries, the stated goals in this case being to encourage the spread of Islam and to fight "Zionist penetration."

Since most of these plans were never implemented, the Committee for Cultural and Technical Action is of interest primarily as an example of institutional development and Moroccan-Libyan consultation. Yet there were also some concrete accomplishments relating to social and, above all, economic cooperation. By the end of 1984, three hundred Moroccan medical personnel had been put to work in Libya, where there are serious shortages in almost all health care fields, and the minister of health in Rabat announced that arrangements had been made to provide Libya with Moroccan pharmaceutical products. In addition, the number of Moroccan workers finding employment in Libya increased steadily during this period and throughout 1985, and in May 1985 Tripoli loaned Rabat $100 million as a sign of friendship between the two countries. Still another area of economic cooperation that benefitted Morocco was Libya's provision of oil at preferential prices. By the end of 1985, Morocco was receiving five hundred thousand tons annually at concessionary rates.

Plans for additional cooperative economic ventures were announced during 1985. In September, the two countries agreed to set up a joint investment company to undertake development projects, with $40 million of capital to be provided in equal shares by the Moroccan Ministry of Finance and the Libyan Foreign Investment Company. In November, the Moroccan and Libyan central banks signed a payments agreement, one purpose of which was to facilitate the transfer of remittances by citizens of one country working in the other. By year's end, Morocco and Libya had also agreed to establish a joint construction company and negotiations concerning yet additional projects were under way as well. Among the other areas in which cooperative action was envisioned were oil exploration and the production of fertilizer and steel.

Statements by Moroccan and Libyan officials during this period further reflected the development of ties between the two countries. In a March 1985 interview, Hassan stressed the importance Morocco attached to the Arab-African Union and stated that it was even possible Rabat and Tripoli would in the future agree to some military cooperation. At a press conference in July, the king coupled praise for the union with support of Libya's position in Chad. He asserted that the majority of Chad's population is Arab and that it might therefore be appropriate for that country to become the third member of the Arab-African Union. Several months later, in October, Libya returned the favor; Foreign Minister Ali Triki endorsed Rabat's goals in the Western Sahara by telling the General Assembly of the United Nations that the solution to the conflict lay in creation of a "union" between Morocco and the Western Sahara.

Modest gestures of mutual good will, occasionally substantive but for the most part symbolic, continued in the months that followed and were visible during the first part of 1986. In February, for example, the secretary of the Libyan General People's Committee paid a visit to Fez and held discussions aimed at increasing economic cooperation. Talks focused in particular on matters relating to labor and employment. There was also a proposal to establish a "twin-city" relationship between Fez and an as yet undetermined town in Libya. In light of these and other developments, *Maroc Soir*, a pro-government newspaper, at the time editorialized that "the example of the Arab-African Union is something to watch. This union of detente, understanding and cooperation is not partial but global. In effect, the economic and social cooperation between the two countries is going forward, and one witnesses daily the consolidation of this union in every sector" (February 9, 1986, p. 1).

These developments, as noted, caught observers in Washington and elsewhere by surprise. Among those whom the Reagan administration blamed for failing to foresee the alliance between Hassan and Qadhafi was Joseph Verner Reed, the American ambassador in Rabat. Reed's glowing praise of the king had given a distorted picture of the Moroccan political scene. Yet Hassan and Qadhafi are strange political bedfellows, and the 1984 Oujda agreement did indeed have an implausible appearance. The radical Libyan leader had repeatedly denounced Hassan as a lackey of imperialism, berating the Moroccan monarch for close ties to the West and for moderation toward Israel. Libya had also been a major backer of the Popular Front for the Liberation of Saguia el Hamra and Rio de Oro (Polisario), Rabat's adversary in the Saharan war. Hassan, for his part, had vigorously condemned Qadhafi for international terrorism and for his association with radical regimes and movements. The Libyan colonel, he asserted, was a regional troublemaker with an unstable personality. In addition, the king had called Qadhafi's revolutionary visions confused and illogical, made all the more improbable by the backward character of his underpopulated and historically insignificant state. Thus, although Reed and others had apparently failed to attach proper significance to the rapprochement between Rabat and Tripoli that had been in the making for about a year, it must be said in their defense that Hassan and Qadhafi were indeed unlikely allies.

Patterns of government in Libya and Morocco are fundamentally different and this, too, made a union between the two countries improbable. Morocco has a traditional and patrimonial political system. Power is centralized in the monarchy, which sits atop a national political machine. Political parties, unions, and other national organizations structure inter- action among a fragmented and largely submissive elite, most of which supports and benefits from established patterns of clientelism. Thus, though political competition is sometimes intense, it is for the most part confined to a small and in-grown political class; and members of this class, with few exceptions, are content with the status quo and compete only for personal power and influence. In this conservative political environment, few meaningful choices are offered to the electorate, and political institutions rarely play the role of linking masses and elites or of giving the former genuine political influence. Moreover, political actors seeking to challenge the system, rather than to enter it and share in its rewards, are often dealt with harshly.

Libya, by contrast, has an institutionally unified political system and high levels of citizen participation. The basic political unit is the "revolutionary committee," which is the local- level section of the political structure created by Qadhafi in the name of popular democracy. The decision-making councils of these local committees are known as "basic congresses," and through them the committees do exercise some influence in the conduct of community affairs. The revolutionary committees are unified in a national movement, which regularly convenes a General People's Congress composed of delegates from the basic committees.

In practice, however, despite the relatively high level of popular involvement and the appearance of considerable decentralization, real power is concentrated at the top of the structure and is held by Qadhafi loyalists. The Revolutionary Committees movement thus serves mainly to mobilize segments of the populace for regime purposes and is only very secondarily an instrument of either grass-roots democracy or independent political expression. Further, by working through the bureaucracy of various ministries, Qadhafi's government frequently bypasses the revolutionary committees entirely in the formulation and implemen- tation of public policy. Dissent is suppressed in this controlled and sometimes totalitarian political environment. On the other hand, Qadhafi has until recently remained popular with the average citizen because he spends heavily on development projects and public welfare.

In addition to the ideological antagonisms and structural differences between the two re- gimes, each has a history of providing active support to opponents of the other. This increased the enmity between Hassan and Qadhafi and made the 1984 agreement between them all the more unexpected. Libya, for example, had harbored Moroccan dissidents and, according to authorities in Rabat, occasionally sent agents into the country for the purpose of sowing unrest. Libya had also for many years been one of Polisario's principal backers. Although Tripoli's support for the Saharan rebels had declined somewhat by the time of the Oujda treaty, Libya was a principal supplier of arms to Polisario in the late 1970s and early 1980s. Qadhafi was also active, along with Algeria, in promoting international recognition of Poli- sario's proclaimed Saharan Arab Democratic Republic (SADR).

Morocco, for its part, had provided assistance to the National Front for the Salvation of Libya (NFSL), the organization of Libyan exiles opposed to the regime in Tripoli. NFSL personnel received military training in Morocco in 1981 and 1982, and possibly even later. The NFSL also held its first congress of anti-Qadhafi forces in Morocco, in May 1982. In addition, a number of individual Libyan dissidents had found refuge in Morocco and from there written articles or made radio broadcasts denouncing the Qadhafi regime. The most prominent was probably Omar Muhayshi, a childhood friend of Qadhafi who had initially been part of the Libyan colonel's revolutionary government but had broken with the Tripoli regime in 1974.

Domestic Pressures

Despite all these factors making the Morocco-Libya union unlikely, it was a highly logical response to the situation in which both countries found themselves in mid-1984. Moreover, these same factors had been driving the two countries toward a tactical rapprochement for more than a year. As a result, historic antagonism between Hassan and Qadhafi notwith-standing, what is truly surprising was not the union itself but the fact that so few observers had seen something of the sort coming. To understand the logic of the Oujda agreement, it is accordingly necessary to examine both the domestic pressures and the regional conflicts by which North African political life was marked in 1984. Tunisia and to some extent Algeria, as well as Libya and Morocco, were buffetted by tensions and uncertainties that pervaded the entire region; and it is in response to this situation that the Arab-African Union was formed. Both Qadhafi and Hassan were pursuing a strategy of containment. Each hoped the union would reverse his sagging political fortunes and give him the means to undermine opponents and put critics on the defensive.

A convenient point of departure for the analysis of domestic pressures is provided by the riots that occurred in Tunisia and Morocco in January 1984. Although there had for several years been signs of unrest in each of the two countries, the explosion of violence that greeted the new year left both societies badly shaken. Rioting in Tunisia was particularly intense, spreading rapidly from one part of the country to another and continuing for a week. Knowl-edgeable Tunisians described the mood of the rioters as one of "rage," or even "hatred." In the capital, for example, thousands of students, workers, and unemployed slum dwellers roamed the streets, shouting antigovernment slogans and attacking symbols of authority and wealth. Thousands more shouted encouragement from open windows and rooftops. Protes-tors attacked cars and buses, tore up street signs, looted and set fire to shops, and, in some areas, attacked public buildings. They also fought police and military units, which had brought in tanks, armored personnel carriers and even helicopters in an effort to restore order. Security forces killed over 150 persons and wounded hundreds more.

While a rise in the government-controlled price of bread and semolina provided the catalyst for the outbreak of violence, the scope and intensity of the rioting showed that public frus-tration was the result of more fundamental grievances. Much anger was directed at the consumption-oriented middle and upper classes, population categories perceived to be pros-pering at a time when the economic circumstances of the masses were deteriorating and the government was asking the poor to tighten their belts even more. In the view of many, the nation's elite was prospering mainly as a result of personal and political connections, gaining access to and spending frivolously resources that should be devoted to national development.

Public alienation and cynicism also reflected a widespread belief that Tunisia's political leaders were more interested in struggling for power among themselves than in addressing the nation's pressing problems. Prime Minister Mohammed Mzali and Interior Minister Driss Guiga, longtime rivals, each sought to discredit the other by blaming him for the disturbances; and to many this power struggle confirmed their worst suspicions. Instead of seeing the recent violence as a national cry for help and as the public's demand for new development policies, Tunisian leaders appeared to view the riots first and foremost as an opportunity to neutralize opponents. While the country appeared to be on the brink of disaster, its leaders seemed to be limited in their vision to the rarefied and largely irrelevant world of intra-elite politics and to be concerned with little more than their personal political fortunes.

January 1984 was also a time of violence in Morocco, and both the immediate catalyst and the underlying popular grievances were strikingly similar to those observed in Tunisia. Late in December 1983, King Hassan addressed the Moroccan people on television and announced new austerity measures in the context of an effort to promote economic recovery. The king also affirmed that the burden of new efforts would fall primarily on the rich, but in fact it was the working class and the poor who were hurt most by the price increases announced at the beginning of January. Many Moroccans thus felt betrayed by Hassan, and in the rioting that ensued some carried placards denouncing the monarch personally.

The first disturbances were relatively limited. They involved high school students in Marrakesh, whose immediate concern was a spreading rumor that school registration fees would be increased substantially. The youthful protesters were soon joined by university students, however, and there were also instances of adults from poorer neighborhoods joining the students. Marches and demonstrations occurred frequently between the beginning of January and the middle of the month, and property damage was extensive in some areas. Moreover, the disturbances soon spread beyond Marrakesh, with student-based demonstrations also flaring up in Agadir, Safi, and Kasbah-Tadla in the south and in Rabat and Meknes in the central part of the country.

By mid-January the disturbances had spread to the northern part of the country, the most neglected and underdeveloped region of Morocco. Here students were joined by adults in what became riots of much greater intensity. The worst violence was in Nador, but there were also serious disturbances in El-Hoceima, Tetouan, Oujda, and Berkane. In Nador, there were attacks on banks and the agency of the national airline, Royal Air Maroc, indicating anger at the government and special bitterness at institutions symbolizing elite privilege. The sentiments heard were similar to those recorded in the Tunisian case, where many saw their own plight as linked to the waste, corruption, and indulgence of the privileged classes and their accomplices within the government. Some protesters carried pink parasols to express their disdain for royal pomp and their indignation at the excesses of the king and the elite.

Moroccan security forces used considerable violence in quelling the riots, increasing public anger even as calm was restored. The government's official report stated that 29 demonstrators had been killed and 114 wounded, but most observers placed the numbers far higher. Press reports from Spain spoke of 150 to 200 deaths, or in some cases even more, as well as hundreds of injured; and diplomatic sources also confirmed that the number of casualties was almost certainly far in excess of official figures. Almost all of the deaths were in the north, with the greatest number of casualties being in Nador.

The restoration of public order was followed by numerous arrests, with both the government and external human rights groups putting the figure at fifteen hundred to two thousand. Although some detainees were subsequently released, stiff prison sentences were handed out to many others. Repressive measures were also taken in other areas, including the closing of several opposition newspapers. Finally, on January 22, the king delivered a television address to the nation, expressing anger at what he deemed to be a personal affront and making additional threats which added to the nation's somber mood. His message to the north was particularly stern. He reminded inhabitants that he had not hesitated in the past to use military force against the region and made it clear that he was prepared to do so again, should this prove to be the only language that would-be dissidents understand.

As in Tunisia, sustained political uncertainty was connected to economic problems and added further to the national malaise. Although Morocco had held parliamentary elections in 1977, the government had been unwilling to call elections since that time. In 1981, the king asked the nation to postpone for two years the legislative elections scheduled for that year. Hassan said the request was associated with Morocco's war against Polisario guerrillas in the Western Sahara, but many believed the action was in fact motivated by a fear of growing opposition to the government's policies. And indeed the king was correct in his assessment of the public mood; major riots broke out in Casablanca a few weeks later, smaller in scope but just as intense as anything seen in January 1984. Police confronted roving bands of protestors in some neighborhoods, occasionally firing directly into the crowd and killing at least two hundred, possibly many more.

Pressure mounted throughout 1982 and 1983, and yet another source of uncertainty was the loyalty of the military. The Royal Armed Forces (FAR) had grown to over two hundred thousand men, largely as a result of the war in the Western Sahara, and Hassan and his associates had become increasingly concerned about political consciousness and possible discontent within its ranks, especially among younger officers. In January 1983, sixteen senior officers were arrested amidst rumors that a military plot against the king had been discovered. About the same time, General Ahmed Dlimi, commander of Morocco's forces in the Sahara, was killed in a bizarre car crash, it being widely believed that Hassan's supporters had arranged the "accident." Following these developments, Hassan fragmented the FAR command structure and took other steps to reduce the autonomy of the military.

In the wake of these and other developments, Hassan did not call parliamentary elections when the two-year postponement expired in 1983, and at the time of the 1984 riots it was still not known whether or when a new national assembly would be chosen. Elections for provincial and prefectural assemblies were postponed as well. Elections for municipal and rural councils did take place in 1983. Unfortunately, however, they were accompanied by serious irregularities, making the victory of Hassan's supporters meaningless and, in the end, serving only to deepen public discontent and uncertainty. Widespread intimidation and fraud, as well as occasional violence, accompanied the balloting. Many also complained that candidate registration, voter registration, and campaign procedures were deliberately designed to favor parties aligned with the palace and to permit irregularities on their behalf. Amidst general agreement that the election had accordingly been "cooked," even government courts upheld several challenges later brought by opposition parties. Thus, in sum, concern about the political situation in the country reinforced economic grievances and added significantly to the public anger which burst forth in January 1984.

Though the situation in Libya was very different, that country, too, experienced unrest in 1984. Blessed with substantial revenues from petroleum exports, Libya has had ample resources with which to meet the needs of its small population. Moreover, the regime of Colonel Muammar Qadhafi has spent heavily on projects designed to promote national development and enhance the welfare of the common citizen. Thus, in contrast to Tunisia and Morocco, grievances related to poverty and relative deprivation have not been a major source of tension in Libya. On the other hand, the Qadhafi regime is highly authoritarian, imposing its political and cultural visions on a sometimes reluctant populace and, when necessary, using force to suppress any hint of criticism or dissent. It is this repressive and sometimes brutal political climate that has spawned most of the tension in Libya.

High school and university students have been among the most active of Qadhafi's domestic opponents. This is not unlike the pattern in Tunisia and Morocco, despite the very different character of the regimes in Tripoli and those in Tunis and Rabat. In April 1984, authorities executed two students in Tripoli and three more in Benghazi after finding them guilty of treason. Although the alleged traitors were hanged in public in a move calculated to discourage further acts of dissent, the executions were in fact followed by student strikes and boycotts and by several acts of sabotage. Among the latter were explosions early in May at two military camps near Benghazi.

Much of the opposition to Qadhafi is articulated by Libyans residing outside the country, some of whom have also been the target of attacks by agents of the Tripoli government. The major organization of opposition is the National Front for the Salvation of Libya (NFSL), which in 1984 was based in the Sudan. Another dissident group is the Muslim Brotherhood, a militant Islamic-tendency organization that has ties to its namesake in other Arab countries, most notably in Egypt, and that accuses Qadhafi, despite his Muslim rhetoric, of abandoning and betraying the true path of Islam. Some of the students executed in April were accused of being members of the Muslim Brotherhood, which, ironically, Qadhafi then described as an American-backed terrorist organization.

In May 1984, a coalition of dissident groups, including the NFSL and the Muslim Brotherhood, launched an armed attack in Tripoli designed to overturn the Qadhafi government. On the eighth, at 7:30 A.M., about two dozen commandos struck at Bab al-Azziziya barracks, the headquarters of the regime's movement of Revolutionary Committees. The compound also frequently serves as Qadhafi's personal residence, although the Libyan leader was elsewhere on this particular morning. The attackers succeeded in penetrating the heavily guarded compound but, once inside, they were eventually defeated in a fierce battle with Libyan soldiers. There was substantial damage to offices and living quarters within the compound, and reports indicate that as many as eighty Libyan soldiers may have been killed. Nine commandos were also killed at Bab al-Azziziya, and the remainder fled with Qadhafi's forces in pursuit.

Authorities attempted to seal off central Tripoli to prevent any escape, with major traffic tie-ups being one immediate result. This was followed by a house-to-house search in the southern part of the city and in a number of other areas, in which weapons and sympathizers as well as the perpetrators of the attack on Bab al-Azziziya were sought. Some reports place the number arrested as high as five thousand, which is probably an exaggeration but nonetheless indicates a sweep of substantial magnitude. On May 12, the leader of the attempted coup, Wadji es-Shwehdi, was killed along with six of his comrades in a Tripoli residential neighborhood. By the seventeenth, all known commandos had been caught and killed. According to press reports, the bodies of the slain commandos were displayed in Tripoli and also shown on Libyan television.

At the same time, local "congresses," which are the basic units of the national organization of Revolutionary Committees, began dispensing popular justice to many of those apprehended in the roundup of elements deemed hostile to the regime. In a number of instances this involved death sentences carried out only hours after an arrest had been made. Public hangings took place not only in Tripoli and Benghazi but in a number of smaller towns as well. Furthermore, this campaign, which some observers described as a reign of terror, was extended to opponents of the regime living outside the country. In June, four Libyan dissidents were killed in Greece by a Tripoli-sponsored assassination team. Other attacks followed in July, with two Libyan students being shot in downtown Athens.

Despite the primacy of political issues, economic concerns also began to emerge during this period. For the first time since Qadhafi came to power in 1969, there had been a serious decline in the nation's revenue from petroleum exports. Falling oil prices, coupled with a drop in production from about 2 million barrels per day in 1981 to approximately six hundred thousand per day in 1984, had cut this revenue by more than half. Earnings had shrunk from $22 billion in the former year to $10 billion in 1983 and $9 billion in 1984; per capita income, though still quite high in absolute terms, had fallen from $11,000 to $8,000 during the same period. None of this created the kind of poverty that was visible in Tunisia and Morocco. On the other hand, Libya's changing economic fortunes were reflected in a significant reduction in imported goods, including foodstuffs, and in a dwindling supply of many consumer products. Given the likelihood of a continuation and perhaps even an intensification of these trends, Qadhafi had reason to worry that his popular base would erode and that the appeals of his many political opponents would strike an increasingly responsive chord among the Libyan masses.

Algeria, the largest state in Arab North Africa, appeared orderly and stable in comparison to its neighbors to the east and the west. The government of President Chedli Benjedid, which had come to power in 1978, enjoyed widespread legitimacy and appeared to be receiving high marks for the relative absence of corruption and a genuine commitment to national development. Nevertheless, there were also a number of incidents that raised questions about Algeria's future.

Among these incidents were disturbances provoked by militant Islamic groups in 1982 and 1983; and in March 1984 approximately twenty-five thousand people attended the funeral of Sheikh Abdellatif Soliani, a leader of the Algerian Islamic movement who had died while under house arrest. In September, responding to the challenge of Islamic-tendency movements, the government sentenced seven Muslim extremists to prison terms ranging up to eight years. Seven months later, in April 1985, it tried 135 men accused of membership in underground Muslim organizations. Eighty-three were condemned to prison, of whom three received life sentences, and the rest were released. In August of 1985, a group of extremists broke into a police compound at Souma and stole a supply of weapons, and two weeks later a number of "Muslim zealots" were arrested in connection with the incident. In October there were yet additional clashes between Muslim militants and police, one of which resulted in the death of five policemen.

There were also demonstrations over poor housing conditions in Algiers in both 1984 and 1985. In April of the latter year, for example, following rumors that homes being built for the poor would be allocated instead to government bureaucrats, there were riots in the casbah which brought police units into the streets. The disturbances continued for several days, and following the restoration of order thirty-three persons were condemned to prison for their part in the riots. In addition, this period also witnessed a growth in the number, visibility, and activity levels of opposition movements based outside the country. The most important of these is the Paris-based Movement for Democracy in Algeria, headed by former president

Ahmed Ben Bella. Ben Bella, who had led the country from the time of its independence until 1965, is a former socialist who has embraced an Islamic political agenda in recent years.

This collection of domestic political and economic pressures created a climate of uncertainty to which Hassan and Qadhafi sought to respond. Both men were prompted to action by the tensions within their own country, and both also felt the cumulative impact of mounting uncertainty within the region as a whole. The rapprochement between Libya and Morocco was therefore conceived as an effort at containment, a political strategy by which Qadhafi and Hassan hoped to revive their political fortunes and regain the initiative in the struggle with domestic opponents.

Regional Conflicts

The political climate of North Africa in the mid-1980s was shaped not only by events within Libya, Morocco, Tunisia, and Algeria but also by relations and rivalries among various combinations of these four states. Regional conflicts were the source of considerable tension in the months preceding the Oujda agreement, and a desire to contain external challenges was thus an additional factor in the political calculations of Hassan and Qadhafi. Libya and Morocco were both at odds with their neighbors in the Maghreb. Both countries also felt themselves disadvantaged by the pattern of alliances taking shape in the region. For these reasons, as well as those associated with domestic unrest, Qadhafi and Hassan were led to the conclusion that a union between their two states would be mutually beneficial.

One important source of regional tension has been the war in the Western Sahara, which pits Morocco's enormous and well-equipped army against roughly five to seven thousand Polisario guerrillas.* Morocco claims the vast Saharan territory as its own, having invaded and annexed it following the termination of Spanish colonial rule in 1975. Rabat insists that the region had been illegally detached from the rest of Morocco during the colonial era. In annexing the former Spanish Sahara, King Hassan accordingly declared that his country was merely seeking to reestablish its territorial integrity. Polisario, by contrast, claims to represent the indigenous population of the Sahara; and, in the name of self-determination, the rebel organization calls for the creation of an independent Saharan Arab Democratic Republic (SADR).

The war in the Sahara began in 1976, when Polisario guerrillas took up arms against Morocco's forces in the territory, and it has been dragging on ever since in spite of numerous regional and international attempts to bring about a diplomatic solution. Although Morocco has had a distinct military advantage in recent years, it has proved costly and difficult to secure the vast stretches of desert. The Royal Armed Forces of King Hassan have thus been unable to suppress Polisario resistance and remain open to periodic hit and run attacks and other forms of harassment from rebel units. Moreover, the cost of Morocco's war effort, and of politically-motivated civilian construction in the disputed territory, have contributed significantly to the nation's economic problems.

Much of Polisario's staying power is the result of assistance received from other North

---

*A few sources judge the number of guerrillas to be substantially higher, with estimates by Polisario sympathizers ranging as high as twenty thousand.

African powers, especially Algeria and also, until recently, Libya. Both countries have provided Polisario with weapons and, according to Morocco, military advisors. Algeria, which shares a small border with the Western Sahara, has also at times permitted Polisario fighters to operate from its territory. Finally, Algiers has led an effective diplomatic campaign on Polisario's behalf. One result is that a majority of the member states of the Organization of African Unity have recognized the SADR, leading Morocco to withdraw from the OAU in 1984.

Algeria claims that its support for Polisario is motivated by adherence to the principle of self-determination. But while this may be true to a degree, the explanation of Algeria's active involvement in the Saharan conflict is in large measure to be found in its longstanding rivalry with Morocco and in past conflicts involving the two countries. In any event, regional diplomacy related to the Saharan war and, more broadly, to the competition between Algeria and Morocco became particularly intense during 1983. The year began on a promising note, with Benjedid and Hassan meeting in February to discuss the Saharan issue. Benjedid was motivated, in part, by his own country's deteriorating relations with Libya. Also, Polisario spokesmen reacted favorably to the Hassan-Benjedid talks, generating additional optimism. Nevertheless, the Moroccan-Algerian dialogue turned out to be short on substance. Benjedid insisted that he had no mandate to speak for the Saharawis, whereupon Hassan reiterated his longstanding opposition to direct negotiations with Polisario.

In March 1983, the North African political scene became further polarized with the conclusion of a Treaty of Fraternity and Concord between Algeria and Tunisia. This treaty brought Tunisia, which had heretofore striven for neutrality in the competition between Morocco and Algeria, into the political orbit of the latter country. Morocco, by contrast, was left in relative isolation, sharing exclusion from the new alliance with the unpredictable regime of Muammar Qadhafi. To deepen their cooperation, Tunisia and Algeria in April convened the mixed commission that coordinates relations between the two countries and agreed on a number of measures involving enhanced economic and cultural cooperation. In May, for example, they established a new banking convention. In the same month, Habib Bourguiba and Chedli Benjedid met in a ceremony at the border between the two countries, and at the end of May Bourguiba paid a highly publicized state visit to Algiers.

Benjedid and Bourguiba sought to use the new friendship treaty as a foundation for the pursuit of broader unity in North Africa, for movement toward what North Africans call "Le Grand Maghreb." Morocco was not to be excluded from this effort, and Hassan was accordingly invited to join Bourguiba on the Tunisian president's state visit to Algiers. But Rabat was expected to give tacit recognition to Algeria's leadership role and, more specifically, to modify its uncompromising attitude toward the Saharan conflict. Thus Hassan declined the invitation to come to Algiers. His most immediate concern was to avoid pressure for direct negotiations with Polisario, which is a measure of the degree to which Tunisia's position had evolved in a direction favorable to the Algerians. Whereas Tunisia had in the past spoken somewhat vaguely of a need for negotiations between Morocco and Algeria, improving relations with Algiers now inclined the government in Tunis toward the thesis that direct negotiations with Polisario representatives were necessary.

Khouna Ould Haydala, president of Mauritania, traveled to Algiers in December 1983, at which time his country became a signatory to the Treaty of Fraternity and Concord. Mauritania's participation extended and solidified the new alliance, which appeared more than ever to leave Morocco and Libya on the sidelines. Moreover, Mauritania's inclusion in the alliance was important for practical as well as symbolic reasons. Although a poor country and a marginal player in North African international relations, Mauritania shares borders with both the Western Sahara and Algeria, and thus its attitude toward the Polisario and the war is a matter of some consequence. Initially allied with Morocco, the country had more recently steered a neutral course, and the friendship treaty with Algeria now moved the country away from its declared neutrality. Early in 1984, Nouakchott recognized the SADR, giving additional support to the Algerian position not only in the OAU but also in the Arab League and within North Africa itself.

Although Algeria's support for Polisario and its friendship treaty with Tunisia and Mauritania were the most important manifestations of the rivalry between Algiers and Rabat, the potential for conflict between the two North African states was also reflected in other arenas. Perhaps most significant were the acts of sabotage and infiltration with which Morocco charged Algeria in 1985. Moroccan authorities claimed that Algerian intelligence operatives were training a large group of Moroccan dissidents and preparing them to carry out acts of "collective terrorism" inside Morocco. The Moroccans also captured and put on trial a number of alleged saboteurs (including some charged with plotting to assassinate the king), whom they said had been trained and supported by Algeria.

Also adding to the tension were several clashes between Moroccan and Algerian military forces. Though limited in number and intensity, these encounters reflected yet another dimension of the severe strain in relations between the two countries. In June 1984, for example, Algeria reported that sixty Moroccan troops had crossed into its territory. The invaders had been intercepted by the Algerian military, the report continued, with two Moroccans killed, two more wounded and thirty-one captured. Other encounters were reported by Morocco in February 1985. According to Rabat, several Algerian troops stationed on the border between the two countries had been wounded in a series of recent clashes.

A totally different set of regional conflicts revolved around Libya and its relations with neighboring states. First, Libya was embroiled in Chad. Although not usually regarded as a North African state, Chad is Libya's neighbor to the south and its involvement with Libya has important regional implications. Second, there were important strains in relations between Tripoli and Tunis. Finally, relations between Libya and Algeria became increasingly tense during this period, even though both countries had in the past sided with Polisario against Morocco.

Libyan involvement in Chad is motivated by Tripoli's territorial claims in northern Chad and by its desire to see the latter country governed by a friendly regime, one willing to operate within Libya's sphere of influence. This connection is further influenced and complicated by the civil war in Chad, which has been going on with varying degrees of intensity for almost twenty-five years. In 1972, Tripoli began to send soldiers into the Aouzou Strip, a seventy-mile-wide territorial band running the width of the country along the northern border; and in 1973 Libya annexed the territory.

Although Chad seeks to recover the Aouzou Strip, which allegedly is rich in uranium, this claim has in recent years been superseded by matters of greater urgency. Enmeshed in a protracted civil war, Chad's political leaders have been preoccupied with internal conflicts, and it is particularly significant in this connection that the faction led by Oueddei Goukhouni has sought assistance from Qadhafi in its struggle with rivals. Several thousand Libyan troops moved into Chad late in 1980 at the request of Goukhouni, who issued the call for assistance in his capacity as President of the Transitional National Unity Government (GUNT). Within a few weeks the Libyans had routed the forces of Goukhouni's principal adversary, Hissene Habre; and shortly thereafter, in a move that caused alarm among Chad's African neighbors, Goukhouni and Qadhafi announced a "prospective merger" of their two countries. France, which had its own troops in Chad until May 1980, also expressed concern about Libyan involvement in Chad.

The Libyans left Chad at Goukhouni's request in November 1981. But Goukhouni was ousted by Habre in summer 1982, and the following year Libyan forces reentered the country on behalf of the GUNT. Qadhafi's troops drove south across the Libya-Chad border, occupying the northern portion of the latter country. Again there were protests, however, and in August 1983 France sent three thousand troops into the country in support of the Habre government. With the French in the south and the Libyans in the north, the Chadian civil war now had the potential to become a major international conflict. Regional actors scrambled to defuse the crisis as French and Libyan-backed forces clashed late in 1983 and in 1984. In January of the latter year, Paris charged Tripoli with responsibility for downing one of its fighter planes and moved its troops further north in response to recent skirmishes.

Strains in Libya's relations with Tunisia were another source of regional tension at this time. In January 1984, a few days after the rioting stopped in Tunisia, commandos blew up a section of the Tunisian-Algerian natural gas pipeline. Tunisian officials charged Libya with involvement, alleging that Tripoli was hoping to take advantage of the disorder in Tunisia to weaken the regime. According to some analysts, Qadhafi's government was expressing its unhappiness over the new alliance between Tunis and Algiers. In addition, Libya undoubtedly saw the disorder in Tunisia as an opportunity to press the Bourguiba regime to reduce its close ties to the United States and other western allies. Finally, some observers suggested that Qadhafi was still smarting over Tunisia's failure to implement a unity agreement that the two countries had concluded a decade earlier. Tripoli denied any involvement in the attack on the pipeline but nonetheless offered to pay for repairs.

Libya, for its part, charged that Tunisia was one of the foreign powers conspiring against it and accused Bourguiba's government of providing support to the NFSL and other dissident movements. Two days before the May 8 attack on Bab al-Azziziya barracks, a leading Libyan dissident, Ahmed Ahwas, crossed into Libya from Tunisia along with two colleagues. Ahwas was killed at the town of Zuwarah, apparently shortly after having entered the country, and his two companions were captured.

Libyan officials contended, most probably with reason, that Ahwas's infiltration was linked to the plan that resulted in disturbances two days later. They also claimed that dissidents had used Tunisia as a base, adding that one of the participants in the May 8 attack had taken refuge in the Tunisian embassy in Tripoli. Later on the eighth, Libyan border police seized three of their Tunisian counterparts at the Ras Ajdir crossing point and Qadhafi's government then stated that these men would be held until the dissident alleged to be hiding in the Tunisian embassy was surrendered. Several days later Libyan border forces carried out a series of military maneuvers, reportedly entering Tunisia briefly on two occasions. Other actions included Libyan radio broadcasts denouncing the regime in Tunis and Tripoli's refusal to permit several hundred Tunisians working in Libya to cross the border and return home.

Tunisia's firm protests, and its refusal to resume normal relations until the border guards were released and other provocative actions stopped, led to a temporary moderating of Libya's aggressiveness. Indeed, high-level Tunisian-Libyan contacts during the latter part of 1984 led to new cooperation between the two countries. But tension flared up again in 1985. In mid-January, Tunisia arrested seven heavily armed Libyan commandos who had infiltrated the country through Algeria. Although Qadhafi denied that they were agents of his government, the infiltrators were apparently intent on carrying out sabotage operations and sowing unrest in order to put pressure on the Tunisian government.

Tension increased during the spring and summer of 1985 as Tripoli began to expel tens of thousands of Tunisians working in Libya. The reason for the expulsions was economic as well as political; with a decline in the price of oil, there had been a slowdown in construction and other economic activity inside Libya. Thus Egyptians and other foreign workers, as well as Tunisians, were told to leave. Yet Tripoli also continued to allege that Tunisia had harbored Libyan dissidents and, most important, Qadhafi was unhappy about Tunisia's continuing movement into the political orbit of Algeria. Like King Hassan of Morocco, he felt himself isolated by the 1983 friendship treaty between Algeria, Tunisia, and Mauritania.

Libya fired at least one-third of the ninety to one hundred thousand Tunisians working in that country. Moreover, many were held in detention camps for several weeks until their exit papers were deemed to be in order, intervention by Morocco and Kuwait having been necessary to facilitate their eventual departure. Finally, Tripoli imposed restrictions on the remittances that those Tunisians still employed could send out of the country, thereby creating additional hardship for a number of communities in southern Tunisia. Other aspects of the renewed tension involved Tunisia's expulsion of several hundred Libyan nationals, including about thirty diplomats whom it accused of spying, and Libyan threats of military action in southern Tunisia. Some Tunisians also worried that Qadhafi might be planting agents among the Tunisian workers being deported.

There were also difficulties in Libyan-Algerian relations. Having signed a defense agreement with Tunisia in October 1983, Algeria warned Tripoli in the spring of 1984 that it was prepared to respond militarily should there be incursions into Tunisian territory. This warning, issued in connection with the events on the Tunisian-Libyan border that followed the attack on Bab al-Azziziya barracks, was reiterated when a Libyan air force jet flew into Tunisian airspace in August 1985. Libya apologized for the incident, stating that an inexperienced pilot on a training exercise had mistakenly flown off course.

An even more important source of tension was the situation along Algeria's own border with Libya, particularly in the extreme south, near the Libyan town of Ghat. Early in 1985 Algiers protested that a Libyan air force plane, stationed at the Ghat airbase, had flown into Algerian territory. Qadhafi dismissed the incident, however, stating that in view of Arab solidarity the border between the two countries was in fact artificial. Further complicating the situation was Algeria's longstanding claim to Libyan territory in this region, a claim made more significant by the area's richness in natural gas. Algiers insists that the region was inappropriately handed to Libya during the colonial era. Ironically, it complains of the same Franco-Italian accords which Qadhafi denounces in connection with his own country's claims in northern Chad.

In the spring of 1985, Algerian troops occupied a portion of the disputed territory, taking up positions around the Ghat airbase. Some reports placed Algerian troops as much as twenty-five miles inside Libya. Despite previous statements about the border's artificial character,

Tripoli vigorously protested the incursion and threatened to take the case to the United Nations. These threats and other appeals did not lead Algeria to remove its forces, however.

Finally, Libya was concerned about the significant improvement in Algeria's relations with the United States, a development that was indeed motivated, in substantial measure, by U.S. concern over Libyan adventurism. In addition to its displeasure over Libyan threats to Tunisia, Washington had been angered by Libyan terrorism in Europe and the Middle East. Of special concern was a plot uncovered by Egyptian authorities in November 1984, in which Qadhafi's agents in Cairo had planned both to assassinate political opponents and to steal a U.S.-made F-16 jet. For this reason, and also because of growing commercial relations between Algeria and the United States, Chedli Benjedid was received in Washington in April 1985. Among the results of his visit was an agreement to sell American weapons to Algiers and to increase military cooperation between the two countries.

The Logic of Oujda

In response to this constellation of domestic pressures and regional conflicts, a new relationship between Libya and Morocco began to take shape in 1983. In June, about a month after Chedli Benjedid and Habib Bourguiba had met in Algiers, the Libyan colonel paid a visit to Rabat and discussed possible responses to the new Algerian-Tunisian alliance. On the one hand, mindful that Hassan had also been invited to the summit meeting in Algiers, Qadhafi sought to discuss Libya's inclusion in any genuine movement toward North African unity that might grow out of the recently signed Treaty of Fraternity and Concord. On the other, since Hassan had declined the invitation and reiterated that Algeria's terms were unacceptable, the Moroccan and Libyan leaders both apparently reached the same conclusion—namely, that cooperation between their two countries would be effective in checking Algeria's growing regional influence. A tactical alliance between Libya and Morocco would in effect outflank the Algerian-Tunisian compact. And, more specifically, it would put pressure on Tunisia to resume a position of relative neutrality in regional affairs.

Hassan and Qadhafi found other common interests as well, and, in particular, each concluded that he could benefit from the support of the other in his own country's territorial dispute. As a major backer of Polisario guerrillas in the Sahara, Qadhafi obviously held a strong negotiating position. Hassan, though not in a position to make an equally tangible contribution to Libya's struggle in Chad, could nonetheless confer a measure of legitimacy on Tripoli's territorial claims in the latter country. Moreover, Rabat's diplomatic support might carry weight where Tripoli needed it most, among conservative Arab states, in Black Africa, and in France. Qadhafi thus agreed to end arms shipments to Polisario and to cease his country's active participation in the diplomatic campaign on behalf of the SADR, and in return Hassan offered public acceptance of Libya's involvement in Chad.

This arrangement did not lead to a resolution either of the war in the Sahara or of the conflict in Chad. But both parties nevertheless stuck to the bargain and each took action that proved beneficial to the other. Libya withdrew its support from Polisario, forcing Algeria to increase its own assistance to the rebels. Also, although the change in Libyan policy was only one among a number of pertinent factors, Morocco was able to improve its military position in the Sahara during the latter half of 1983. As a result, fighting in the disputed territory became more intermittent and the war itself evolved into something of a military stalemate. By constructing an extended network of defensive fortifications, manned by approximately eighty thousand RAF troops, Rabat established itself as the militarily dominant adversary and forced Polisario to limit itself to a long-term "war of attrition." Yet Moroccan forces have been unable to destroy the rebel units, leading Polisario spokesmen to assert that Hassan's regime will eventually be forced to compromise because of the heavy and continuing economic cost of the war. At the time of the Oujda agreement, Rabat was spending on its military and construction efforts in the Sahara an amount equal to 40 to 45 percent of the national budget.

Morocco, for its part, issued a number of statements explaining the legitimacy of Tripoli's involvement in Chad. For example, early in 1984, Hassan told France's *Le Figaro Magazine* that colonial powers had "amputated" a portion of Libya's historic territory, just as they had illegally detached the Western Sahara from Morocco. He also stressed "blood ties" between northern Chad and southern Libya. These statements, of course, did not alter the nature of the conflict, or even its evolution. Yet, like the Libyan-Moroccan rapprochement more generally, they did reduce somewhat Qadhafi's international isolation and his reputation as a regional troublemaker. More specifically, they helped Qadhafi to argue that his country's involvement in Chad was motivated by more than adventurism and, accordingly, that he was a legitimate participant in any attempts to negotiate an end to the fighting in that country.

All of these factors that contributed to the rapprochement between Morocco and Libya in 1983 help to explain the logic of the Oujda agreement. There is another set of motivations that was even more compelling, however. Given that Morocco and Libya had both experienced serious unrest during the first part of 1984, Hassan and Qadhafi came to Oujda preoccupied, above all, with the domestic challenges confronting their respective regimes. Qadhafi was eager to secure an end to Moroccan assistance to the NFSL, which only a few months earlier had demonstrated its ability to strike at the Libyan colonel's headquarters in Tripoli. Qadhafi also sought to deny asylum in Morocco to prominent critics of his regime, the most notable example being Omar Muhayshi. Moreover, the Libyan leader did indeed realize benefits in each of these areas. Although only secondarily because of actions related to the Oujda treaty, the NFSL experienced important setbacks in the months after its unsuccessful attack on the Bab al-Azziziya barracks. The fate of Muhayshi, by contrast, was directly linked to the Libya-Morocco agreement: Hassan arranged for the Libyan dissident to be returned to Tripoli, whereupon he was immediately executed.

Qadhafi may also have hoped to receive several other benefits from the treaty with Morocco. In addition to the May coup attempt, which demonstrated the strength and determination of the organized opposition, there had recently appeared cracks in the popular support that Qadhafi's regime had long enjoyed. A decline in oil prices and production had severely damaged Libya's economy, with earnings from oil exports having dropped significantly between 1980 and 1984 and per capita income having also declined sharply during this period. By 1984 the country was thus being asked to tighten its belt for the first time since Qadhafi had come to power. Imports had been reduced and the availability of consumer goods in particular had declined sharply. In addition, as noted earlier, many of the foreign workers on whom Libya's economic development depends had been dismissed. Finally, Qadhafi's growing isolation abroad, especially in the Arab world and in Africa, added to doubts about the colonel's ability as a leader and, in this context, assumed domestic significance as well.

As long as Libyans were prospering, many seem to have been willing to overlook the regime's authoritarian character and its dubious foreign adventures. In more difficult economic times, however, Libyan dissidents and others who opposed the regime in the name of its political excesses could expect to find greater support inside the country. The union with Morocco may thus have appealed to Qadhafi because of the possibility that it would enhance his legitimacy and reduce his isolation. If the Libyan leader were indeed the pariah that his enemies claimed, would the conservative and pro-Western Hassan have been willing to make common cause with him? Moreover, temporarily at least, the Oujda accord diverted public attention from pressing domestic problems and fostered a hope, plausible if somewhat naive, that the Moroccan connection might both moderate Qadhafi's political extremism and contribute to Libyan development.

Hassan's calculus regarding domestic political challenges was more elaborate, and particularly important were the direct economic benefits that he hoped would result from the union with Libya. Remittances from Moroccans working overseas are a major source of revenue and hard currency for the economically depressed country, yet opportunities for Moroccans to find work in Western Europe had begun to decline. Overseas employment is also an important source of jobs for young Moroccans, a consideration made critical by the fact that domestic unemployment was approximately 20 percent and may have been as high as 35 to 40 percent among the young. Another indication of the nation's difficult economic situation is that the number of Moroccans living in "absolute poverty" was variously estimated to be 35 to 45 percent in 1984, based on World Bank figures, which define such poverty as an income of less than $1600 per year for an urban family of six. This situation, as well as the disparities between rich and poor, contributed significantly to the rioting that took place in January 1984. Nor had the king forgotten that these same considerations also gave rise to the Casablanca riots of June 1981.

The union with Libya offered Morocco an opportunity to address some of its economic problems and, in particular, to increase the number of jobs available to its citizens. Libya is a labor-importing country, which had roughly half a million foreign nationals working within its borders in 1984. The majority of these workers were Egyptian, and approximately one hundred thousand more were Tunisian. Given Libya's strained relations with both Egypt and Tunisia, however, Hassan saw his accord with Qadhafi as providing an opportunity to replace many of these laborers with unemployed Moroccans. Further, at least in the short run, this goal was realized to a meaningful, albeit comparatively modest degree. Declining oil revenues forced Libya to reduce its overall demand for imported labor. Yet, even as many Egyptians, Tunisians, and others were being deported, the number of Moroccans working in Libya increased from ten thousand to fourteen thousand during the year following the signing of the Oujda agreement.

Other potential economic benefits to Morocco included the possibility of purchasing oil at preferential prices, energy costs having been 28 percent of the country's import bill in 1983. Hassan also looked to increased trade and investment as a result of his country's new Libyan connection. Indeed, the rapprochement with Tripoli in 1983 had already led to a number of new commercial agreements and to an increase in Moroccan exports to Libya. Thus there were exchanges of trade and other delegations between the two countries late in 1983 and early in 1984. In January 1984, for example, an eighteen-member Libyan delegation visited Rabat and concluded a series of cooperative agreements dealing with commerce, scientific and cultural exchanges, joint business ventures, and other matters. Finally, Rabat looked to direct economic aid from Tripoli as well, and in May 1985, roughly nine months after the accord reached in Oujda, Libya provided Morocco with a loan package of $100 million.

Although the possibility of economic relief was Hassan's principal domestic motivation for the Oujda agreement, he may also have hoped to reap some ideological and symbolic benefits that could be translated into political capital. In particular, a link with Qadhafi might be seen as contributing to his campaign against militant Islamic movements in Morocco. Hassan had charged local Islamic-tendency organizations with partial responsibility for the January 1984 riots; and even though these charges were greatly exaggerated, underlying economic and political grievances having been the principal cause of the disturbances, the intensity of opposition from militant Islamic groups had indeed increased in recent years.

For this reason, in February 1984, Moroccan religious officials announced an educational campaign to reinforce Morocco's "legitimate" Islamic character and to call attention to the king's historic role as the spiritual leader of both orthodox and popular Islam in Morocco. The union with Libya offered Hassan another opportunity to associate himself with Islam in the eyes of his people. While fundamentalists do not view Libya's revolution as truly Islamic, Qadhafi is identified with militant Islam in the popular mind and, like Iran, is a symbol to many of an Islamic alternative to domination by either the West or the East. Thus, allied with Libya, Hassan's regime might be less vulnerable to criticism by Muslim opponents.

It is ironic that Hassan and Qadhafi each sought to use the radically differing image and ideology of the other to shore up his own sagging popularity at home. Yet Morocco's economic circumstances gave Hassan an additional reason for seeking to narrow the symbolic distance between himself and Qadhafi. The Moroccan monarch appears to have reasoned that he could demonstrate his independence from conservative Western powers, particularly the United States, by embracing Qadhafi; and this may have been especially important to the king at a time when Western creditors were pressing for economic changes that, whatever their long-term value, would in the near term further erode the living standards of the Moroccan poor. Indeed, the price rises that served as catalyst for the January 1984 rioting had been decreed in response to pressure from the World Bank and the International Monetary Fund. Thus the king may have reasoned that a Libyan connection would undermine the argument, put forward by opposition parties of the left, that the regime in Rabat was unduly subservient to the interests of Western capitalist powers and that this was in large measure responsible for Morocco's economic troubles.

The logic of this assessment is reinforced by some of the ideological positions that Hassan has staked out in the past during periods of domestic tension. In the early 1960s, for example, Morocco entered the political competition between radical and conservative forces in Africa on the side of the former. Although it was clamping down strongly on leftists at home, the Moroccan regime played an active role in organizing the "Casablanca Bloc," a coalition of African states declaring themselves in favor of socialism and pan-Africanism. Similarly, in the early 1970s, Hassan responded to two attempted military coups and other manifestations of domestic unrest by championing various Third World causes and by projecting a more militant and nationalist posture in matters of foreign policy. Seen from this historical perspective, the king's willingness to identify himself with radical policies abroad in order to fortify his position at home appears less improbable.

In Qadhafi's case, by contrast, it was a reduction rather than an increase in militant international independence that may have held out the promise of political gain. The Libyan leader apparently concluded that he could shore up his popularity in the domestic political arena by reducing his ideological distance from the conservative and pro-Western regime in Rabat. Not only could he tell the Libyan people that he had made progress toward achieving his frequently-proclaimed goal of Arab unity, he could also present himself as a respected international statesman, one whose influence and appeal were not limited to a single ideological camp. Further, by appearing less radical and philosophically uncompromising in general, and by embracing a conservative and pro-Western monarch in particular, he could raise hopes that a greater diversity of political views might soon be tolerated inside Libya. This, in the short run at least, would reduce domestic tensions and diffuse the criticism of his government.

Similarly, in the international arena, Qadhafi may have sought to reduce his country's isolation by shedding his own negative image and by presenting a more moderate face to his Arab and African neighbors. Having incurred the wrath of many African states because of his involvement in Chad, and being regarded as a troublemaker and even an outlaw by a number of Arab governments, the Libyan colonel was in need of a political connection that would enable him to claim that these labels were undeserved. Moreover, should the union with Morocco indeed lead to reduced isolation and greater respectability abroad, this would undoubtedly contribute further to the improvement of Qadhafi's popular standing at home. Thus, both domestic and international considerations may have led the Libyan leader to reason that he could benefit from an association with the very ideological tendencies that had become a domestic liability for the Moroccan monarch.

In neither the Moroccan nor the Libyan case were these symbolic considerations as central as the direct political and economic benefits that the new union portended. In both instances, however, a conscious desire to manipulate poltical symbols may well have provided an additional incentive and rationale for the accord reached at Oujda. Moreover, for Hassan, there were gains to be made not only from the manipulation of symbols about his own country and regime but also from the new image that he was helping Qadhafi to project.

To the extent that Hassan could present himself as capable of moderating Qadhafi's international behavior, he hoped to score points of his own in the diplomatic arena, especially with the United States and with those Arab, African, and European countries most concerned about Qadhafi's foreign entanglements. Thus, about a month after the signing of the Oujda treaty, Hassan called attention to the possibility of delivering a more moderate and responsible Qadhafi by brokering an agreement between Libya and France for the mutual withdrawal of foreign troops in Chad. Hassan's initiative was of course designed to win favor with the French, whose attitude toward North Africa's regional conflicts is important to all participants. It also was intended as a signal to the United States, both to allay fears that Moroccan foreign policy would change and, in addition, to give Washington the impression that one of its bitterest enemies in the Middle East might even be partially neutralized.

Since the removal of Libyan troops from Chad is sought not only by France and the United States but by many sub-Saharan African states as well, Hassan also hoped that the agreement he had brokered between Tripoli and Paris would increase support for Morocco within the Organization of African Unity. Black African attitudes are important to Morocco because diplomatic efforts to end the Saharan war have been centered in the OAU. In September 1984, a slight majority of OAU members supported Polisario and favored admitting the Saharan Arab Democratic Republic it claims to represent. If Morocco could claim credit for Libya's withdrawal from Chad, however, it might be able to make new gains within the OAU.

Repercussions inside Morocco and Libya

Shortly after the Oujda summit, the Libyan General People's Congress convened to consider and approve the treaty with Morocco. The process of ratification in Morocco, by contrast, was more prolonged and deliberate and was carried out in a manner consistent with Hassan's political strategy for coping with the domestic challenges to his regime. In order to derive the maximum degree of political capital from the new accord, the Moroccan government organized a national referendum on the treaty, preceded by an intense two-week campaign of public information and discussion during which hundreds of meetings and rallies were held throughout the country. All of Morocco's political parties, including those in the opposition, endorsed the proposed union, and most took an active part in organizing the rallies held on behalf of ratification.

Like the agreement itself, this activity was designed both to mobilize popular support for the Moroccan government and to undermine the position of opposition parties and groups. Moreover, the tactic was highly successful. The palace claimed to have received thousands of letters and telegrams endorsing the treaty, and the electorate endorsed the union overwhelmingly when the referendum was held at the end of August. Given the nature of Moroccan political life, national plebiscites of this sort may not necessarily be a true indication of popular sentiment. In this instance, however, observers agreed that public reaction to the union with Libya was indeed highly favorable. Thus, for King Hassan, the Oujda agreement had achieved its short-term goals. It had diverted attention from immediate problems, raised hopes of economic benefit, and boosted the popularity of the Rabat regime.

Even more significant is the fact that Hassan then used his newly-won popularity to put the country back on the road toward democracy. Morocco's twice-postponed parliamentary elections were finally held in September 1984, provincial and prefectural elections having been conducted the month before. Moreover, and equally important, the elections appear to have been reasonably fair. There were some complaints, but these were not excessive. Also, Hassan released 354 political prisoners shortly before the balloting. Finally, the parliament elected in 1984 is more representative and contains a greater diversity of views than the one it replaced. All of this served to increase public confidence in national political institutions, to enhance the legitimacy of Hassan's government and to buy time for the regime to address other pressing problems.

The election results did not undermine the dominance of politicians loyal to the king but they did produce a few significant changes. The leftist Union Socialiste des Forces Populaires (USFP), the largest opposition party and a major victim of electoral interference in the past, doubled its representation in parliament. It won 17 percent of the popular vote, ranking third among the parties. The USFP's improved showing indicated tolerance of dissent during the election and brought greater political diversity into the new parliament. The biggest winner was the Union Constitutionelle (UC), a new party formed in 1983, which received 27 percent of the popular vote. UC leaders are closely aligned with the king. Moreover, since the party is not highly institutionalized and has no secure electoral constituency, it is particularly dependent on ties to the palace. Nevertheless, it is a party of the moderate center with many young technocrats in its ranks, and its success was largely at the expense of electoral fronts controlled by conservative barons with years of participation in patrimonial politics.

Hassan's critics correctly point out that these actions did not introduce fundamental political and economic change. A small and in-grown political class remained dominant and movement toward democracy had not been institutionalized, meaning that it remained dependent on the king's popularity and political calculations and could be withdrawn any time he deemed it counter to his personal interest. Similarly, though economic problems were not all the result of government policies and, in any event, could not be solved overnight, fundamental needs in this domain remained unaddressed, too. These included the corruption and extravagance of the elite and a need to distribute more equitably the nation's economic burden. The Oujda treaty and the elections of 1984 raised hopes that these issues would now receive attention. But it remained to be seen whether this would indeed be the case, and many Moroccans recalled that similar hopes, generated in the mid-1970s, had not been fulfilled.

Despite these critical questions about Morocco's future beyond the short-term, Hassan had again proved himself to be a skillful politician. Temporarily at least, he had reversed his political fortunes at home and those of his domestic opponents as well, gaining needed breathing space and buying time for strategic thinking of a more long-range sort. In the Libyan case, by contrast, it was difficult to see a coherent plan for employing anything other than continuing repression against domestic opponents. Nor, therefore, did the political mood inside the country change appreciably in the wake of the Oujda accord. Whatever the mix of motivations that led Qadhafi to seek an agreement with Hassan, and whatever the potential for symbol and image manipulation that the treaty might have offered the regime in Tripoli, there was no Libyan equivalent of Hassan's mobilization of popular support or of his opening up of domestic political life. As a result, the Arab-African Union did not produce even short-term changes of any significance so far as the domestic scene in Libya was concerned; and Qadhafi's gains, if any, would have to be sought in the international and diplomatic arena.

There was no movement inside Libya either toward the development of greater institutional autonomy and pluralism or toward increased tolerance of differing political views. From the latter part of 1984 through 1985 and 1986, political life in Libya remained as authoritarian and closed as it had been before the conclusion of the Oujda accord. In addition, the regime in Tripoli continued to face challenges and to be confronted with expressions of political opposition and popular discontent. Thus, in contrast to Morocco, the political outlook of neither government elites, counter elites, nor the Libyan masses changed very much as a result of developments set in motion by the formation of the Arab-African Union. Under these circumstances, tensions continued, and if anything increased, in the domestic political arena.

A continuing deterioration of Libya's economic situation added to the country's bleak national mood and interacted with political considerations to produce uncertainty and discontent. One area where this was visible was the recall of students enrolled in foreign universities. The General People's Congress decided on this action after the attack on Bab al-Azziziya barracks in May 1984, and the first phase of the new policy was implemented in February 1985. Students receiving state support for study in England and several other European countries were ordered home at this time, it being expected that more recall notices would be issued later and that these would also be sent to students who were not studying on government scholarships. This action reflected both the economic and the political exigencies to which the regime was seeking to respond. On the one hand, steadily declining revenues from petroleum exports meant the government could no longer afford the cost of educating several thousand students abroad. On the other, the regime had concluded, evidently with reason, that Libyan students overseas were increasingly receptive to the appeals of Qadhafi's opponents.

Tension was also reflected in the contentious mood that prevailed at the General People's Congress convened in February 1985. A number of government policies generated criticism and resistance, including some related to proposed changes in the structure of the GPC and in the number of basic congresses, the local-level units making up the Revolutionary Committees Movement. There were also concerns about the deteriorating economic situation, which had required deep cuts in consumer imports and in domestic spending on education and public welfare. Finally, behind-the-scenes power struggles, centered in particular around control of the state bureau for external security, added an additional element of uncertainty. One result of this collection of concerns was that the assembled delegates refused to approve reelection of the General People's Committee, as the Libyans call their country's cabinet, and this matter remained unresolved until an extraordinary session of the the GPC was convened in May.

The Tripoli regime's greatest concern during the first half of 1985 was undoubtedly the discovery of opposition within the armed forces. The military challenge from the NFSL had abated in the wake of the failed raid on Bab al-Azziziya barracks in May 1984. The group, which shifted its base to Egypt in 1985, for the time being was capable only of launching verbal salvos at Qadhafi. Yet a new and potentially much more serious military threat emerged in April 1985. According to press accounts, a plan to overthrow Qadhafi was discovered within the armed forces, among conservative officers who were said to be disturbed by the growing power of the regime's revolutionary committees. The Movement of Revolutionary Committees had increasingly been used by Qadhafi to limit the power of the military; and, as noted earlier, these committees had been given the power to investigate political offenses, to make arrests, and even to conduct trials and impose sentence on those judged guilty.

Details of the plot discovered in April 1985 are sketchy, as are accounts of the government's response. Some reports indicate that there may actually have been two different attempts to assassinate Qadhafi which took place about the same time, and available sources also indicate that the government may have executed as many as seventy-five officers in retaliation for the alleged plots. In September, there were reports of yet additional disturbances within the military. Egyptian newspaper accounts assert that Qadhafi had ordered the army to prepare for an invasion of Tunisia, in response to the crisis provoked by Tripoli's expulsion of Tunisian workers and the related developments discussed above. According to the account, however, senior army officers refused to obey Qadhafi's order.

A final indication of Qadhafi's troubles with the armed forces was the death in November of Colonel Hassan Ishkal, military commander of the central region of Libya. Although the government claims that Ishkal died in an automobile accident, Libyan dissidents and a number of foreign press sources report that he was shot on Qadhafi's orders. Some of these accounts suggest that Ishkal had been found to be helping the Egyptians plan an invasion of Libya, while others indicate that he had fallen from favor because he advocated the withdrawal of Libyan forces from Chad. There are also some reports which assert that the colonel was killed as part of a power struggle taking place within the Libyan military, in which revolutionary officers sought to remove those whom they believed were interested in rapprochement with Libya's enemies.

Although there were other events that indicated the tense political mood that prevailed during the course of 1985, a fuller review of the domestic scene in Libya is beyond the scope of the present report. The point to be noted, however, is the clear and dramatic contrast between the political climate in Libya and that in Morocco during the year and a half following the Oujda agreement. Whereas Hassan had made impressive, albeit short-term gains, Qadhafi was as beset by domestic challenges as ever.

The International Dimension

Both Hassan and Qadhafi had an international as well as a domestic political agenda; and, as noted, both hoped that the formation of an alliance between their two countries would lead to gains in the area of foreign policy and diplomacy. Of particular concern to Rabat and Tripoli was a desire to counter the growing regional prominence of Algeria, whose 1983 Treaty of Fraternity and Concord with Tunisia and Mauritania appeared to consolidate a central political bloc in the Maghreb and to leave Morocco and Libya isolated on their respective sidelines. As discussed earlier, the rivalry between Algeria and Morocco was particularly intense and was fueled both by Algiers' support of the Polisario cause in the Western Sahara and by a broader competition for leadership in North Africa. There was also, as noted, tension between Libya and both Algeria and Tunisia during this period. A major objective of the Oujda treaty was therefore to counter the perceived challenge from Algeria and its allies; and some analysts argue that these regional considerations were as important a goal as the containment of domestic pressures.

Part of Hassan's and Qadhafi's strategy was to force Tunisia to distance itself from Algeria, putting pressure on the government in Tunis to assume a more neutral posture with respect to both regional affairs in general and the Saharan conflict in particular. Moreover, for a few months at least, the architects of the Arab-African Union realized gains in this regard. For one thing, there was a dramatic improvement in relations between Tunisia and Libya late in 1984 and early in 1985. The two countries announced a series of cooperative economic measures at the end of 1984. Among them were an agreement to guarantee minimum levels of trade and the removal of customs barriers on locally manufactured products. In addition, in January 1985, the Tunisian foreign minister visited Tripoli for political talks. Yet another Tunisian response to the new constellation of political forces in North Africa was an attempt to convene a Maghreb summit early in 1985. Although Tunis obtained agreement in principle from Morocco, Algeria, Libya, and Mauritania, the proposed summit was never convened. Nevertheless, this flurry of Tunisian diplomatic activity showed that the government in Tunis was concerned about the intensifying struggle for power in the region.

These developments led some observers to conclude that Morocco and Libya had indeed succeeded in neutralizing the effects of the 1983 alliance among Algeria, Tunisia, and Mauritania; and Algeria, for its part, was understandably concerned about Tunisia's new attitude toward regional politics. Early in 1985, for example, the Algerian foreign minister told the French-language magazine, *Jeune Afrique*, that the Tunisian government's commitment to the 1983 Treaty of Fraternity and Concord had in recent weeks become suspect. This remark embarrassed the regime in Tunis, which responded by banning the sale of *Jeune Afrique* for the next six months. Nevertheless, the foreign minister's remark accurately reflected both the concerns of Algeria and a conclusion to which many independent observers had come as well.

This situation came rapidly to an end, however, as new strains in relations between Tunisia and Libya emerged during the spring of 1985. By summer, as mentioned earlier, Tripoli had begun the expulsion of thousands of Tunisians working in Libya. Moreover, even the temporary rapprochement between Tunis and Tripoli had not been due solely to the Oujda agreement. Authorities in Tunis, aware of their country's military weakness and political vulnerability, were to a considerable degree motivated by the clashes with Libya that had followed the attack on Bab al-Azziziya barracks the preceding spring. Finally, in any event, the cautious attitude that Tunisia displayed toward regional affairs was a response to essentially negative stimuli; rather than being attracted by a new-found moderation and responsibility on the part of Qadhafi, or by a new-found Moroccan willingness to work out a political compromise in the Sahara, Tunisia sought little more than to defend itself against aggressive neighbors in a Maghreb beset by intensifying conflicts. Thus, in sum, though Hassan and Qadhafi could argue that Tunisia had been pushed toward a position of greater neutrality in North African affairs and that this, in turn, had weakened the principal regional alliance of their own rivals in Algiers, the gains realized by Morocco and Libya were in fact quite short-lived and, as will be seen, of limited significance as well.

A potentially important foreign policy cost that the regime in Morocco had to weigh against any gains it might realize from the union with Libya was a deterioration of its relations with the United States. Although a rapprochement between Rabat and Tripoli had been in the making for over a year, the Oujda accord caught Washington off guard and was a source of great concern in the United States. The administration was fearful that the new union might give Qadhafi an opportunity to make mischief in Morocco, exploiting the vulnerability of the Rabat regime in the wake of domestic unrest and rising internal opposition. Of even greater concern was Washington's fear that the new alliance might strengthen the Libyans. The Reagan administration considers Qadhafi an international outlaw and opposes any action that might give him greater legitimacy. The United States also worried that arms provided to Morocco might be transferred to Libya.

To smooth relations, the king sent his senior advisor, Ahmed Reda Guedira, to Washington in September 1984. Guedira met with Vice-President Bush and other senior officials, and later in the month roving ambassador Vernon Walters traveled to Morocco to meet with King Hassan. As a result of these and other discussions, the Reagan administration cautiously accepted Morocco's assurances that its own behavior would not be influenced by Libya. Though skeptical, the administration also listened to arguments about how the behavior of Qadhafi might in fact be moderated. There were no attempts to reduce aid to Morocco; both economic and military assistance packages were funded in full for the 1985 fiscal year. On the other hand, some administration officials continued to feel that the United States had been betrayed by Rabat, and there remained a new element of tension in Moroccan-American relations. For this reason, Hassan was advised early in 1985 that the time was not right for a proposed visit to Washington.

Hassan's claims that the union with Libya would serve to restrain Qadhafi's behavior merit additional attention. Although it is impossible to know for sure, Hassan was apparently sincere in his belief that he could deliver a more moderate Qadhafi to the international community, and he presumably based some of his calculations about the international implications of the Oujda agreement on this assumption. As mentioned earlier, he hoped this would not only allay American concerns but would earn him the thanks and admiration of the United States. Appreciation would similarly be forthcoming from those countries disturbed by Libyan involvement in Chad, most notably France and a number of black African states. Indeed, if Morocco could arrange for the withdrawal of Qadhafi's forces in Chad, Hassan might be able to gain new support within the OAU for his country's cause in the Western Sahara. In the hope of accomplishing some of these objectives, the king helped to broker an agreement in September 1984 for the mutual withdrawal from Chad of Libyan and French troops.

Hassan had little to show for his efforts, however. Morocco not only failed to deliver a Qadhafi who was more responsible in the eyes of its allies, the king was in fact embarrassed by the Libyan colonel's behavior. By November 1984, it became clear that Libya had misled France and had not removed its troops from Chad as promised. The government of President François Mitterrand was embarrassed and angry voices were heard in Washington as well as Paris. There were also denunciations emanating from Sub-Saharan Africa, and in January 1985 Chad itself complained to the UN Security Council about the continuing Libyan presence.

Casting further doubts about whether Hassan would have any influence over Qadhafi was an Egyptian announcement in November 1984 to the effect that Cairo had foiled a Libyan plot to assassinate several Arab and European leaders. Yet another source of international concern about Qadhafi was a deepening confrontation between Libya and Britain, which began with a shootout at the Libyan People's Bureau in London in April 1984 and was followed by the arrest of four Britons in Tripoli. Libya refused to release the detainees, the last of whom was held until February 1985. There were a number of other incidents as well. Disturbing to the United States, for example, was an address that Qadhafi broadcast via satellite to a black Muslim convention in Chicago in February 1985. The following month, a Libyan student was arrested for planting bombs in London; and, a month after this, West Germany recalled its ambassador from Tripoli to protest the murder of a Libyan dissident in Bonn. About the same time, Tunisian authorities accused Libya of anti-Jewish radio broadcasts, in which North African Muslims were urged to kill their Jewish minorities.

With a conflict in the Mediterranean between the United States and Libya also taking shape during the first months of 1985, it rapidly became apparent that the Oujda treaty had done little to change Qadhafi's international behavior and that restraining the Libyan colonel was not an accomplishment for which Hassan could expect to claim credit. Indeed, if anything, Washington's concerns about the Arab-African Union intensified during these months, and it is against this background that the full significance of the Reagan administration's reluctance to receive Hassan in Washington may be seen.

These developments demonstrated that the moderation of Hassan was not about to prevail over Qadhafi's militant radicalism. They also put to rest all speculation that the Libyan colonel himself might be eager to change his international image and the direction of his foreign policy. Qadhafi, for his part, insisted that he was innocent of many of the charges made against him by the United States and others. He denied responsibility for the anti-Jewish radio broadcasts of April 1985, for example. Qadhafi also argued that his country had, in fact, been the target of foreign aggression, such as the "provocative maneuvers" that the U.S. 6th Fleet carried out off the Libyan coast in January 1985; and, to an extent, the validity of his claims was recognized and asserted by Hassan. Balancing his ties to Washington and Tripoli, the Moroccan king issued several cautious statements to the effect that the Reagan administration's fixation on Qadhafi as a major source of international terrorism was both simplistic and inappropriate. Nevertheless, whether totally by design or in part because of constraints imposed by the provocative behavior of others, there did not emerge in the months following the Oujda agreement a more moderate and conciliatory Libyan foreign policy.

Nowhere was this more apparent than in the escalating tension between the United States and Libya. Inside Libya, there were popular demonstrations against the United States following the 6th Fleet's exercises in the Mediterranean in January 1985. In the United States, it was reported in May that a grand jury was investigating charges that Qadhafi's agents planned to assassinate Libyan dissidents in the United States, and a few weeks later the State Department announced the expulsion of a Libyan diplomat at the United Nations in connection with these charges. As the Reagan administration became increasingly preoccupied with Qadhafi's "pattern of aggression" during the course of 1985, the list of offenses with which it charged the Libyan leader grew steadily longer and Qadhafi himself sought new opportunities to strike out at the United States and its interests. A special State Department report issued in January 1986 declared Qadhafi guilty of numerous acts of international terrorism and of assistance to radical groups ranging from the Abu Nidal faction to Muslim extremists in Southeast Asia. Appended to the report was a chronology of "Libyan Support for Terrorism," which listed eleven episodes involving nine countries during 1985 alone.

Many observers of the Middle East and North Africa criticized the Reagan administration for failing to address the underlying political and economic problems to which much of the region's terrorism was a response. They argued that Qadhafi was but a small part of a much more complicated problem. Some also asserted that Washington's campaign against the Libyan colonel was counterproductive. On the one hand, it boosted Qadhafi's prestige in the Arab world and at home by creating the impression that the United States considered him a serious adversary. On the other, it projected U.S. power into the Middle East in a way that embarrassed moderate Arab leaders and generated anti-American sentiments among the masses, both of which in turn worked to Qadhafi's advantage. Even if one accepts these criticisms of U.S. policy, however, it remains the case that Libya did pursue a foreign policy marked by the same radical goals and tactics that had characterized it before the formation of the union with Morocco. Thus, in conclusion, whatever the original intentions of Hassan and Qadhafi, the Oujda treaty did not prove to be a step toward the reduction of Libya's international isolation or toward a significant and sustained change in the character of Libyan foreign policy.

Morocco's most important foreign policy goal was to strengthen its military and diplomatic position with respect to the conflict in the Western Sahara. Should the Oujda agreement lead to gains in this domain, the balance sheet of the accord would be highly favorable from the Moroccan point of view, even if other anticipated benefits were not realized. But while the reconciliation between Hassan and Qadhafi did end Libyan assistance to Polisario guerrillas, the overall military situation in the Sahara did not change significantly with the formation of the Arab-African Union.

Morocco continued to expand the construction of defensive fortifications and thereby solidified the position of general military dominance, which it had already enjoyed for several years. On the other hand, Algeria increased its aid to Polisario in order to compensate for the withdrawal of Libyan support, and Polisario in turn continued and intensified its declared war of attrition, harassing Moroccan forces with hit and run attacks. Polisario and Algerian sources reported that almost six hundred Moroccan soldiers were killed in encounters between mid-October and the end of 1984, and similar claims, including the downing of several Moroccan aircraft, were advanced throughout the course of 1985. While Moroccan officials acknowledged a number of losses during this period, they insisted that rebel claims were grossly exaggerated. Moreover, it is almost certain that this was indeed the case. Nevertheless, whatever the accuracy of various claims and counterclaims about troop losses, the Polisario's war of attrition did continue after Libya's exit from the Saharan conflict and Morocco remained unable to bring about a qualitative change in the overall military situation. Moreover, the conduct of the war continued to place a heavy burden on Morocco's deteriorating economy, forcing Rabat to spend approximately $500 million a year in order to maintain seventy-five to eighty thousand troops along its expanding defensive perimeter.

Morocco's balance sheet in the diplomatic confrontation with Polisario has been even more unsatisfactory. Polisario claims to represent the desire for self-determination of the Saharan people, who accordingly aspire to establish an independent Saharan Arab Democratic Republic, and in November 1984 the SADR was admitted to membership by the Organization of African Unity. Morocco walked out of the OAU summit conference at which this decision was taken, although, notably, it was not accompanied by Libya. Only Zaire joined Morocco and that country announced that its absence would be temporary. A year later, in November 1985, the OAU secretariat in Addis Ababa reported that Morocco had formally ceased membership in the organization.

It is difficult to say whether the OAU's action was influenced by Morocco's union with Libya and by related concerns about Chad. While some black African states were angry at Morocco for giving legitimacy to Libyan involvement in Chad, and for Qadhafi's broken promise to withdraw his troops from that country, it is quite likely the principal motivations of the OAU lay elsewhere. Many delegates consider the Saharan conflict an inter-Arab quarrel that in recent years has diverted attention from more pressing problems, and thus they may simply have sought to rid themselves of this troublesome and divisive issue. In any event, whether or not the Oujda agreement was a contributing factor, November 1984 brought to an unsuccessful conclusion Morocco's four-year struggle to fight the SADR to a draw in the arena of African diplomacy.

The number of countries granting diplomatic recognition to the SADR continued to mount. In November 1984, such recognition was accorded by Nigeria and Yugoslavia. The latter was the first European country to make such a move, and Rabat immediately responded by breaking its own diplomatic relations with Belgrade. Additional countries recognized the SADR during the course of 1985 and 1986, and, in particular, new gains were made in Latin America. In April 1986, for example, Guatemala became the sixty-fourth state to give such recognition, and two months later the Dominican Republic became the sixty-fifth country to do so. Algeria and Polisario also took their case to the United Nations and achieved additional results. In December 1985, the UN adopted an Algerian-backed resolution calling on Morocco to negotiate with Polisario, which King Hassan adamantly refuses to do.

It is again impossible to say whether these developments were influenced in any way by the Moroccan-Libyan connection. Although there was genuine concern about the Oujda agreement, especially in Africa, it is unlikely that many countries turned against Morocco on the Saharan question simply because they disapproved of the union with Qadhafi. It is more plausible to suggest that Hassan could have harvested diplomatic benefits in Africa and elsewhere had he been able to moderate Qadhafi's international behavior. This, too, is an untestable proposition, however. Nor is it any longer of practical significance, given that Libya's involvement in Chad and Qadhafi's other foreign adventures did not diminish as a result of the union with Morocco.

None of Morocco's diplomatic setbacks are likely to force King Hassan to reexamine his policy toward the Sahara. Thus, as in the conduct of the war itself, the next few years will probably see much more continuity than change in the Saharan conflict. But since the conflict is costing Morocco heavily, both in economic terms and in diplomatic isolation, Rabat remains in need of a strategy that will enable it to make new gains and to conclude the Saharan war on a basis it deems acceptable. The Oujda treaty offered such a strategy, and things might have turned out differently had Libya, and to a lesser extent Algeria, behaved differently. Since this was not the case, however, and since the accord produced few other lasting benefits in the international arena, the case for maintaining the Arab-African Union was not nearly so strong in 1985 and 1986 as had been the case for establishing it in 1984.

The End of the Story

The alliance between Morocco and Libya began with much fanfare and its ratification by the two countries was followed by a short-lived period of near euphoria. Ambitious plans were laid for economic and political cooperation, and, in Morocco at least, these were accompanied by new elections and the revival of parliamentary democracy. In addition, with the termination of Libyan support for the Polisario war effort, the prospect of developments favorable to Morocco in the Sahara appeared to improve substantially. Similarly, the conclusion of an agreement between Libya and France for the withdrawal of their respective forces in Chad raised the possibility of a breakthrough in that conflict as well. Finally, Tunisia began to show signs of greater neutrality in inter-Maghreb politics, suggesting that Hassan and Qadhafi might have found a way to counter the growing influence of Algeria.

As discussed, all of this was indeed short-lived. Within a few months, Polisario had launched a series of new attacks on King Hassan's forces in the Sahara, and Morocco had walked out of the OAU summit conference in the wake of that organization's decision to grant membership to the SADR. The agreement between Libya and France also proved to be without substance. Moreover, by the fall of 1984 Qadhafi was being charged not only with misleading the French and others about his intentions in Chad but also with responsibility for new acts of international terrorism. A Libyan-sponsored assassination plot uncovered in Egypt was the most important of these incidents during the latter part of 1984. There were other important problems, too. On the one hand, new strains between Libya and Tunisia emerged early in 1985, pushing the latter country back toward closer cooperation with Algeria. On the other, and ultimately most important of all, Washington's anger at Rabat for concluding the Oujda agreement in the first place was compounded by deepening U.S. concern about Qadhafi's foreign adventures. Finally, there continued to be political unrest and opposition inside Libya.

In view of this situation, it is not surprising that tensions and mutual disappointment soon became prominent in Libyan-Moroccan relations. The construction of the Arab-African Union, though modest in absolute terms, was real enough as far as it went. Moreover, as noted, progress continued to be made through the early months of 1986. Nevertheless, gains were increasingly overshadowed by the disenchantment with the alliance that both parties clearly felt.

In this connection, observers attached significance to the fact that Hassan had not visited Libya since the formation of Arab-African Union and that Qadhafi had not returned to Morocco since his original Oujda meeting with the Moroccan monarch. Hassan was, of course, disappointed by Qadhafi's continuing radicalism and, in particular, by renewed tension between Libya and Tunisia, which pushed the latter country back toward closer cooperation with Algeria. Morocco was seriously concerned as well about an improvement in relations between Libya and revolutionary Iran. Rabat's own relations with Tehran were badly strained, with Hassan having received the Shah after his overthrow and with Moroccans opposed to the monarchical regime having visited Iran following Khomeini's ascent to power. Yet ties between Tripoli and Tehran were upgraded in June 1985, following the visit to Libya of a high-ranking Iranian delegation. To show his displeasure, Hassan delayed for one week the inaugural session of the federal legislature, which was to be held in Rabat with the king presiding.

Most problematic of all for Hassan was Qadhafi's continuing involvement in international terrorism and the deepening hostility between the United States and Libya to which this led. On the one hand, Hassan was cross-pressured by his ties to both Washington and Tripoli. On the other, this situation gave Algeria an opportunity to improve its own relations with Libya and, thereby, to weaken Morocco's position in North African affairs. With respect to the latter development, Algerian President Chedli Benjedid in November 1985 offered to support Libya in the event of American aggression and this was followed by the visit to Algiers of a high-ranking Libyan delegation. The Libyans were careful to brief Morocco about these developments, but King Hassan was nevertheless concerned that his country's regional influence relative to that of Algeria would diminish.

Hassan's concerns intensified when Qadhafi and Benjedid held a summit meeting in Amenas, in eastern Algeria, in January 1986. Although no communique was issued, unofficial reports from Algeria hinted that Libya might soon be ready to resume support for Polisario guerrillas in the Sahara. A month later, in February, Algiers and Tripoli announced that they had signed an agreement to enhance bilateral cooperation. Algeria's motivation for these overtures derived in large measure from a desire to undermine the Moroccan-Libyan alliance and to weaken the Rabat government's position in North African affairs. In addition, however, Algeria was concerned about the escalation of its own conflict with Tripoli, as discussed earlier; and Benjedid was also embarrassed by press reports in the United States to the effect that Algeria might participate in American efforts to destabilize the Qadhafi regime. Libya, for its part, sought a rapprochement with Algeria both to gain support in the event of a confrontation with the United States and to reduce tensions created by its own recent hostility toward Tunisia.

The conflict between Washington and Tripoli worsened after the United States charged Libya with involvement in terrorist bombings at the Rome and Vienna airports in December 1985. A few weeks later, the Reagan administration responded with a package of economic sanctions against the Qadhafi regime, suspending virtually all direct economic ties between the United States and Libya. Increasingly concerned, Hassan offered to mediate between his two warring allies. At the same time, although he maintained a public posture of neutrality and even made several statements urging the United States not to escalate the conflict further, the king in fact began to give evidence that his ties to Washington would take precedence should he be required to choose between continued cooperation with Libya and good relations with the United States.

One indication of Hassan's attitude was to be found in statements he made about Israel. In November 1985, the king told French interviewers that he was prepared to meet with Israeli prime minister, Shimon Peres, and in March 1986 he urged an Arab summit meeting to explore Israel's readiness to negotiate on the basis of the Arabs' own peace proposals, a plan adopted at the Fez summit conference of September 1982. Such moves were designed, at least in part, to show Washington that Morocco could be a valuable Arab ally. Such moves were particularly significant in view of Libya's well-known opposition to any accommodation with the Jewish state. Tripoli belongs to a small group of rejectionist Arab states that do not support the Fez Plan. In addition, Hassan's statements were all the more notable because Israel had bombed the Tunis headquarters of the Palestine Liberation Organization the preceding October. This attack produced condemnation of both Israel and the United States throughout the Arab world and was a special embarrassment to pro-American Arab regimes advocating moderation toward Jerusalem.

Another important gesture made to the United States by Morocco was an invitation that the king extended to CIA director William Casey and American ambassador to the United Nations Vernon Walters. Both men were honored guests at Throne Day ceremonies in March, which in 1986 commemorated twenty-five years of rule by King Hassan. The choice of Casey and Walters was particularly significant and made Hassan's action an unusually clear signal to both Tripoli and Washington. By inviting the head of the Central Intelligence Agency, the king showed his disdain for Arab criticism of covert American operations, including those that may have been designed to topple Qadhafi. Walters, formerly a roving U.S. ambassador and troubleshooter for the Reagan administration, was the man whom Washington had sent to Rabat in the fall of 1984 to register its disapproval of the Oujda agreement.

The U.S. bombing raid on Libya in April increased anti-American sentiment throughout the Arab world and even brought condemnation from most of Washington's Arab allies. The bombing was also an embarrassment to Hassan; and, since Morocco's interests would be served neither by a defense of U.S. action nor by public support for Qadhafi, the king accordingly maintained his silence. Yet the die of Moroccan foreign policy had already been cast, and it was not long before Hassan found new opportunities to show that he deemed good relations with the United States to be his first priority. For one thing, he made plans to visit Washington early in the summer. Most important, however, the king again used an overture toward Israel to signal his foreign policy orientation. Hassan caught virtually all observers unawares by inviting Shimon Peres to Morocco in July, in effect producing another of his famous political "surprises."

Already moribund for several months, the Arab-African Union now suffered a fatal blow. Qadhafi responded to the Hassan-Peres summit by accusing the Moroccan king of treason, and Hassan then replied by stating that the Libyan leader had defamed the honor and dignity of his country. Morocco is a sovereign state, the king insisted, free to determine its own foreign policy. Moreover, since this had been precisely his response to earlier U.S. criticism of the Oujda agreement, Hassan was hardly about to agree that his alliance with Qadhafi should now bring to an end the very independence that had made a Libyan connection possible. Delivering these remarks in a national radio and television address on August 29, the king announced that he was terminating the Oujda agreement and thus brought to an end the two-year-old experiment in Moroccan-Libyan unity.

The life and death of the Arab-African Union has not left any lasting imprint on the political map of North Africa. The short-term significance of the Oujda agreement is rather different, however, although it is only the regime of King Hassan II of Morocco that was able to translate the agreement into meaningful, albeit temporary, political gain.

Some of the gains that Morocco hoped to derive from the union with Libya were not realized. Rabat's fortunes in the Saharan conflict did not improve, Algeria's influence in North Africa was not seriously eroded, and there occurred significant strains in Morocco's important relationship with the United States. On the other hand, the Oujda agreement helped Hassan to accomplish important objectives in the domestic political arena, and the king undoubtedly considered tension in the foreign policy sphere an acceptable price for his vastly improved position at home. In this connection, Hassan's overture to Libya showed itself to be a bold and masterful political stroke, a calculated "surprise" that achieved the most important of the objectives for which it had been designed.

Judged from a short-term perspective, Hassan's political strategy was thus highly successful, producing far more benefits than costs. Whereas the king and his supporters had been under intense pressure during 1983 and the first part of 1984, Hassan subsequently regained the initiative and proved, once again, that his ability to control events should not be underestimated. By the end of 1984, defying predictions of his downfall made barely six months earlier, the king's popularity had been restored and his domestic critics placed on the defensive.

The situation in Libya was different, however. Even in the short-term, during the two years of its existence, the Arab-African Union was not associated with any important changes in the circumstances of Libya or in any significant improvement in the fortunes of the regime in Tripoli. Qadhafi's radical direction in matters of foreign policy continued, as did his conflicts with a growing number of countries. Similarly, Libya achieved little of substance in Chad during this period. Even more serious from Qadhafi's viewpoint were the internal challenges confronting his regime. Deepening economic troubles accelerated the erosion of his regime's popular base. There was also an intensification of political discontent, with opposition coming from students, Islamic activists, and elements within the military. The Oujda agreement was not responsible for these problems, of course, all of which were both visible and serious before the rapprochement with Morocco. But it is also clear that the treaty did little to alter the course of their evolution.

Qadhafi's gains from the alliance with Hassan were thus modest. They were limited to a number of Moroccan statements endorsing Libyan involvement in Chad, an increased ability to put pressure on Tunisia, and the termination of Moroccan assistance to the NFSL and a few other opponents of the regime in Tripoli. But it is possible that Qadhafi could have used his Rabat connection to better advantage.

Hassan had hopes that the Libyan colonel was genuinely interested in moderating his behavior, and had he done so it would certainly have been to the advantage of the king. This course of action would probably have been in Qadhafi's interest as well. Neither Libya nor its leaders have benefitted by strained relations with moderate Arab and African states, to say nothing of Tripoli's conflict with the United States, Britain, and other Western powers. The regime has achieved few of its foreign policy objectives, and the situation inside Libya has become less rather than more secure. This is in contrast to Algeria, for example. Like Libya, its political orientation is radical and its posture frequently militant. But the Algiers government has shown that responsibility and predictability are useful and perhaps even necessary ingredients in the effective pursuit of national interest.

It is impossible to know whether Hassan had reasonable grounds for his expectation that Qadhafi's behavior would become more restrained with the formation of the Arab-African Union, and whether this was in fact the Libyan colonel's intention at the time of the Oujda accord. It did appear that Qadhafi saw Hassan's move toward rapprochement as offering a valuable opportunity for the manipulation of political symbols and the remaking of political images. Specifically, as discussed earlier, it provided Qadhafi with a chance to enhance his international legitimacy and reduce his country's isolation. Moreover, by projecting a more moderate and responsible image, Qadhafi might also have hoped to diffuse opposition at home. All of this must remain speculation, however. While such possibilities are consistent with the logic of the Oujda accord, and with the events that drove Qadhafi to make common cause with Hassan in the first place, subsequent developments make it impossible to advance definitive conclusions either about the Libyan leader's original intentions or about how things would have turned out had Qadhafi followed the scenario scripted for him by Hassan.

BIBLIOGRAPHIC NOTE

Readers seeking a comprehensive introduction to political life in contemporary North Africa are directed to I. William Zartman et al., *Political Elites in Arab North Africa* (New York: Longman, 1982). Other important sources include Richard Parker, *North Africa: Regional Tensions and Strategic Concerns* (New York: Praeger, 1984), and Halim Barakat (ed.), *Contemporary North Africa: Issues of Development and Integration* (London: Croom Helm, 1985). Factual information about the union between Libya and Morocco is provided by a wide variety of journalistic sources, some of which are identified below. In addition, several articles offer more focused and scholarly analyses. These include Mark Tessler, "The Uses and Limits of Populism: The Political Strategy of King Hassan II of Morocco," *The Middle East Review* (Spring 1985); Richard Parker, "Appointment in Oujda," *Foreign Affairs* (Summer 1985); and John Damis, "Morocco, Libya and the Treaty of Union," *American-Arab Affairs* (Summer 1985).

A useful overview of the domestic tensions and regional conflicts to which the Arab-African Union was a response is provided by the May 1985 issue of *Current History*, which is devoted entirely to the countries of North Africa. Additional information is to be found in a collection of articles on the theme "North Africa in Transition," which appeared in the Fall 1983 issue of *American-Arab Affairs*, and, more recently, in Mark Tessler, "Explaining the 'Surprises' of King Hassan II: The Link Between Domestic and Foreign Policy in Morocco—Part I: Tensions in North Africa in the Mid-1980s," *Universities Field Staff International Reports* (1986/No. 38). Readers seeking other English-language sources dealing with recent developments in North Africa are directed to the articles which regularly appear in *Africa Confidential, Middle East International, Middle East Economic Digest,* and *MERIP Reports*. Also helpful are the chronologies and summaries of current events found in each issue of *The Middle East Journal* and *Africa Report*. Finally, the Economist Intelligence Unit publishes the valuable *Quarterly Economic Review of Libya* and *Quarterly Economic Review of of Morocco*, as well as quarterly economic reviews of the other North African states.

VI.

THE CASE OF CHAD

René Lemarchand

The emergence of Chad as a top priority on Qadhafi's agenda does more than explain its growing visibility as a festering crisis area; it brings into focus certain enduring characteristics of his foreign policy orientation—his obsessive concern with Arab unity, his utter disdain for the legacy of colonial boundaries, and his inveterate propensity to engage in destabilization activities through the use of proxies—as well as some rather atypical traits.

To judge by the scale and duration of Libyan involvement in Chad no other state figures more prominently on Qadhafi's "hit list"; measured by the severity of the losses suffered by Tripoli at the hands of the Chadian army since January 1987, no other state, one might add, has as yet exacted a higher price for Libyan adventurism. Between 1973, when a handful of Libyan troops crossed the Libyan-Chadian border into Aouzou, and 1987 when, following a series of decisive engagements, the Libyan army was forced back into Aouzou, leaving behind over 3,600 killed, 1,165 prisoners, and one billion dollars worth of military equipment, Tripoli has consistently upped the ante in terms of ground forces, defense systems, armory, and infrastructural developments. From 1980 to 1987 anywhere from 5,000 to 7,000 Libyan troops saw military action in Chad in engagements ranging from isolated skirmishes to pitched battles involving T-54 and T-62 tanks, heavy artillery, and air strikes against enemy positions. Only in Chad has Libya made a sustained effort to export its *mission civilisatrice* through people's revolutionary committees, the Green Book, and the compulsory use of Arabic as a medium of instruction and communication. Only in Chad has Qadhafi made such an extensive and deliberate use of proxies, and with as much sensitivity to the international recognition of his surrogates. Of all the issues confronting the Organization of African Unity (OAU), none has proved more delicate to handle, or more profoundly divisive, than the Chadian imbroglio (see Pondi, in this volume).

What accounts for the relative success of Qadhafi's adventurism in Chad is not so much the scale of Libyan intervention, or the motives behind it, as the unparalleled set of opportunities that lies in the background of such intervention. These are not reducible to any single set of factors. Some are the product of history; others are directly traceable to the internal convulsions suffered by the Chadian state; others still have to do with Qadhafi's own astuteness in manipulating political actors within and outside the boundaries of the Chadian state. Appreciation of the significance and interrelatedness of these different contexts—the history of the region, the internal politics of Chad, and Qadhafi's manipulative skills and domestic resources—is central to an understanding of the dynamics of Libyan intervention.

Background to Intervention: The Geopolitical Dimension

"Each country responds to its unique geography by arriving at a unique set of geopolitical perceptions and preoccupations" (Brown 1987, 47). Libya is no exception. The forces that have shaped Libya's perception of its national interest in northern Chad were present in the area long before Qadhafi's time: they are inscribed in the history and geography of the Tibesti and the Fezzan, and continue to this day to set the basic parameters of Libyan expansion into this perennially contested region.

The case for the obliteration of colonial boundaries is nowhere more compelling than in this vast no-man's-land that stretches across miles between Chad and Libya, north and south of the so-called Aouzou strip. Population movements back and forth across the Chad-Libyan frontier—some traceable to the caravan trade, others to the rhythm of seasonal migrations and the exigencies of nomadic life, others still to the spread of Islam—have been going on for centuries. The history of the region is preeminently the story of societies in movement. The concept of frontier as a precise, identifiable line of demarcation between territorial units is thoroughly alien to Sahelian societies (Muller 1982, 167); not only does it do violence to the mode of life as nomads or semi-nomads, but to their mode of production and mode of transportation (camels are notoriously unmindful of geographical boundaries).[1] And so, also, is the corollary concept of territoriality: "in nomadic communities the right to move prevails over the right to camp, and ownership means in effect the title to a cycle of migration" (Kratochwil 1986, 29).

Qadhafi's denunciations of colonial boundaries are not just the product of cultural perceptions. Historical precedents are also worth bearing in mind. Libyan claims to northern Chad have a long pedigree, going back at least to the Ottoman period. A Turkish presence was established at Ain Galaka, the Borkou stronghold, in 1911, and prior to that the Senussiya brotherhood was the principal vector of Libyan influence in the region (Latrémolière 1985b). Partly to evade Turkish pressures in Cyrenaica, and also to strengthen its hold over the trans-Saharan caravan trade, in the late nineteenth century the Senussiya moved the focus of its activities southward into Chad, with some of its lodges (*zawiyyas*) reaching as far south as Lake Chad. By then its influence was widely felt in Borkou, Ennedi, Kanem, and Ouaddai, whose King Ali, according to Nachtigal, became one of the brotherhood's "most ardent supporters" (Morsy 1984, 277). The same cannot be said of Qadhafi. Yet there can be little doubt that the history of the Senussiya has contributed to strengthening his conviction that northern Chad is indeed a legitimate sphere of Libyan influence (Al-Hendiri 1984). As much as the scope of its territorial expansion, the active resistance of the brotherhood to French and Italian penetration is a central element in Libyan perceptions of their history.[2]

So, also, are the countless litigations that have arisen between France and Italy over the demarcation of their colonial boundaries. "Certain regions," according to one observer, "were still considered to bear only a provisional demarcation as late as 1950; throughout the whole of the interwar period, up to 1939, French and Italian expeditions attempted to rectify this situation, the final attempt on the French side being the Larroque Mission" (Muller 1982,

170). Ever since 1919, when Italy explicitly laid claim to the Tibesti and Borkou regions, France and Italy had been continually at odds over the international status of the Aouzou strip, an elongated stretch of desert 450 miles long and 90 miles wide, running parallel to the Chadian-Libyan border, on the Chadian side. By assigning the Aouzou strip to Italy, the Mussolini-Laval accords of January 7, 1935 (also referred to as the Rome Treaty) provided the basis for what the signatories hoped would be the final settlement of their *contentieux*. Yet the treaty, though unanimously approved by the French Senate and overwhelmingly so by the Chamber of Deputies (555 votes against 9), was never formally ratified by the French president (Lanne 1982). The matter would hardly deserve mention if it were not for the fact that the Libyan claim to Aouzou is specifically based on the Mussolini-Laval accords; despite or because of it never being ratified the Rome Treaty is one of the very few instruments that Qadhafi considers legally binding.

Shifting the locus of international boundaries was only one of the strategies used by France and Italy to resolve their differences; another involved "the manipulation of the *function* of boundaries through untying the bundle of rights conventionally associated with full territorial sovereignty" (Kratochwill 1986, 29), a strategy by no means limited to the case under consideration. Illustrative of this "functional" solution are the terms of the Franco-Libyan treaty of 1955, where the signatories agreed "to provide facilities for the transhumance of nomads from tribes that traditionally migrate across the Algerian-Libyan frontier." Although this was the "first time that concern for the problems of nomads had actually been enshrined in a treaty" (Muller 1982, 176), this departure from the rights of territoriality was in fact widely tolerated during and after the colonial era. While adding to the imprecision surrounding the tracing of the Chadian-Libyan boundary, it also enhanced its porosity. On both counts the result has been to encourage Qadhafi to use the argument of ethnicity in support of his territorial claims (in much the same way that the French, in the mid-fifties, laid claim to the Ghat region of the Fezzan by stressing "the fact that the same ethnic group inhabited both sides of the frontier" [Muller 1982]).

The Libyan case is convincingly set forth in Qadhafi's statement at the time of the abortive Libya-Chad merger, in January 1981:

> There is a very old historical interaction between the Libyan and the Chadian peoples, and between the Chadian people and the Arab nation, and the borders are open between the two countries. . . . Eastern and southeastern Chad is entirely Arab. . . . A very large number of Libyans emigrated to Chad, settled there and became Chadians. . . . (quoted in Wright 1983, 91)

Among "the large number of Libyans [who] emigrated to Chad" awareness of the Libyan "homeland" persisted throughout and long after the colonial period, thus providing a convenient vehicle for the diffusion of Libyan influences in northern Chad.

Of particular significance here is the role played by the Awlad Sulayman. This is not the place for an extended discussion of their history—"one of movement and maneuvering, a tumultuous existence best analyzed in terms of the Saharan environment that nurtured and threatened them in turn" (Cordell 1985, 322). Suffice it to note that, from their original homeland around the Gulf of Syrte, the Awlad Sulayman moved southward over an extended period of time reaching as far back as the eighteenth century and always under the pressure of external forces. The most recent of such migrations took place during the Italian conquest, when, after a fierce resistance, thousands of Awlad Sulayman found refuge in Chad. Though representing a small minority of Chad's total Arab population of approximately half a million, their relative wealth, military skills, and fluent knowledge of Arabic gave them an influence out of all proportion to their numbers.

Like many Arab "tribes," the Awlad Sulayman face a dilemma that is perhaps best captured by the concept of "situational diaspora," to borrow John Armstrong's phrase. Reinforcing their collective awareness as part of an ethnic diaspora is the special position they held in the Chadian arena as a minority that "does not have a general status advantage" and yet "enjoys many cultural and material advantages compared to other groups in the multiethnic polity" (Armstrong 1976, 394). This does not imply endorsement of political unification with Libya; on the other hand "the situational diaspora's rejection of ethnic political unification has not saved it from the suspicion of the dominant elites of their multiethnic polities" (Armstrong 1976, 395). This is where a vicious circle sets in: because of their cultural and commercial links with Libya, the Awlad Sulayman did incur the suspicion of other groups, and as these suspicions turned into discrimination many felt they had no other alternative but to turn to Libya. Identification with the Libyan homeland increased in proportion to their sense of exclusion. From a "situational diaspora" the Awlad Sulayman rapidly converted themselves into a "mobilized diaspora," providing Qadhafi with one of several sources of support in northern Chad.

Pursuing this theme would take us too far afield. Suffice it to note that Qadhafi's perceptions of the Libyan national interest are solidly anchored in his awareness of the complex interplay of history and geopolitics; as much as his commitment to Afro-Arab unity, his sense of history has contributed in no small way to shape the rationale of his Chadian policies. What helped translate this rationale into reality were the specific circumstances of Chadian politics in the years following independence.

The Chadian Crisis: Threats and Opportunities

If one can speak of a "logic of opportunity" to describe the dynamics of Libyan policies, no less pertinent is the "logic of security" that underlies the formulation of these policies: together they lend an aura of rationality to what otherwise might be dismissed as adventurist folly. To put the matter differently, the interventionist thrust of Libyan policies in Chad can best be seen as a series of calculated responses to specific threats and opportunities.

The threats originated from two separate sources: from the abortive attempt made in 1970 by a group of Libyan opponents to use Chad as a "privileged sanctuary" to overthrow the Libyan regime, and from the Israeli presence in Chad, the second apparently not unrelated to the first.

It is ironic and of no small significance that threats to Libyan security arose from Chad *before* Libya emerged as the most immediate and mortal danger to Chadian security. Though largely forgotten, the so-called "Black Prince conspiracy" must have awakened Qadhafi to the strategic importance of Chad as a springboard for subversive activities. In the summer of 1970 two of his most bitter opponents, Omar Shalhi and "Prince" Abdallah al-Abid al-Senussi ("The Black Prince"), proceeded to use Chad as a base for organizing a raid against Sebha, in southern Libya, as a first step toward the destabilization of the regime. With the help of a mixed bag of "retired officers of the old Libyan security forces, and some businessmen and contractors who had prospered under the old regime" (Cooley 1982, 98), some two hundred mercenaries were recruited, later to be flown into Libya. As John Cooley reports:

> Chartered aircraft were to lift the troops and weapons to an airstrip near Sebha. From there, with local complicity assured by the Seif al-Nasr clan, the rebel force was to make their pronunciamento on Sebha radio. Then they would distribute arms to the local tribes and march northward, hoping to touch off anti-Qadhafi revolts in Tripoli and Benghazi. (Cooley 1982, 99)

The Black Prince conspiracy ended with the landing of an advance planeload of his mercenaries in Sebha, where Qadhafi's troops gave them an unexpected welcome. But the lesson of the conspiracy was not lost on Qadhafi: "The story of this attempt to repeat the feat of the Free French Forces of entering Libya by its southern borders is certainly one of the reasons for Qadhafi's obsession with Chad and his 1980–81 military occupation of the country. With reason, he has always regarded any hostile presence there as a major threat to his security" (Cooley 1982, 98).

If so, it is easy to see why the Israeli connection in Chad should have caused even greater anxieties in Tripoli, particularly in view of the alleged involvement of the Mossad in the Black Prince machinations (Cooley 1982, 98). By 1970 Israel's technical assistance to Chad covered a wider range of activities than anywhere else on the continent; in the aggregate only Uganda received a larger aid package. Until 1972, according to Decalo:

> the Israeli role in Chad . . . included assistance in civic formation (the Mouvement de la Jeunesse Tchadienne), the erection of model pilot farms (Koundoul, near Ndjamena), health and educational aid, surveys and exploitation of natural resources, a loan ($400,000) for the Sarh refrigerated slaughterhouse, and training of Chadian paratroopers at the Zaire Israel-staffed Paratroopers' School. (Decalo 1977, 150)

To which must be added the training of Chad's crack security unit, the *Compagnies Tchadiennes de Sécurité* (CTS). To this day, curiously enough, Libyan military intelligence operates on the assumption of a continuing Israeli connection with the Chadian armed forces.[3]

The rather extensive scale of Israeli aid activities carried implications that went far beyond the Chadian arena. Suspicions of Israeli involvement in the ongoing civil war in neighboring Sudan raised the specter of the Christian south gaining the upper hand over the Muslim north, thereby endangering a critical link in Qadhafi's regional alliance system. From a still broader perspective Qadhafi's effort to counter Israeli influence in Chad may be viewed as part of a global strategy aimed at eliminating all forms of Zionist influence from the continent, a precondition for the realization of the more distant goal of pan-Arab unity on a Sahelian scale.

Irrespective of their broader geopolitical implications, Libyan security interests are a fundamental aspect of Qadhafi's Chadian policy mold; they are explicitly set forth in the statement issued by the Libyan ambassador to Paris, Said Hafiana, in 1983: "We consider that the stability and security of Chad are linked to our stability and security. . . . This means that there must not be in Chad a political regime which is hostile to Libya and which might use Chad as a base for direct action" (*Le Monde*, July 13, 1983). Predictably missing from Hafiana's statement is the recognition that Libyan security has been largely predicated on the destabilization of the Chadian state.

This became tangibly evident, when in the wake of these threats, a host of opportunities arose for turning the tide against Ndjamena; in an ironic reversal of roles, from 1970 onward it was Libya's turn to offer a privileged sanctuary to the Chadian opposition. Drawn into the maelstrom of Chadian politics as much by the fragility of the Chadian state as by the links forged with its enemies, Libya rapidly emerged as the dominant force in northern Chad.

This is hardly the place for a sustained account of Chad's tortuous descent into chaos; what follows is merely intended to provide certain basic reference points for our subsequent discussion of Libyan strategies. The first and most obvious point of reference is the extraordinarily rapid disintegration of the Chadian state in the years following independence. Few other states have been confronted with a more formidable array of obstacles in their efforts to achieve a measure of socio-political integration: the immensity of its national territory (twice the size of metropolitan France), the sheer diversity of ethnocultural aggregates comprised within its boundaries, the persistence of religious discontinuities between north and south, the very superficial impact of French colonial rule beyond the country's southern tier, along with the forbidding nature of the physical environment in the northern half of the country—all of this would have made the task of state-building extraordinarily arduous even under the best of circumstances. Further complicating this task was the combination of ineptitude and ethnic prejudice displayed by the government of François Tombalbaye from 1960 until its overthrow by the Chadian military in 1974: By more or less systematically excluding the northern sectors from political participation Tombalbaye sowed the seeds of a rebellion that in time tended to gravitate increasingly toward Libya, for cultural and practical reasons (Bouquet 1982; Thompson and Adloff 1981; Buijtenhuijs 1978). French efforts to shore up the Chadian state and crush the rebellion—through the joint intervention of the Administrative Reform Mission (MRA) and the Foreign Legion—proved utterly fruitless on both counts. As counter-insurgency operations dragged on, tensions multiplied between the French civilian and military authorities, on the one hand, and their Chadian hosts, on the other; in the metropole, French enthusiasm for their client state dwindled; and the sheer brutality employed by the Legion in dealing with the rebels and their presumed sympathizers played into the hands of the insurgents. Though ostensibly designed to strengthen the capability of the Chadian state and help root out the insurgency, the French intervention only hastened the decomposition of the first and stimulated the spread of the other.

As much as the internal debility of the Chadian state, the sheer fractiousness of the rebellion presented Qadhafi with yet another set of opportunities for interference and manipulation. Born in the Sudan in 1966, the *Front de Libération National Tchadien* (Frolinat) was from the very beginning torn asunder by factional rivalries and personal conflicts. As its bases of recruitment expanded, its ethnic profile became more diversified. To the heavy proportion of Arabs from the east (Salamat), who initially formed the bulk of the Frolinat's fighting force, were subsequently added a variety of Sahelian elements from the central and eastern prefectures, and after the focus of the rebellion shifted to the Borkou-Ennedi-Tibesti (BET), in 1969, the Toubou component (Chapelle 1982) gained decisive weight in the leadership and operational units of the Frolinat. At this point intra-Toubou squabbles rapidly superseded the Arab-Toubou cleavage, with Goukouni Oueddeye (normally referred to in Chad as "Goukouni") and Hissene Habre emerging as the key protagonists in the struggle for leadership.

Though never fully eclipsed by the variety of sideshows revolving around their satellite factions, the Goukouni-Habre struggle went through many different phases, culminating in 1982 with a drastic transformation of their war aims and bases of support. From an internecine feud among warlords, the conflict escalated into a trial of strength between incumbent (Habre) and rebel (Goukouni), fueled by the backing of external actors.

At the root of the endless fragmentation suffered by the Frolinat lies a complex dialectic between the dynamics of segmentation and the incessant quest for external support generated by factional rivalries. Like most segmentary societies, Arabs and Toubou are notable for their tendency to fragment into competing segments, for in such societies "there is no center at which the means of cohesion are concentrated and which can impose its will on other groups" (Gellner 1973, 4). Oppositions and alliances are thus constantly recalculated, commitments reconsidered, alternative combinations explored—a pattern richly illustrated by the fluidity of factional alignments within the Frolinat. What is involved here, however, is not just a carry-over of the segmentary model into the framework of the rebellion. In the context of the bitter rivalries unleashed by factional competition, the procurement of external support is a *sine qua non* of political survival. And in the process of bargaining that normally attends the quest for external patronage new issues arise, around which new forms of conflict tend to develop. This is where Libya played a determining role: by constantly playing one group against another it has decisively contributed to intensifying factional rivalries while at the same time creating the conditions that led to its growing military involvement on the side of its most loyal clients.

Coping with factional strife while holding their ground against the Habre forces proved an impossible task for the Libyans. Recourse to coercion rather than negotiation became increasingly frequent in dealing with recalcitrant factions. As we shall see, Libyan efforts to keep their Chadian allies under control ran into countless obstacles, and as the costs of the war appeared to many Chadians to exceed the benefits of the alliance, their loyalty to the Libyan patron began to falter, culminating in late 1986 with massive defections. What had begun for Libya as a unique opportunity for penetrating the Chadian arena suddenly turned into a crippling liability.

In the range of opportunities—and constraints—faced by Libya, French policies played an equally crucial role, confronting Qadhafi with a counterforce whose weight and deterrent capabilities varied substantially from one period to the next. In the twenty years that have elapsed since the beginning of the French intervention in 1968, French policies went through fundamental shifts and reappraisals. Reassessments of the purpose and scale of France's military commitments were in part a reflection of the many ups and downs that have accompanied its uneasy relationships with its client state, and in part the result of external pressures, some emanating from the metropole, others from African states, Libya included.

But if French policies have been anything but consistent, there is an undeniable logic to Libyan responses: Each time the French withdrew or scaled down their military presence, Qadhafi pressed for advantage, only to engage in a tactical retreat upon their return. A major scaling down of French forces followed the withdrawal of the Foreign Legion in 1972, and its replacement by fifteen hundred regular troops under the umbrella of the so-called *Forces Françaises de l'Escale d'Afrique Centrale* (FFEAC): A year later Qadhafi moved into Aouzou. Again, when the FFEAC pulled out, in September 1975, in the wake of the Claustre affair,[4] and at the request of the Malloum government, Qadhafi quickly took advantage of the situation to maneuver his surrogates into strategic locations.

Qadhafi did not wait for opportunities to happen; some came into being through deliberate pressure and bargaining, others through double-dealing. At least part of the credit goes to Libya for the resolution adopted at the Lagos conference of August 1979, to the effect that French troops in Chad were an "obstacle to peace." By April 1980 the obstacle had been removed; eight months later Libyan troops stormed into the capital city. Full credit, however, must be given to Qadhafi for "snookering" the French into the mutual withdrawal agreement of September 1984, a little over a year after the deployment of a thirty-two-hundred-strong French contingent under the code name Operation Manta (Sting-Ray): only France honored its commitment, thus leaving the Chadian government fully exposed to Libyan attacks.

Insuring a continuing flow of French arms and aircraft to Tripoli in return for specific concessions—ranging from promises of non-interference in Chad to the liberation of hostages held by the Frolinat and oil contracts—has been a crucial element in Qadhafi's tortuous bargaining with the French, and this as late as 1981. It is ironic to note in this connection that Mitterrand's arms transfer policy has not always been significantly less restrictive than his predecessor's: "An arms embargo on Libya that had been imposed by Giscard d'Estaing in the wake of Qadhafi's intervention in Chad was lifted, thus permitting the delivery of previously ordered Mirage F-1 fighters, helicopters, and fast patrol boats. The lifting of the embargo cleared the way for renewed oil exploration by the French government-owned company Elf-Aquitaine. No new arms would be sold to Libya, however, until it had withdrawn its troops from Chad" (Pierre 1982, 96, 97). By then, however, the Soviet Union had effectively supplanted France as Libya's main arms supplier.

As the foregoing makes plain, the forms and timing of Libyan intervention must be seen in the light of the changing structure of opportunities within and outside the Chadian arena. What remains to be spelled out are the specific strategies used by Qadhafi to penetrate and subvert the Chadian state.

Strategies of Penetration

No single strategy or master plan accounts for the relative success (until 1987) met by Qadhafi in carving out for himself a sphere of influence in northern Chad; nor is there anything like a discernible chronological sequence in his choice of strategies—even though the trend has been clearly in the direction of an ever greater reliance on force. In trying to identify the principal patterns of Libyan intervention from 1973 to 1987 our aim is to convey a sense of the variety of tactics and strategies employed by Qadhafi, rather than to present a blow-by-blow account of such intervention.

Bargaining from Strength: Aouzou (1973)

Qadhafi's readiness to use force if necessary to stake out his claims was dramatically brought to light in August 1987, when the oasis town of Aouzou became the focus of a major military confrontation between Chad and Libya. After capturing the town on August 8 the Chadian army held its ground against Libyan counterattacks for twenty days, until a massive land and air assault of the Jamahiriya delivered the oasis back into Libyan hands. A closer look at the recent history of Libyan penetration in this long-contested area reveals an equally crucial feature of Qadhafi's modus operandi—his adeptness at negotiating from a position of strength.

Although the exact circumstances of the occupation of the Aouzou strip by Libya in 1973 are still clouded in mystery, the consensus of informed opinion is that it came about as a result of a secret arrangement between Tombalbaye and Qadhafi, at a time when the Chadian army had practically lost what little capacity it once had to effectively control the area. But there was more to it than mere acknowledgement of a *fait accompli*.

The Aouzou "accord" was part of a package deal brokered by Niger's President Hamani Diori to bring about a rapprochement between Tripoli and Ndjamena. Briefly stated, Libya agreed to desist from giving further aid to the Frolinat and put a stop to its anti-Chadian radio broadcasts; on top of this, Tombalbaye was offered a CFAfrs. 23 billion aid program. In return, Tombalbaye agreed to resume diplomatic relations with Libya (severed in August 1971) and break its ties with Israel. Recognition of the Palestinian Liberation Organization (PLO), of Vietnam's National Liberation Front (NLF), and Communist China immediately followed the break with Israel. As an additional concession to Qadhafi, however, a secret "understanding" was reached that gave Libya a virtually free hand in policing the Aouzou strip (Lanne 1982; Berri and Kebzabo 1975).

On the occasion of Qadhafi's visit to Ndjamena, in March 1974, officially described as a "dazzling success," Tombalbaye gave a broad hint of this understanding when he told the Executive Bureau of the *Mouvement National pour la Révolution Culturelle et Sociale* (MNRCS): "Chad's borders with Libya are a most difficult area to secure because of the geographical configuration and the desert; and now that Libya and Chad share common interests, now that discord no longer exists between our two countries, we shall together secure our borders" (*nous allons ensemble garder nos frontières*) (*Le Canard Déchaîné*, March 15, 1974). As it turned out, Libya did the "securing" single-handedly, and with no opposition from Ndjamena.

Tombalbaye's compliance is hardly surprising given the state of affairs in Aouzou following the Toubou insurrection of March 1968 (Buijtenhuijs 1978, 145–61). Inspired by the Derdei—the traditional authority figure of the Toubou—and fueled by a group of Frolinat emissaries operating from Libya, the 1968 insurrection brought to a head the growing resentment of the local populations in the face of the countless exactions and brutalities perpetrated by the Chadian army. Unrest rapidly spread through much of the Tibesti. In Aouzou, Bardai and Zouar units of the Chadian National Army found themselves under siege and remained at the mercy of the insurgents until early September, when a joint Franco-Chadian rescue operation finally got under way. Subsequent efforts to "pacify" the area proved unavailing. With Aouzou now formally claimed by the Frolinat as a "liberated area," and the French increasingly reticent to tangle with the Toubou insurgents, Tombalbaye's hopes of ever regaining control over the palmeraie quickly evaporated. By 1973 he had no other choice but to accept Qadhafi's offer.

Equally noteworthy, by April 1972 Franco-Chadian relations had reached their lowest ebb, with the French being blamed for their poor performance in dealing with the rebellion, their niggardly aid package, and at one point (in July 1971) for supposedly seeking to overthrow the Tombalbaye government. More significantly, the French expeditionary corps was about to be withdrawn, to be replaced by a smaller contingent under the FFEAC umbrella. Finally, growing pressures were being exercised by the French to induce Tombalbaye to seek a normalization of diplomatic relations with Libya—with Hamani Diori of Niger seen as the ideal go-between. All of which argued for a drastic reversal of Chadian-Libyan relations.

While demonstrating Qadhafi's skill at bargaining from a position of strength, the 1973 rapprochement makes equally plain his ability to relate his Chadian policies to more global objectives. Tombalbaye's break with Israel and subsequent recognition of the PLO was clearly a major diplomatic victory. Furthermore, in return for his commitment to stop aiding the Frolinat Qadhafi was able to clinch a major arms deal with Paris, in the form of a delivery of Mirage fighter bombers.

Within Chad, however, the Aouzou deal quickly backfired, causing a profound and persistent rift between the two leading figures of the Toubou-dominated "Second Army" of the Frolinat, Habre and Goukouni, over the legitimacy of the Libyan take-over (of which more in a moment).

The Use of Proxies: Playing One Faction against Another

"Clients are like the sides of our tents, which we fasten around us or discard to suit the vagaries of the wind . . . " (Peters 1968, 173). As among the Bedouin pastoralists of Cyrenaica, Qadhafi's use of proxies (or clients) has been nothing short of opportunistic, though at times tempered by his undiminished awareness of cultural affinities with Arab-speaking elements.

A key feature of his Chadian policies, the manipulation of client factions, proved reasonably effective in facilitating Libyan expansion as long as the terms of the *quid pro quo* between patron and clients were acceptable to both. Though generally acceptable to some clients some of the time, Qadhafi's terms changed drastically over the years, prompting one "realignment" after another and culminating in 1986 with massive defections. The spectacular routing of the Libyan army in 1987 must be seen in part as dramatic evidence of the failure of Libyan-linked clientelism.

"Issues" and "context" are critical reference points for unraveling the complexities of factionalism within the Frolinat. For if the first have often precipitated factional splits, the second helps us understand the logic behind Qadhafi's choice of factional allies. Thus a crucial element behind the emergence of Toubou-Arab tensions in 1971 was the decision of the Tripoli-based Frolinat leadership under Abba Siddik, to set up a unified command structure to coordinate the operations of the Second and First Armies, respectively identified with Toubou and Arab elements. The move was immediately perceived by Goukouni (then in charge of the Second Army) as a thinly veiled attempt to bring the BET-centered Toubou wing of the rebellion under Arab control. Ethnic tensions eventually spilled over into the streets. In Beida (Libya) Toubou students organized a protest march against Siddik, soon followed by similar manifestations on the part of Chadian migrant workers, also of Toubou origins (Buijtenhuijs 1978, 243).

As the situation threatened to get out of hand following Goukouni's attempt, in November 1971, to arrest some key members of the Siddik faction, Qadhafi promptly turned against the Toubou leadership. Goukouni was placed under house arrest (not to be released until April

1972) while Habre was ordered to leave the country. Giving in to Goukouni's demand for greater decisional and operational autonomy for the Second Army would have resulted in a major setback for the Siddik faction and by the same token caused a lessening of Libyan influence in the affairs of the Frolinat. From Qadhafi's perspective, supporting Siddik against Goukouni, that is Arabs against Toubou, was the only sensible course.

For a variety of reasons, including the relative success of counter-insurgency measures in the Center-East region, the closure of the Sudanese sanctuary[5] and the emergence of the Second Army as a force that had to be reckoned with, by 1972 the center of gravity of the rebellion shifted to the Tibesti—precisely when Qadhafi was about to make good his claim to Aouzou. From then on, and largely as the unintended consequence of the Libyan thrust into the Tibesti, intra-Toubou rivalries increasingly tended to eclipse Toubou-Arab polarities (the latter to reappear in a new guise in 1977).

The continuing personal enmity between Habre and Goukouni is more than a reflection of cultural differences between their respective subgroups, Daza (Habre) and Teda (Goukouni). Nor is Goukouni's claim to greater social recognition as the son of the Derdei of determining significance. Irreducible differences of opinion between the two men over the legitimacy of the Libyan claim to Aouzou is what drew them apart. Unlike Goukouni who saw the Libyan take-over as a necessary (though perhaps temporary) concession to the exigencies of Libyan support, Habre has consistently and categorically expressed his opposition to this and other manifestations of Libyan "imperialism." While the Libyan move into Aouzou drove a deep wedge within the Second Army, the split was further aggravated by similar disagreements over the Claustre affair. Goukouni's willingness to play the Libyan card and surrender the French hostage to Tripoli (as indeed happened in January 1977) decisively strengthened his credentials as Qadhafi's most trusted and obedient client, leaving Habre no other option but to turn to Egypt and the Sudan (and ultimately the United States) for help. Predictably, Goukouni's faction—now known as the *Forces Armées Populaires* (FAP), to distinguish it from Habre's *Forces Armées du Nord* (FAN)—received the lion's share of Libyan military assistance. For his part, Qadhafi could claim much of the credit for handing Claustre over to the French, and in return extract another arms deal from Paris. Within Chad the FAP served increasingly as a vehicle of Libyan penetration.

With the rise of a new batch of claimants for Libyan patronage, however, serious strains entered this heretofore privileged relationship. Thus, by 1977, a new twist was added to an already complex situation by the active involvement of Sahelian Arabs in the rebellion (Buijtenhuijs 1984, 19–20). Unlike the first generation of Frolinat combatants, they were recruited for the most part from the nomadic and semi-nomadic "tribes" of the Central and Center-West regions. Their staunchly pro-Libyan sentiments came to be identified with the *Comité Démocratique Révolutionnaire* (CDR), itself a lineal descendant of Ahmed Acyl's *Armée du Volcan* (whose leadership he inherited from Mohammed al-Baghlani, after his death in March 1977). It was now Acyl's turn to act as Qadhafi's "man" in Chad. Acyl's accidental death in 1980, and his replacement by Acheikh Ibn Oumar, did little to diminish Libyan sympathies for the CDR and the CDR's loyalty to Libya. Ironically, although the CDR eventually turned against Goukouni's FAP—notably in Faya in August 1978, shortly after the capture of the oasis by Goukouni—it was in no small way as a result of the spectacular victories scored by the FAP in 1977 and 1978 that the political mobilization of ethnic Arabs from the Center-West and

Borkou regions became a distinct possibility. Two additional factors played a critically important role in the mobilization of Arab elements: the presence of a large number of Libyan "advisers" in the liberated zones of northern Chad, and at least from 1977 onwards, the persistent efforts made by Qadhafi to propagate the ideas of the Green Book among Arab "brothers." Both factors helped strengthen the Libyan connection with the CDR, giving it a special ideological aura that was largely missing from the instrumental relationship struck with other client groups.[6]

A full discussion of the Byzantine twists and turns that have accompanied Libya's relations with its Chadian surrogates is beyond the scope of this chapter. Suffice it to note that by 1979 the context of Chadian politics underwent a drastic alteration as a result of Nigerian peace initiatives. Four reconciliation conferences were held under Nigerian auspices, the first two in Kano (March–April 1979), and the other in Lagos (May–August 1979). Though ostensibly aimed at breaking the deadlock among warring factions, the net result of the Nigerian-sponsored initiatives has been to greatly complicate the quest for a settlement, and ultimately to pave the way for a further escalation of the crisis.

Several points here deserve attention. To begin with, the need to insure a fair representation of Chadian interests led to a phenomenal proliferation of presumptive spokesmen for such interests. As has been noted, "with a view to reducing all possible sources of tension, the number of factional leaders invited to attend the various conferences was progressively increased until, by the time that of August 1979 was held, no dissident organization in Chad could complain of being ignored" (Thompson and Adloff 1981, 90). The transitional government that emerged from the Lagos conference, the so-called *Gouvernement d'Union Nationale Transitoire* (GUNT), comprised no less than eleven factions, thus presenting Qadhafi with fresh opportunities to play one group against another. By then, however, Nigeria had emerged as a major participant in the treacherous game of foreign-linked factionalism. By casting his lot with Abdel-Rahmane's Third Liberation Army, Obasanjo gave further impetus to intra-factional rivalries while at the same time prompting Qadhafi to up the ante. Last but not least, the impending withdrawal of French troops, in accordance with the resolution adopted at Lagos II, made it all the more tempting for Qadhafi to throw the full force of his army behind his surrogates in an effort to consolidate his position on the ground. Partly because of the new competitiveness arising from the proliferation of clients in search of external patrons, and partly bcause Libya felt fewer inhibitions to use its military backing on behalf of its allies, the risk of escalation had never been greater than on the eve of the French pull-out.

The Projection of Force

What began as a limited effort to shore up his surrogates rapidly escalated into a situation where Qadhafi chose to rely increasingly on direct military action. Evidence of direct Libyan involvement south of Aouzou goes back to 1977, when a handful of Libyan advisers was sent into the Tibesti to instruct Goukouni's FAP in the use of heavy weaponry, consisting mainly of bazookas and 81 and 82mm mortars. By 1978, however, the number of Libyan instructors was estimated at anywhere from five hundred to one thousand, to the stock of weapons delivered in 1977, were added multiple rocket-launchers (Stalin organs) and SA-7 surface-to-air missiles (Buijtenhuijs 1984, 18). The new weapons were used with devastating effect against the Chadian army. After the fall of Bardai and Zouar in 1977, came the capture of Ounianga-Kebir. The battle of Faya, in February 1978, during which approximately twenty-five hundred men—that is, half of the Chadian armed forces—were taken prisoner, marked a turning point in what was now evolving into a war by proxy. From then on, the Libyan presence on the ground had to be recognized as a decisive factor in the equation of power among Chadian warlords.

Just how decisive this factor turned out to be was dramatically brought to light on December 14, 1980, when Libyan tanks, backed by units of the Islamic Legion and the Libyan army, delivered the capital into Goukouni's hands (see Foltz in this volume). Overwhelmed by Libyan fire power, Habre's FAN virtually disintegrated. It is estimated that at least a thousand troops of the Islamic Legion were thrown into the battle, along with five or six armored companies equipped with Soviet-supplied T-54 and T-55 tanks. Not least impressive was the demonstrated Libyan capability to project its armory thousands of miles from its home base, across forbidding terrain.

After this conclusive demonstration of Libyan military power, Habre had no other choice but to seek the backing of external allies. Egypt, the Sudan, and the United States emerged as his strongest supporters: the first provided shelter and logistical support, the second "technical advisers" and equipment, the third an estimated $10 million in covert assistance funneled through CIA networks (with or without the "good offices" of Admiral Secord). While planning his next move from the Sudan, Habre knew that his anti-Libyan stance would probably continue to pay off. Thanks in part to this timely assistance the FAN leader eventually won the day, after successfully fighting his way back into Ndjamena in June 1982—and at this point the GUNT, still headed by Goukouni, heaved off to Bardai, in the heart of the Tibesti, to seek Libyan protection and continuing support.

What Habre had managed to accomplish with covert U.S. aid, Goukouni was now determined to do with Qadhafi's military backing, thus setting the stage for a reenactment of the 1980 Libyan intervention.

The second Libyan intervention (1983) differed from the first (1980) in one fundamental respect: The Libyan assault against Ndjamena in 1980 was at the request of the GUNT, to bring an end to Habre's "dissidence"; the 1983 intervention, on the other hand, was clearly directed against a government that enjoyed the official recognition of the majority of the OAU. Furthermore, at least twice as many Libyan troops were thrown into the battle, consisting primarily of armored units and mechanized infantry; a far more sophisticated arsenal was now available to both Libyan and GUNT forces; and the latter were now beefed up by thousands of southerners—the remnants of Kamougue's *Forces Nationales Tchadiennes* (FAT)—who had recently rallied to Goukouni.

On June 23, 1983, Goukouni's Libyan-backed forces launched their first major attack on Faya. The assault lasted twenty-four hours and involved anywhere from fifteen to twenty-five hundred "rebels" assisted by an estimated two-thousand-strong mobile column consisting of Libyan regulars and elements of the Islamic Legion equipped with B-12 and B-13 multiple rocket launchers and SAM-7 surface-to-air missiles. On June 24, Habre's troops fell back before the massive firepower of the insurgents who quickly pushed their way into the southeast, scoring one victory after another. On July 8, the strategic border town of Abeche fell into their hands. Almost immediately Habre launched a brilliant counteroffensive. Realizing the vulnerabilities of his opponents, now hundreds of miles from their lines of supply, he struck back on July 12. Abeche, Biltine, Kalait, and Oum Chalouba were recaptured in a matter of days. On July 13, against heavy odds, the FAN successfully fought their way back into Faya. Yet on August 10, a massive assault against the FAN positions delivered the oasis back into Goukouni's hands. Against the heavy pounding by Libyan artillery and the bombing raids of MIG-23 and SU-22 fighter-bombers, Habre's desert warriors caved in. One-third of his troops, that is about one thousand, were killed or captured during the assault; the rest miraculously escaped moments before the oasis fell.

Only through the eleventh-hour decision of President Mitterrand to send in French paratroopers and air support was the Libyan advance brought to a stop. The deployment of some three thousand French troops under the umbrella of Operation Sting-Ray froze the status quo along the sixteenth parallel, on a line running from Abeche in the east to Salal, Moussoro, and Mao in the west; and as Libyan troops, tanks, and artillery consolidated their hold on the northern half of the country, the military stand-off led to a de facto partition of the country (see Foltz in this volume).

Sting-Ray brought to an end a process of escalation in which diplomatic pressures and counterpressures played a crucial role in shaping the outcome of the struggle on the ground. No less important to bear in mind is that it also paved the way for a fundamental transformation of the balance of forces on each side of the sixteenth parallel. In the south it gave Habre the security guarantees he needed to consolidate his power base and reorganize his army; in the north, on the other hand, the result has been to force Libya into the inevitable role of a neocolonial power. The growing visibility of the Libyan presence on the ground, along with the unrelenting pressure brought to bear on Qadhafi's Chadian allies to endorse his Green Book philosophy, imposed insuperable strains on the partnership. What had begun as a Libyan-sponsored rescue operation turned into a full-fledged annexation, with the Chadians acting as auxiliaries on behalf of a new imperial power.

Even in the best of circumstances, the sheer number and diversity of factions under the GUNT would have made it difficult for Qadhafi to exercise effective control over this extraordinarily mixed bag of clients; with many of them now questioning the utility and long-term implications of their Libyan connection, the task proved quite beyond any of the recipes found in the Green Book. With one faction after another defecting to the "enemy," the GUNT began unraveling at the seams, laying bare in the process its utter lack of credibility as a politico-military organization. By late 1986 only the CDR was still hanging tough. As the majority of the GUNT forces switched sides, an entirely new situation developed on the ground, in which the Libyans were left to confront their former allies, now working hand in hand with the Chadian army. The army was set for the crushing defeat of Libyan forces at Fada and Ouadi Doum on March 19 and 22, 1987—"the biggest desert battles since the Second World War" (*Africa Confidential* 1987, 2)—followed by the evacuation of the Libyan garrison from Faya on March 25.

With Aouzou still in Libyan hands, Qadhafi appeared willing to shift course. Following a meeting of Sudanese Prime Minister Saddiq al-Mahdi with the Chadian Minister of State for Foreign Affairs, the quest for "a peaceful settlement of the Libya-Chad dispute" seemed no longer excluded from his agenda. Qadhafi's "two-track" policy was once again being tested.

Qadhafi's "Two Track" Policy: Diplomacy as an Adjunct to Force

"Pacta sunt servanda" is not one of Qadhafi's most cherished principles of international behavior. As in a zero-sum game, when too much sanctity inheres in Islam, there is presumably too little left to be conferred on treaties. Only those rules of international behavior that serve Libyan interests are binding, and only as long as they correspond to such interests.

So, also, with diplomacy. If the use of force proves unavailing in furthering Libyan interests, diplomacy is the next best thing; alternatively, if diplomacy fails, recourse to force is a likely response. So far from being mutually exclusive, force and diplomacy are but two faces of the same coin. They are mutually supportive and strategically related to each other. Just as the use of force may set the stage for diplomatic advantage, diplomacy is intended to create those very conditions that will enable Qadhafi to draw maximum benefits from the application of force, or, when the going gets rough, cut his losses.

Such is the essence of Qadhafi's "two-track" policy, for which the case of Chad provides graphic illustrations. The Aouzou deal is not untypical: By promising Tombalbaye to desist from giving aid to the Frolinat, Qadhafi not only scored a major diplomatic victory, but was given a free hand to "police" the Aouzou strip—a unique opportunity to move his troops into a strategic area, eventually to become a stepping stone for further advances into northern Chad. Perhaps no other diplomatic coup brought Libya higher dividends. Without the jumping-off point provided by Aouzou, and the military facilities subsequently installed in the oasis, it is hard to imagine how the Libyans could have staged their massive attacks against Ndjamena in 1980, and Faya in 1983.

The interrelatedness of force and diplomacy is again plainly demonstrated by the circumstances leading to the 1983 intervention on behalf of Goukouni. In a fundamental sense, the timing of the Libyan intervention testified to the egregious failure of Qadhafi's OAU diplomacy. For it was the repeated failure of Qadhafi to gain for his client the recognition of the OAU, first at the Tripoli summits of 1982 and then at Addis Ababa in 1983, that convinced him that force was indeed the only alternative to diplomacy. And yet, diplomacy also played a supportive role in his decision to use force. After leaving the Addis summit he traveled to Saudi Arabia, Morocco, Algeria, and Tunisia, and in the course of these visits, according to one observer, "a deal was struck whereby Saudi Arabia and Morocco would look the other way when the Qadhafi-Goukouni team made its move into Chad if Libya would reduce its arms and cash supplies to the Polisario fighting Moroccan troops in the Western Sahara" (Cooley 1983). Thus, only after securing the "neutrality" of Morocco and Saudi Arabia did Qadhafi give his full military backing to Goukouni.

Further evidence of how diplomatic maneuvering enhanced Qadhafi's military objectives followed the Franco-Libyan negotiations of September 1984, exactly a year after Operation Sting-Ray got under way. On November 11, France and Libya announced a joint withdrawal of their troops: "The evacuation of operations of French forces in Chad and the Libyan units ended to-day, following the intervention of mixed teams of observers as foreseen under the agreement signed between the two countries" (*Le Monde* November 11, 1984). What turned out to be a Libyan ploy designed to force the French out of Chad would soon be denounced by foreign observers as France's "destructive disengagement" (*The Economist* December 15, 1984). As France withdrew its thirty-two-hundred-strong contingent it became patently clear that Libya would not honor its obligations under the terms of the agreement. Initially hailed as a major victory for the Mitterrand government, it became a source of considerable embarrassment for the French and the occasion for bitter recriminations between Paris and Ndjamena. In time the metamorphosis of Sting-Ray into Sparrowhawk, involving the redeployment of French troops from Bangui, in the Central African Republic, to Ndjamena, restored a measure of credibility to the French shield—but not until renewed attacks by the GUNT drove home to the French the full implications of Libyan deception.

The Crunch

A thousand kilometers northeast of Ndjamena, in a setting reminiscent of a Beau Geste movie, is where Libyan adventurism eventually met its nemesis: The capture of Fada, "capital" of the Ennedi, marked the first of several crushing blows suffered by the Libyans at the hands of the Chadians. Held by four Libyan mechanized infantry battalions, totalling twelve hundred men, and approximately four hundred CDR "auxiliaries," Fada fell to the combined forces of Habre's Chadian National Armed Forces (FANT) and Goukouni's FAP on January 2, 1987, after a series of engagements begun three days earlier from the Kalait and Ito staging areas (Soudan 1987, 16). In a brilliant display of desert *blitzkrieg* —involving rapid pincer movements against Libyan columns—the Chadians stormed the Libyan stronghold, killing 784 and capturing 81. The Libyan commander (Colonel Al Mabrouk) and his staff, however, miraculously flew out of Fada moments before the Chadians captured the airstrip, leaving behind an impressive amount of equipment and intelligence (see Foltz in this volume).

An even more devastating blow was landed on the Libyan positions in Ouadi Doum on March 22. Located in the Borkou region, one hundred kilometers northeast of Fada, the oasis was the nerve center of the Libyan occupation forces in the BET as well as a major supply base for neighboring outposts. With its twelve-thousand-foot concrete runway, radar and communication sites, massive quantities of sophisticated weaponry and three-thousand-strong garrison, Ouadi Doum seemed impregnable. The turning of the tide began with a Libyan attempt to recapture Fada, a move that led to the near annihilation of two armored columns near Bir Kora on March 19 and 20. Hot pursuit operations quickly followed. Finally, after three days of heavy fighting, the twenty-five-hundred-strong Chadian forces overran the outpost, using the same desert tactics displayed with such good effect three months earlier. These tactics, as has been noted, are

> based on extremely rapid movement: the bulk of the force is carried at full speed in light armored cars and in Jeeps and Toyota pickups equipped as gun platforms. Quick concentration of forces and intense fire power are achieved via repeated pincer movements, in which the attacking forces close so tightly with the enemy that high-level air bombardment is useless, while portable ground-to-air missiles (captured SAM-7s and US Redeyes) discourage planes from coming in low enough to be effective. (*The Economist Intelligence Unit, Country Report: Cameroon, CAR, Chad* 1987, 33)

If the Libyan losses, estimated at fifteen hundred bear witness to the violence of the fighting, the volume of the booty testifies to the strategic importance of Ouadi Doum in the Libyan defense system. Included in the Libyan equipment captured were 2 SU-22 bombers, 4 L-39 light bombers, 2 Marchetti SF-260 ground support planes, 7 radar systems, 86 BMP personnel carriers, 232 T-54/55 and T-62 tanks, and 3 MI-25 helicopter gunships, one in mint condition (*Africa Confidential* April 1987, 3). All in all the Chadians were left in possession of an estimated $1 billion worth of weaponry.

With the collapse of Ouadi Doum, Faya appeared a logical target for Habre's forces. Wisely declining to raise the gauntlet, however, the Libyans fled the oasis on March 25, before the Chadians were able to plan their next move. In less than a week the balance of forces in the BET was thus dramatically altered, with the Libyans precariously holding their ground in the extreme north, along the Aouzou strip.

Tempting as it is to blame Libyan reverses on Qadhafi's hubris, his efforts foundered on two specific errors. By simultaneously overestimating the willingness of his Chadian allies to act as obedient surrogates, and vastly underestimating Habre's military capabilities once he had joined forces with his former opponents, Qadhafi took a gamble against odds. While the Libyans fought a war of position, the Chadians fought a war of movement, and in so doing exposed the basic flaw behind the Libyan defeat, that is, the notion that the military superiority normally derived from the use of highly sophisticated weaponry would also obtain in a desert theater. As one observer shrewdly noted,

> In defeating the Libyans, the Chadians did more than achieve a major victory. They also showed that the weapons and tactics of advanced industrial nations are not necessarily appropriate, offensively or defensively, for poorly trained armies of less developed countries. The Chadians fought the desert battles in their own fashion, using weapons and tactics with which they were comfortable, such as charges in armed pickup trucks. However unorthodox their approach to warfare may appear to others, to them it was a modernized version of tactics they have used in the desert for centuries. The Libyans, for their part, apparently believed that by simply transferring Soviet technology and tactics to their army, they had a magic formula for military success without the need for hard fighting. (Trainor 1987)

Although Qadhafi has never been unwilling to operate a strategic retreat when the circumstances required, his long-term goals in Chad, whether of a maximalist or minimalist variety, will remain unchanged. The same applies to his tactics. Seizing the opportunity whenever it arises, exploiting divisions whenever and wherever they occur, pushing his luck to the limit of the feasible, and more often than not in blatant disregard of international conventions, are all part of his modus operandi. And they will probably remain an integral part of his Chadian policies long after Ouadi Doum.

1. These facts are well established and universally recognized by historians of Sahelian Africa—except by Bernard Lanne, whose position on this issue is surprisingly unorthodox and singularly misleading. "Une première constatation s'impose," writes Lanne, "la frontière (tchado-libyenne) sépare des populations différentes. . . . Une chose est certaine: la notion de frontière préexistait à la colonisation" (Lanne 1984, 241). For a far more convincing case, see Al-Hendiri 1984, 25ff.
2. For a wealth of interesting insights into Libyan perceptions of the historical connections between Libya

and Chad, the reader should consult Said Abderrahmane Al-Hendiri's *Chadian-Libyan Relations* (1984), published under the auspices of Al-Fatha University in Tripoli. The author took advantage of the 1980–81 Libyan occupation to conduct interviews in Abeche with Chadians who took part in the Senussiya-led resistance against Italy in the 1920s. A recurrent theme in Al-Hendiri's book is that "you cannot tell the differences between Chadians and Libyans." I am grateful to François Burgat for drawing my attention to this source, and to Omar Sefiane for helping me with the translation of relevant passages.

3. One of the most intriguing documents left by the Libyan forces on the battlefield of Fada, in January 1987, is the organizational chart of an Israeli infantry brigade. "Why Tsahal in the Chadian desert?" asked one observer. "Because Libyan military analysts are convinced that Israeli instructors serve with the Chadian forces." (Soudan 1987, 12).

4. Habre's kidnapping of Françoise Claustre, a *bona fide* anthropologist and wife of the head of the *Mission de Réforme Administrative* (MRA), in Bardai in 1974, along with several other hostages including a German national, marked a turning point in Franco-Tchadian relations as well as another source of tension in the Habre-Goukouni feud. By its decision to negotiate the release of Françoise Claustre through direct contacts with the "rebels" the French government incurred the wrath of the Ndjamena authorities who soon requested the withdrawal of French forces from Chad. Furthermore, "it was a basic disagreement over how to handle the Claustre case that caused the fatal rift between Habre and Goukouni in October 1976" (Thompson and Adloff 1981, 63). If it did not specifically "cause" the rift, it nevertheless contributed to it in a major way, for in the end it was Goukouni who, against Habre's wishes, decided to turn the French hostage over to the Libyan authorities who then released her to the French—for a price.

5. Libyan-Sudanese relations began to deteriorate as early as September 1971, when the Federation of Arab Republics was officially proclaimed. Numeiry's decision to stay out of the federation—reflecting his conviction that "southern non-Arab leadership could not contemplate accommodation with the north if Khartoum were bent on integrating the Sudan into some larger Arab entity" (Waterbury 1979, 76)—was bitterly resented by Qadhafi. From then on things went from bad to worse. Thus Qadhafi was openly accused of having instigated the abortive September 5, 1975, coup against Numeiry; again, when another attempt was made to overthrow Numeiry in July 1976, it was said that the plotters had enlisted the support of mercenaries of various origins "trained in Libya and then infiltrated into Khartoum over several months" (Waterbury 1979, 207). In view of these developments it is easy to see why in 1981 Habre had little trouble convincing Numeiry that he stood as his most loyal ally in their fight against Libyan "subversion."

6. Contrary to what the preceding discussion might suggest, the CDR suffered major splits, being in this sense very much within the norm of Chadian factionalism. For a particularly astute commentary on the origins and ethnic components of the CDR, see Latrémolière (1985a, 2672-73). On this and other convulsions of Chad's recent history, Buijtenhuijs's companion volume (1988) provides the indispensable backdrop.

REFERENCES

Africa Confidential. 1987. Vol. 28, nos. 2, 8:1-2, 3–6.

Armstrong, John A. 1976. "Mobilized and Proletarian Diasporas." *American Political Science Review* 70, no. 2 (June): 393–408

Berri, Younes, and Saleh Kebzabo. 1975. "Que Fait Qadhafi au Tchad?" *Jeune Afrique*, no. 768 (September):3–6.

Bouquet, Christian. 1982. *Tchad: Genèse d'un Conflit.* Paris: L'Harmattan.

Brown, Seyom. 1987. *The Causes and Prevention of War.* New York: St. Martin's Press.

Buijtenhuijs, Robert. 1978. *Le Frolinat et les Révoltes Populaires du Tchad: 1965-1976.* Paris: Mouton.

———. 1984. "Le Frolinat à l'Epreuve du Pouvoir." *Politique Africaine* 16 (December):15–29.

———. 1988. *Le Frolinat et les guerres civiles du Tchad (1977-1984).* Paris: Karthala.

Le Canard Déchaîné. 1974. March 15.

Chapelle, Jean. 1982. *Les Nomades Noirs du Sahara.* Paris: L'Harmattan.

Cooley, John. 1982. *Libyan Sandstorm.* New York: Holt, Rinehart and Winston.

———. 1983. "Qaddafi's War." *The New Republic* (September 5).

Cordell, Dennis D. 1985. "The Awlad Sulayman of Libya and Chad: Power and Adaptation in the Sahara and the Sahel." *Canadian Journal of African Studies* 19, no. 2:319–44.

Decalo, Samuel. 1977. *Historical Dictionary of Chad*. Methuen, NJ: The Scarecrow Press.

———. 1980. "Chad: The Roots of Center-Periphery Strife." *African Affairs* 79, no. 317 (October):491–509.

The Economist. 1984. December 15.

The Economist Intelligence Unit. 1987. Country Report: Cameroun, CAR, Chad, no. 2:32–38.

Gellner, Ernest. 1973. "Introduction to Nomadism." In *The Desert and the Sown*, edited by Cynthia Nelson, 1–9. Berkeley: The University of California Press.

Al-Hendiri, Said Abderrahmane. 1984. *Libyan-Chadian Relations: 1843–1975 (Al-Alaqat al-Libiyya al-Tchadiyya)*. Tripoli: Markaz dirasat jihad Libiyyin didda ghazou al-Itali.

Kratochwill, Friedrich. 1986. "Of Systems, Boundaries and Territoriality: An Inquiry into the Formation of the State System." *World Politics* 39, no.1 (October):27–52.

Lanne, Bernard. 1982. *Tchad-Libye: La Querelle des Frontières*. Paris: Karthala.

———. 1984. "Les Relations entre le Tchad et la Libya." In *Enjeux Sahariens*, 241–48. Paris: Centre National de la Recherche Scientifique.

Latremolière, Jacques. 1985a. "De l'affaire Achek à l'affaire Goukouni." *Marchés Tropicaux*, November 1:2672–73.

———. 1985b. "Tchad: Le Lent Cheminement des Evidences." *Marchés Tropicaux*, January 4:9–10.

Lemarchand, René. 1985. "The Crisis in Chad." In *African Crisis Areas*, edited by Gerald Bender, James Coleman, and Richard Sklar, 238–56. Berkeley: The University of California Press.

Le Monde. 1983. July 13.

———. 1984. November 11.

Morsy, Magali. 1984. *North Africa: 1800–1900*. London: Longman.

Muller, Martine. 1982. "Frontiers: An Imported Concept." In *Libya since Independence*, edited by J. A. Allen, 165–80. New York: St. Martin's Press.

Peters, Emrys. 1968. "The Tied and the Free (Libya)." In *Contributions to Mediterannean Society*, edited by J. G. Peristiany, 167–90. Paris: Mouton.

Pierre, Andrew. 1982. *The Global Politics of Arms Sales*. Princeton: Princeton University Press.

Rondos, Alex. 1983. "Why Chad?" CSIS *Africa Notes*, no. 18 (August 31):1–10.

Soudan, François. 1987. "Les documents de l'état-major libyen de Fada." *Jeune Afrique*, no. 1366 (March 11):12–13.

Thompson, Virginia, and Richard Adloff. 1981. *Conflict in Chad*. Berkeley: The University of California Press.

Trainor, Bernard. 1987. "In Desert, Much Evidence of Chad's Rout of Libyans." *The New York Times*, April 13.

Waterbury, John. 1979. *Hydropolitics of the Nile Valley*. Syracuse: Syracuse University Press.

Wright, John. 1983. "Chad and Libya: Some Historical Connections." *The Maghreb Review* 8, nos. 3–4 (May–August):91–95.

VII.

THE LIBYAN DEBACLE IN SUB-SAHARAN AFRICA 1969–1987

Ronald Bruce St John

Although Libyan foreign policy has invited increasing consideration and reflection in recent years, surprisingly little emphasis has been placed on its sub-Saharan dimension.[1] Our aim in this chapter is to offer a corrective to this situation, and in so doing draw attention to the elements of change and continuity that have marked Libyan policies in Africa since the revolution of September 1969, when the Revolutionary Command Council (RCC), under Qadhafi's leadership, took power from the monarchy.

Qadhafi's revolutionary message, heavy with Nassirist overtones, marked a sharp break in the pattern of Libyan-African relations established under the monarchy. In the early 1970s sub-Saharan Africa was the scene of intense diplomatic and propaganda activity, eventually becoming the arena where the regime scored its earliest and most stunning diplomatic victories. In view of these early successes, the subsequent setbacks and ultimate collapse of Libya's African policies are all the more intriguing, and raise obvious questions about the nature of implications of such policies.

While departing in some fundamental ways from the relative passivity of the monarchy toward Africa, Libya's policies under Qadhafi bore the stamp of its historic interactions with the societies of sub-Saharan Africa. As even cursory acquaintance with the historical record shows, trade and religion were critical vehicles of Libyan influence south of the Sahara long before Qadhafi proceeded to reactivate them in the name of Afro-Arab unity. Precolonial trade routes, several of which passed through Libya, forged powerful links between Sahelian and sub-Saharan Africa on the one hand, and the Maghreb on the other, and these in turn helped nurture Libya's continuing interest in the affairs of Central and East Africa. Commercial intercourse received further impetus from the spread of Islam. Centuries ago Sufi holy men and Muslim traders acted as the carriers of Islam to Central and West Africa, and in the late nineteenth century the Libyan-based Senussi Order further expanded the scope of Islamic influence by setting up lodges (*zawiyya*) as far south as Lake Chad.

Predictably, the French saw in the spread of the Senussi brotherhood a major obstacle to their penetration into Sahelian Africa, as did Italy after 1911, and the fierce resistance to European conquest put up by Senussists could not but profoundly influence Libyan perceptions of the West. That Libya once shared with black Africa the indignities of colonial rule, and the arbitrariness of colonial boundaries, is central to an understanding of Qadhafi's self-image as ideologue and activist.

In view of the long-standing historic and geopolitical ties between Chad and Libya, it is not by pure coincidence that after Libya's independence, in December 1951, Chad enjoyed a relatively high priority on its foreign policy agenda, a fact all the more notable when one considers how little attention was at first paid to other African states. There were significant historical precedents for continued Libyan interest in Chad, going back to the Ottoman period (Lemarchand in this volume). Long before Qadhafi asserted his claims to Aouzou, northern Chad had emerged as a distinctive sphere of Libyan influence. In 1955 Libyan motorized units briefly penetrated into the Aouzou strip, only to be repulsed by French troops, and with the outbreak of the Chadian rebellion a decade later, monarchical Libya gave support and shelter to the *Front de Libération National Tchadien (Frolinat)* rebels. Yet relations between Tripoli and Ndjamena later improved, and a few months before the ouster of the monarchy Libya and Chad signed a number of bilateral agreements aimed at improving communication facilities, maintaining Islamic institutions in Chad, and regulating the status of Chadian workers in Libya (Thompson and Adloff 1981, 121–22; Neuberger 1982, 15–20, 22–24).

The overthrow of the Idrissian regime marked the beginning of a new epoch in which Qadhafi's vision of the past merged with his vaulting ambitions to give an entirely different texture to Libyan-African relations. To properly grasp the dynamics of this transformation, attention must be paid to the sequence of events that have accompanied Qadhafi's efforts to translate his vision into reality.

First Steps

With the attention of the RCC riveted on the Mashriq (Arab east), its African policy began tentatively with diplomatic overtures to African, and largely Muslim, neighbors like Niger and Mauritania. The primary objective of this early diplomatic offensive was a reduction in Israeli influence in Africa. In Qadhafi's eyes, Israel's presence in Africa was as a fifth column behind the Arab front lines, sapping its strength at the back door. Secondary objectives included opposition to Western interests and influence, the elimination of foreign military bases, opposition to apartheid and white minority regimes, support for African liberation movements, the propagation of Islam, and enhancing African and Libyan control over the continent's natural resources (First 1974, 222; Nelson 1979, 191–92; Otayek 1987, 77–79).

In the late 1950s, Israel initiated an intense diplomatic effort in sub-Saharan Africa that aimed to counterbalance the hostility of its Arab neighbors as well as Arab influence in the Third World. Israel's African policy focused on diplomatic relations, trade, and aid. In the decade after 1957, Israel established diplomatic representation in twenty-nine African countries. By 1965, Israel had the world's fourth largest diplomatic corps; and by 1970, it had more diplomatic missions in Africa than all the Arab states combined. Israel's diplomatic efforts were complemented by a modest but steadily increasing volume of trade relations. While trade with Africa represented only a fraction of Israel's total world trade, it increased by 42 percent from 1966 to 1969. Moreover, expanding Israeli-African trade relations were establishing important links between infant economies. At the same time, the Republic of South

Africa remained Israel's most important trading partner followed by the Central African Republic, Ethiopia, Uganda, and Gabon. Israeli aid, while modest in financial terms, centered on small-scale, practical projects that were immediately beneficial to the recipient country. The 1967 Arab-Israeli war provided a measure of the effectiveness of Israeli diplomacy. During the war, the majority of African states remained silent. Only seven openly took sides, with six supporting the Arab position and Malawi supporting Israel. In effect, Israeli diplomacy had neutralized the continent in terms of the Arab-Israeli conflict (Ismael 1974, 175–78; Habib 1975, 356).

The strategy of the RCC was to establish diplomatic relations with African states, offer one or more forms of aid, and then urge the recipients to break relations with Israel. At the same time, Libya moved to reduce Western power and influence on the continent by eliminating Western military bases and undermining moderate African governments opposed to Libyan policies. Support was provided to African liberation movements as well as radical, anti-Western governments; and the white minority regimes in southern Africa were repeatedly denounced. Libya provided significant military assistance to liberation movements in Angola, Guinea-Bissau, and Mozambique, for example, and in 1973, it closed Libyan air space to South African over-flights. In many instances, Libyan foreign policy assumed an Islamic hue as preference was given to governments and groups that expressed their opposition to the status quo in religious terms (Libyan Arab Republic 1973, 262–65; Shembesh 1975, 212–13; Mertz and Mertz 1983, 97–98).

Under Qadhafi's guidance a variety of institutions were set up to support his sub-Saharan policies. A Jihad Fund was established in 1970 to strengthen the Libyan Armed Forces and to support the Arab nation in its struggle against Zionist forces and "imperialist perils." At the Fourth Conference of Foreign Ministers of Islamic Countries, held in Benghazi in March 1973, the Jihad Fund assumed both an Islamic and African coloration. A central objective of the fund was described as African liberation through assistance to Islamic liberation movements and aid to Islamic welfare associations. Direct action groups, like the Bureau to Export Revolution, were formed to train non-Arab Africans in guerrilla tactics. An Islamic Call Society was also established in the early 1970s. Ostensibly an instrument for propagation of the faith, the society was also used increasingly for political propaganda and subversion. Finally, toward the end of the last decade, Libya organized an Islamic Legion, largely consisting of recruits from African states, to further its Saharan and Sahelian objectives (Harris 1987, 85; Cooley 1982, 188; Hottinger 1981, 145–47).

Although Islam is a key element of Qadhafi's African policies, it is important to keep it in perspective. The Islamic dimension is only one of several elements—including Arab nationalism, positive neutrality, Arab unity, and a pragmatic assessment of Libya's political and strategic interests—that have motivated and constrained the conduct of Libya's external relations. Qadhafi's policy was never Islamic to the extent of automatically taking the Muslim side in any dispute, and the role of Islam differed from that of conservative Arab states, like Saudi Arabia, in that Libya did not equate Islamic revival with anticommunism. For example, Libya supported the Marxist regime in Ethiopia against the predominantly Muslim Eritrean independence movement as well as the Soviet intervention in Afghanistan. While Libya actively supported Islam, the most distinctive and controversial feature of Libya's approach to Africa was not the amount of Islamic aid given, but rather the extent to which religious assistance was linked to the development of economic relations, the provision of secular economic support, and the pursuit of often aggressive political goals (Libyan Arab Republic 1973, 174–81; Ghariani 1979, 118–21, and 139; Mertz and Mertz 1983, 89–91; Otayek 1987, 79–84).

Growing oil revenues, especially after the price increases of 1971 to 1974, enhanced the ability of Arab states in general and Libya in particular to influence other Third World leaders. African states were anxious for economic aid and thus receptive to Libyan overtures. It was under the RCC regime that Libya's economic resources were for the first time used as a political and diplomatic weapon. Even after the discovery of oil, the monarchy assumed a defensive posture using its resources to reduce or thwart political agitation from surrounding countries. In contrast, the RCC quickly initiated an aggressive policy based on the disbursement of oil revenues to support friends, attack enemies, and further its foreign policy objectives (Ghariani 1979, 57; Abid 1982, 220–21).

Of all Arab donors, Libya was the most actively involved, politically and economically, in sub-Saharan Africa, especially among states with dominant or large Muslim communities (Beshir 1985, 233). Unfortunately, the exact nature, level, or impact of Arab or Libyan aid is difficult to assess. There are serious discrepancies between aid commitments and aid disbursements because many Arab states, particularly Libya, did not translate commitments into disbursements. Nevertheless, it appears that Libya contributed at least $500 million through bilateral and multilateral channels from 1973 to 1979. Zaire and Uganda were the largest individual recipients of aid, receiving almost half of total Libyan bilateral aid to sub-Saharan Africa from 1973 to 1980. In terms of recorded sums, Libya ranked second to Saudi Arabia as an Arab donor of African aid. Overall, Africa was a far more important region, relatively speaking, to Libya than to any other Arab donor (Mertz and Mertz 1983, 10, 87, 94; Otayek 1987, 93; Mattes 1987, 95).

A prominent feature of Libya's growing economic intercourse with Africa during this period was its participation in the ownership and management of companies engaged in African trade and development. With the first such company established as early as 1972, Libya developed no fewer than fifty joint venture companies in a wide variety of economic sectors. Such companies were established in Benin, Burundi, the Central African Republic, Chad, Gabon, Gambia, Mali, Niger, Sierra Leone, Togo, Uganda, and Upper Volta, usually as part of wide-ranging economic, financial, and commercial agreements. Although the capital of each company seldom exceeded a few million dollars, Libyan ownership tended to be at least 51 percent so that effective management control rested with the Libyan government. The second type of aid that Libya practiced widely was the allocation of loans in the form of protocol agreements, often promoting Islamic culture or the Arabic language. Such economic-cum-cultural agreements were concluded with the governments of Gambia, Niger, Mali, Burundi, the Central African Republic, Gabon, Liberia, Togo, and Uganda. The amount disbursed annually by Libya for purely Islamic purposes does not appear to have been large, but it was often highly visible, politically oriented economic assistance (Howe 1981, 16–17; Mertz and Mertz 1983; 90–96; Otayek 1987, 97–100; Mattes 1987, 102–10).

Early Success

Despite the RCC's comparative lack of emphasis on sub-Saharan Africa from 1969 to 1973, its approach to the region was rewarded by a series of early diplomatic victories. Following a late 1971 meeting between Qadhafi and Ugandan President Idi Amin, Uganda expelled several hundred Israeli advisers and later broke diplomatic relations. In September 1972, during Amin's first confrontation with Tanzania, Libya successfully intervened with an airlift of troops, justifying its action as support for the Ugandan struggle against colonialism and Zionism. Nine months later, during the 1973 ceremonies marking the closure of the United States air base outside Tripoli, Qadhafi saluted his honored guest, President Amin, praising him for transforming Uganda from a backward satellite of Zionism into one of the vanguard African countries combating Zionist colonialism and apartheid (Embassy of the Libyan Arab Republic, July 1973, 1 and 6).

Libya scored another early diplomatic victory in Chad. After two years of acrimonious relations, Libya had resumed diplomatic ties with Chad in April 1972. In return for Libyan friendship, a withdrawal of official support for Frolinat, and a promise of aid from Libya and other Arab states, Chad broke relations with Israel in November 1972. The reconciliation between Libya and Chad was crowned by a treaty of friendship signed in December 1972. The following year Libya moved troops into the Aouzou strip (Carvely 1973, 713; Wright 1982, 168; Robinson 1987, 180).[2]

After these early successes, Libya's diplomatic offensive against Israeli influence in Africa gained further momentum, especially in the predominantly Muslim states on the southern rim of the Sahara. By mid-1973, the governments of Mali, Niger, the Congo, and Burundi had severed diplomatic relations with Israel. Libya also raised the issue at meetings of the OAU, a body that had previously been largely neutral on the Arab-Israeli conflict, urging member states to sever their ties with Israel and shift the OAU headquarters from Ethiopia to a country more suitable for achieving the freedom and unity of Africa (Libyan Arab Republic 1973, 265–66).

While African support for the Arab position on Palestine grew in 1972 and 1973, the litmus test for the Libyan approach came during and after the October 1973 Arab-Israeli war. Skillfully exploiting African concerns raised by the oil embargo and oil price increases, Libya and other Arab states pressured African states to abandon their neutrality on the Palestinian issue and rid the continent of Zionism. By the end of 1973, over twenty more African states had broken relations with Israel, with many opening relations with Libya for the first time (Ismael 1974, 178–80; Wright 1982, 166, 168–69).[3] Only four member states of the OAU refused to sever diplomatic links with Israel. Hence, by the beginning of 1974, Libya's foremost goal in Africa, the reduction of Israeli influence, had been achieved, with Libya often supplanting the Israeli presence. The aftermath of the October 1973 war marked the nadir of Israeli authority in Africa and the apogee of Libyan prestige.

The Failure to Consolidate

After 1973, while maintaining the anti-Israeli emphasis of its sub-Saharan policies, the RCC gave increasing attention to the related goals of attacking colonialism and neocolonialism as well as increasing African control of the continent's natural resources (Qadhafi 1975, 118–19, 138). Libya provided both rhetorical and practical support for African liberation movements, including arms and military training. Its favorite targets were the white minority governments in Rhodesia and South Africa, which Qadhafi grouped with Israel as racist regimes (Embassy of the Libyan Arab Republic, July-August 1975, 3). His emphasis on this association helped set the stage for the controversial United Nations General Assembly vote in November 1975 that equated Zionism with apartheid. Twenty-eight African states voted for the resolution with twelve abstaining and only five opposing. Meanwhile, the Libyan government continued to use the OAU as a forum to advocate stronger policies against all forms of imperialism and colonialism. Though already represented on the OAU Liberation Committee, in February 1978 Libya was made a member of a new military committee whose members included the so-called front-line states of southern Africa. The purpose of the committee was to secure and provide sophisticated weaponry for African liberation movements (Legum 1982, 118–21).

While Libya's approach to the Western Sahara conflict has been nothing short of ambivalent, a key element, in addition to the promotion of popular democracy and the development of a wider Saharan Islamic state which Libya would then influence, was its opposition to imperialism and colonialism (Wright 1982, 208–9). As early as February 1972, Qadhafi showed a willingness to provide military support to liberate the Western Sahara; and in June 1972, he announced his decision to back a people's war of liberation if Spain did not leave by the end of the year. When the Polisario campaign began in May 1973, Libya was the only Arab state ready to provide meaningful material support, although its ability to do so was hampered when neighboring states refused to cooperate. At the same time, Libya's policy in the Western Sahara proved erratic, largely because Qadhafi disagreed with the policies of both Algeria and the Polisario. In particular, his emphasis on Arab unity made him reluctant to support the Polisario's goal of creating its own national state (Hodges 1983, 326–28). Libya did not recognize the Saharan Arab Democratic Republic until 1980, four years after its founding; and even then, Qadhafi hoped it would eventually merge with Mauritania, proposing such a union to Mauritania's Prime Minister in 1981. In the end, of course, Libya had no choice but to terminate its support for the Polisario as part of its 1984 merger with Morocco (see Tessler in this volume).

Libyan efforts to enhance African control of the continent's natural resources only met with limited success. Unable to offer technical assistance, its ability to influence African mineral producers was largely confined to being an alternative source of capital. In Zaire, for example, Libya joined the World Bank and the European Investment Bank as a cofinancier of a multi-million dollar loan to finance cobalt and copper production. In Gabon and Niger, Libyan attempts to buy into uranium reserves upon which France relied to reduce its dependence on imported petroleum were largely rebuffed, in part due to the strong opposition of the French government (Mertz and Mertz 1983, 94–95).

Libya's interest in Africa's mineral wealth acted as a stimulus to its territorial ambitions in northern Chad and Niger, while prompting a determined effort to buy into reserves of strategic minerals in Guinea, the Central African Republic, Mauritania, Rwanda, Upper Volta, and Zaire as well as Gabon and Niger (Mertz and Mertz 1983, 95; Robinson 1987, 173–74). As its oil reserves diminished and tentative exploration failed to uncover major non-hydocarbon mineral deposits beyond the iron ore reserves at Wadi Ash Shati, Libya tried to consolidate its position as an energy supplier by seeking access to other natural resources. Anticipated access to mineral reserves in border areas is one reason among others for Libya's efforts to resolve its border disputes on its own terms.

By 1979, at any rate, Libyan influence in sub-Saharan Africa was decidedly on the wane. Nowhere was this more evident than in Uganda and the Central African Republic. Beginning in 1972 Libya provided Idi Amin with considerable financial and military assistance; and when

Uganda was invaded by a mixed force of Ugandan exiles and Tanzanian armed forces in 1978, Qadhafi again responded by sending Libyan troops and supplies to Kampala to repel the invaders. Libyan forces suffered a crushing defeat, and Qadhafi reportedly paid a sizable ransom to secure the release of the survivors.

In the Central African Republic, self-proclaimed emperor Jean Bedel Bokassa was deposed in September 1979 while in Tripoli negotiating for Libyan aid in return for military facilities in the north of his country near the Chadian border. Three days later, the official Libyan news agency denounced the French involvement in the coup as an attempt to thwart the spread of Islam; however, it was abundantly clear that what the French government had really thwarted was Libya's efforts to bolster one of Africa's most bizarre and unpleasant regimes (Wright 1982, 212–13). Uncritical support for notorious regimes like those of Amin and Bokassa reflected badly on Libya but were consistent with Qadhafi's general approach to Africa. Personalities and internal policies were often irrelevant as long as governments professed support for Islam and opposed imperialism, colonialism, and Zionism (Fallaci 1979, 121).

Setbacks

By 1980, Libyan diplomacy in Africa and elsewhere was coming under extreme pressure, in part because of growing French and American opposition.[4] In particular, Libya's ongoing involvement in Chad alarmed Western and African policymakers because they feared success there would encourage intervention elsewhere. In the course of the year, nine nations (including Senegal, Gambia, Ghana, and Gabon) either expelled Libyan diplomats, closed Libyan embassies, or broke diplomatic relations with Libya. In addition, strong tensions or a serious deterioration in relations occurred with at least six other states, including Uganda and Upper Volta.

African governments were especially concerned about the intricate nexus of politics, religion, and foreign aid that characterized Libyan foreign policy. Many African states resented Libya's use of Islam as an instrument of foreign policy (Hasan 1985, 42); even those claiming sizable Muslim communities or a geographic split between Muslims and Christians (or animists) complained that the Libyan emphasis on religion exacerbated sensitive national cleavages. Ongoing recruitment into Libya's Islamic Legion was also a source of widespread concern. In Senegal and Gambia, for example, diplomatic relations with Libya were severed because the latter was allegedly providing military training and support for antiregime forces (Haley 1984, 224; Robinson 1987, 178). Throughout Africa, governments also complained, with apparent justification, that the discrepancy between Libyan aid commitments and disbursements continued to widen.

Events in Chad in 1980–1981 highlighted Libya's diplomatic isolation. Intent on drawing Chad into its sphere of influence, Libya had been deeply involved in Chad's internal affairs for most of the previous decade. In fact, it was largely due to Libya's diplomatic and military intervention that the civil war became irrevocably internationalized as early as 1978 (Thompson and Adloff 1981, 79–80). At that time, Libya hosted a series of international conferences attended by representatives of adjacent states; but an agreement reached in Benghazi in April 1978 was soon breached. A year later, the Nigerian government launched a fresh diplomatic initiative, eventually supported by the OAU, which aimed at bringing peace and unity to Chad; but it met with a similar lack of success. In June 1980, Libya and Chad signed a treaty of friendship which formalized Libyan support of Chadian independence and territorial integrity, thus providing legal justification for the December 1980 Libyan intervention on behalf of Goukouni Oueddeye's *Gouvernement d'Unité Nationale Transitoire* (GUNT). The subsequent still born Libyan-Chadian merger agreement proclaimed in Tripoli on January 6, 1981 (Neuberger 1982, 69–72) marked the limits of Qadhafi's diplomatic efforts in Chad.

Intervention in Chad gave Qadhafi his first taste of military success, but at considerable cost. Five days after the announcement of the proposed merger, the chairman of the OAU called for a withdrawal of Libyan troops from Chad; and an emergency OAU meeting later in the month openly denounced Libya for the first time, condemning the projected union.[5] A more tactful approach was reflected in the carefully worded resolution passed by the OAU in the summer of 1981 thanking Libya for establishing peace in Chad and calling for the withdrawal of Libyan troops and their replacement by a pan-African peacekeeping force (Brewer 1982, 212). The egregious failure of the OAU-sponsored peacekeeping force to carry out its mandate was a major contributory factor to the collapse of the GUNT in June 1982 (Lemarchand 1984, 115).

The reaction of individual African states to the proposed merger varied considerably. The level of indignation seemed to be in direct proportion to their distance from Libya and to the size of the Muslim population claimed by any given state. By January 1981, Mali, Mauritania, Niger, and Nigeria joined the list of African nations having broken diplomatic relations with Libya while other states either expelled Libyan diplomats or closed Libyan embassies. Liberia, the Sudan, and Somalia followed suit later in the year (Neuberger 1982, 53–54). Ironically, about the only African head of state to defend Libya's policy in Chad publicly was the Christian leader of Ethiopia, Mengistu Haile Mariam. Sub-Saharan Africa was thus beginning to show the unity that Qadhafi had long advocated, albeit in opposition to Libya.

Opposition to Libya in 1981 and 1982 reflected many of the concerns raised in 1980 with some larger strategic considerations added. Many African states feared Libya would use control of Chad to increase its influence in the Sahel region and West Africa as well as to harass the Sudan. Around the time of the Chadian-Libyan union announcement, the governments of Niger, Nigeria, Ghana, and Mauritania joined Senegal and Gambia in saying they had found evidence of Libyan interference in their internal affairs. Gabon and Cameroon implied as much (Cooley 1982, 199–203).[6] Concern about Qadhafi's nebulous plans to create an Islamic Republic of the Sahel—and how the Islamic Legion might fit into those plans— intensified these fears; for some, Qadhafi's vision of an Islamic Republic appeared to be little more than a thinly veiled pledge to destabilize Libya's neighbors (Laipson 1983, 52–53).

Adding to these fears and suspicions, the eruption of fundamentalist Islamic unrest in Kano (Nigeria), in December 1980, seemed to offer tangible proof of Libyan conspiracy. Although the sect responsible for the Kano riots (the so-called Maitatsine sect) is indigenous to northern Nigeria, it was nevertheless denounced by Nigerian authorities as a vehicle of Libyan subversion and dealt with accordingly—with extreme brutality. Not until a thousand people were reportedly killed was "peace and order" restored. Meanwhile, "Libyan diplomats were expelled from Lagos in February 1981, after Tripoli announced it was converting its embassy into a 'people's bureau'. . . . Nigeria's deep concerns and frustrations with Libya led it to cooperate with the West in pushing for Tripoli's ouster (from Chad)" (Baker 1987, 85).

To cut his military and political losses as well as buttress his candidacy to the chairmanship of the OAU, Qadhafi abruptly withdrew his forces from Chad in November 1981 (Yost 1983, 978–79). While the withdrawal temporarily reduced his leverage over Chad, Qadhafi's move improved his credibility elsewhere in Africa. Diplomatic relations with Ghana were restored in January 1982 after Libya supported the second successful coup of Jerry Rawlings and provided oil on favorable terms to his new government. Relations with Tanzania also improved after it backed Libya in the latter's dispute with OAU members over seating the Polisario. Relations with Zaire were abruptly severed, however, when Mobutu resumed diplomatic contacts with Israel.

On the multilateral level, the key issue for much of 1982–1983 was the Libyan effort to convene the nineteenth summit meeting of the OAU in Tripoli under Qadhafi's chairmanship. Opposition came from moderate African leaders, acting from personal conviction or under pressure from the United States and European governments, who had no desire to attend a high-level meeting that could appear to vindicate Libyan policy in sub-Saharan Africa (Wright 1981–82, 14). A contributing issue was the war in the Western Sahara and the bitterly divisive question of whether or not to seat a representative of the Polisario. After two attempts to convene the summit in Tripoli failed, an OAU panel recommended moving it to OAU headquarters in Addis Ababa where it eventually opened in June 1983 under the chairmanship of the Ethiopian head of state. Qadhafi attended the summit briefly but soon departed after suffering the double indignity of being denied the chairmanship and seeing his protégé, the Polisario, effectively barred from the meeting. Qadhafi was the first African leader in OAU history to be denied its chairmanship, a dramatic illustration of how limited and indeed counterproductive his influence in Africa had become.

Continuity

After 1983, sub-Saharan Africa continued to enjoy high priority on Qadhafi's agenda, but there was very little new in the policies pursued. Israel remained a central concern. In August 1986, Cameroon became the fourth African country, following Zaire, Liberia, and the Ivory Coast, to resume diplomatic relations with Israel; and there was ongoing speculation that other African states might follow suit. Israel was allowed to operate interest sections in Kenya, Togo, Ghana, and Gabon. As part of the Reagan administration's broad efforts to undermine Qadhafi's regime, the United States became actively involved in helping Israel to restore diplomatic links with African states. In contrast, the French government was reported to be distinctly unhelpful in the promotion of Israeli-African ties, possibly because a wider Israeli role would likely promote American as opposed to French interests in Africa (*The Jerusalem Post*, December 20, 1985).

In response to their Israeli connections, Libya cut its diplomatic ties with Liberia and Zaire. And it refused to participate in the UN/OAU Icara II refugee conference in July 1984 because South African and Israeli delegations were scheduled to attend. In November 1985, Libya announced it was blacklisting Liberian registered vessels, making it the first Arab state to implement a 1984 Arab League decision to boycott Liberian ships because of Liberia's ties with Israel. On a more positive note, Libya restored or normalized diplomatic relations with a number of African states, including Niger, Gambia, Somalia, and Mauritania.

In support of his efforts to improve relations with sub-Saharan Africa, Qadhafi relied heavily on the familiar tools of economic aid and trade. After visiting African states, he doled out Libyan largess to at least a dozen countries in the years 1983 to 1987. Libyan aid took a multitude of forms, including economic and technical agreements with Nigeria, the establishment of joint companies with Benin and Upper Volta, a $1 million check to Mali, and concessionary oil sales to Burkina Faso and Ghana. While considerable publicity often accompanied Libyan aid commitments, it remains extremely difficult to compare commitments to actual aid disbursements; and the probability is that the latter continued to fall short of the former. Although the evidence is admittedly sketchy, it is safe to assume that Libya's growing financial difficulties had a restraining effect on its diplomacy. From a peak of $22.6 billion in 1980, Libya's oil revenues dropped to around $10 billion in 1985, with 1986 estimates at around $4.5 billion (George 1986, 218–20). One small example of the negative effect Libya's plummeting oil revenues had on its foreign policy was the bitterness expressed by the governments of Mali and Mauritania when their nationals were included among the foreign workers expelled in August–September 1985 as part of an austerity program.

In Chad, sporadic outbreaks of fighting continued between 1983 and 1987, prompting renewed intervention by Libyan and French forces. The second Libyan intervention differed from the first in one fundamental aspect. In 1980, Libyan troops moved into the Chadian capital at the request of the GUNT, Chad's only legitimate government; in 1983, by contrast, Libya threw its weight behind a rebel faction and against a government which enjoyed the official recognition of the vast majority of the OAU members (Lemarchand 1984, 116). As Libya reinforced its military presence in northern Chad, Qadhafi aggressively defended Libya's right to intervene in African affairs, terming Chad an extension of Libya (*Le Matin*, Paris, July 1, 1983; *International Herald Tribune*, Zurich, April 27, 1984). In November 1984, Libya and France announced the completion of a mutual phased withdrawal of their armed forces in Chad; however, within a week, France was forced to admit that a sizeable Libyan force had remained in Chad. As the stalemate in Chad continued, many African states displayed an ambivalent attitude. Understandably nervous about Libya's regional objectives, African governments also remained generally reluctant to support openly a former colonial power against an African nation and thus either quietly supported French policy or remained silent.

The second Libyan intervention in Chad was followed by a series of diplomatic realignments, which intensified African concern about the direction of Libyan foreign policy. In June 1984, Libya and Morocco signed an Arab African Federation Treaty, in part to counter a 1983 treaty of fraternity and concord signed by Algeria, Tunisia, and Mauritania (see Tessler in this volume). A year later, following the overthrow of the Numeyri regime, Libya and the Sudan signed a military cooperation agreement in which Libya agreed to stop supporting the Sudanese rebels in the south. In return, Libya had every reason to expect that Khartoum would not oppose its policies in northern Chad. In short, the 1984 and 1985 accords drastically altered pre-existing regional alignments and thus carried disquieting implications for supporters of the regional status quo.

Elsewhere, Libya continued to employ a variety of nondiplomatic means to reassert its former influence in Africa. The Central African Republic, Ghana, Burkina Faso, and Uganda, among others, received substantial quantities of arms and military equipment from 1983 to 1987. At the same time, allegations continued (invariably denied by the Libyan government) of unsolicited Libyan involvement in the internal affairs of African states. Recruitment into the Islamic Legion went unabated, with Djibouti, Ethiopia, the Sudan, Nigeria, Mali, Ghana, and Burkina Faso targeted as prime contributors.[7] By the spring of 1987, the Islamic Legion included thousands of Africans, including twenty-five hundred Sudanese. Meanwhile, speculation heightened as to whether the objectives of the Islamic Legion had been broadened to include the establishment of an international revolutionary force (*Jeune Afrique*, March 19, 1986, 49; Otayek 1987, 88).

Deeply concerned over the renewed fighting in Chad, the OAU in late February 1987 issued an appeal to Libya and Chad, together with all interested parties, to seek a peaceful resolution to what had become a Libya-Chad conflict. A few weeks later, African leaders meeting in Cairo condemned foreign intervention in Chad. Following the aborted attempt at mediation by the Sudan, Chadian troops inflicted a devasting defeat on Libyan forces at Ouadi Doum on March 22, 1987. The Chadian victory marked a major turning point in the war as it rendered Libya's position at Faya Largeau untenable. The Libyan forces there soon began retreating north to the Aouzou strip. Although Libya's ability to make good its claim to the Aouzou strip remains uncertain, Qadhafi declared that the confrontation in Chad would continue as long as French troops remained on Chadian soil. Characteristically, he rejected a Chadian proposal to bring the issue of the Aouzou strip before the International Court of Justice, arguing that the disputed territory had been an indivisible part of Libya since the French and Italian occupations, and that he would consent to arbitration only if he was sure Libya's rights would be confirmed (*Le Monde*, March 24, 1987, and April 14, 1987).

Conclusions

A variety of regional, extra-regional, and domestic interests and concerns combined to frustrate Libyan ambitions in sub-Saharan Africa after 1969. At the root of the problem was Qadhafi's failure to impart a minimum of credibility to his political and ideological aims in the continent. African interests, in the minds of many Africans, came to be perceived as secondary to, if not downright incompatible with, Qadhafi's global political objectives. Especially in the early years of the revolution, the RCC focused on pan-Arab issues, with Africa seen as a subordinate arena for the promotion of the Arab position on Palestine. Later on, when Libya's growing political isolation in the Mashriq and Maghreb gave way to a heightened interest in sub-Saharan Africa, Qadhafi proved unable to develop a credible ideological posture to the region. African responses to Qadhafi's ideology brought to light the same widespread disbelief and disinterest previously accorded to his unification schemes in North Africa and the Middle East. Where the Arab world viewed Qadhafi's ideology as inflexible if not anachronistic, sub-Saharan Africa saw it as simply irrelevant.

Libya's approach to Africa was also mortgaged by its essentially negative character. The key objective was the elimination of Western, especially Israeli, influence in the continent, as opposed to fostering viable long-term socioeconomic and political relationships. The negative motivation of Libyan diplomacy was obvious in the early 1970s and persisted even after Israel's influence had been undermined. In a milieu with limited ideological substance, the ongoing discrepancy between Libyan aid commitments and disbursements was fatal because it reinforced a feeling in Africa that Libyan solicitude was both insincere and self-serving. The ambiguity of Libyan motives, coupled with its long-term commitment to revolutionary change, compounded African anxieties.

Extra-regional pressure came primarily from France and the United States—though not always with the consistency that one might have expected. French opposition to Libyan adventurism in Chad was only the symptom of a wider set of motivations, some having to do with the threats posed to French influence in Francophone Africa, others reflecting the growing pressures brought to bear upon Mitterrand by certain key members of the Franco-phone community, most notably the Ivory Coast, Senegal, and Zaire. American perceptions of Libyan threats developed in a different framework, and in response to different preoc-cupations, not the least being the threat of Libyan-instigated terrorism. And yet, though originating from different concerns and priorities, a remarkable convergence eventually de-veloped between French and American efforts to thwart Libyan adventurism. It is a com-mentary on the extent of the diplomatic leverage available to Washington and Paris that their efforts to contain or reverse Libyan expansion further reinforced African opposition to Qa-dhafi's imperial designs. Qadhafi's debacle in black Africa thus bears testimony not only to the futility of his ideological travail but, more fundamentally, to his inability to take the full measure of the constraints inherent in his wider environment.

NOTES

1. An earlier draft of this chapter appeared in a volume published by the author entitled *Qadhafi's World Design: Libyan Foreign Policy, 1969–1987*, (London: Saqi Books, 1987).
2. While the Tombalbaye government in Chad received some aid from Libya, total disbursements never approached the amount reportedly promised (Neuberger 1982, 28).
3. Several African states were very disappointed with the economic rewards resulting from their support of Libya, especially resenting the fact that little was done to help them meet the greatly increased cost of oil imports. Many of them voiced their displeasure at the first African oil conference convened in Tripoli in February 1974 (Wright 1982, 169).
4. For a more detailed discussion of French and American policies in Africa the reader is referred to Bayart, 1984; Haley, 1984; St John, 1986; St John, 1987; and Yost, 1983.
5. While most Africans viewed Libya's intervention in Chad as a destabilizing influence, there were those few who took the opposite position. In their view, Libya had intervened to restore a degree of order after the Chadians proved unable to govern themselves and then departed when asked to leave (Parker 1984, 73).
6. While there is little question about Qadhafi's willingness to finance and train dissidents, the evidence suggests that some African governments used him as a scapegoat for clamping down on various forms of domestic discontent (Anderson 1982, 528–29).
7. In the spring of 1986, India became the first known government to ask Libya officially to stop local recruitment for the Islamic Legion.

REFERENCES

Abid, N. 1982. "Common Regional Policy for Algeria and Libya: From Maghribi Unity to Saharan Integration." In *Social and Economic Development of Libya*, edited by E. G. H. Joffé and K. S. McLachlan, 215–31. Wisbech, UK: Menas Press.

Alexander, Nathan. 1981. "The Foreign Policy of Libya: Inflexibility Amid Change." *Orbis* 24, no. 4 (Winter):819–46.

Anderson, Lisa. 1982. "Libya and American Foreign Policy." *The Middle East Journal* 36, no. 4 (Autumn):516–34.

Baker, Pauline H. 1987. "A Giant Staggers: Nigeria as an Emerging Regional Power." In *African Security Issues: Sovereignty, Stability and Solidarity*, edited by Bruce Arlinghaus, 76–97. Boulder CO: Westview Press.

Bayart, Jean-François. 1984. *La Politique Africaine de François Mitterrand*. Paris: Editions Karthala.

Bearman, Jonathan. 1986. *Qadhafi's Libya*. London: Zed Books.

Beshir, M. 1985. "The Role of the Arab Group in the Organization of African Unity." In *The Arabs and Africa*, edited by Khair El-Din Haseeb, 223–56. London: Croom Helm and Centre for Arab Unity Studies.

Bessis, Juliette. 1986. *La Libye Contemporaine*. Paris: Editions L'Harmattan.

Brewer, W. 1982. "The Libyan-Sudanese 'Crisis' of 1981: Danger for Darfur and Dilemma for the United States." *The Middle East Journal* 36, no. 2 (Spring):205–16.

Carvely, A. 1973. "Libya: International Relations and Political Purposes." *International Journal* 28, no. 4 (Autumn):707–28.

Cooley, John. 1982. *Libyan Sandstorm*. New York: Holt, Rinehart and Winston.

The Embassy of the Libyan Arab Republic. 1973 and 1975. *Progressive Libya*. Washington: Embassy Press Section.

Evans-Pritchard, E. E. [1949] 1973. *The Sanusi of Cyrenaica*. Oxford: Oxford University Press.

Fadel, Yousef. 1975. "The Historical Roots of Afro-Arab Relations." In *The Arabs and Africa*, edited by Khair El-Din Haseeb, 27–57. London: Croom Helm and Centre for Arab Unity Studies.

Fallaci, Oriana. 1979. "Iranians Are Our Brothers: An Interview with Colonel Muammar el-Qadhafi of Libya." *New York Times Magazine* December 16:40, 116–28.

First, Ruth. 1974. *Libya: The Elusive Revolution*. Harmondsworth: Penguin Books.

George, A. 1986. "Drastic Fall in Oil Revenues." *Petroleum Economist* 53, 6 (June):218–20.

Ghariani, M. 1979. "Libya's Foreign Policy: The Role of the Country's Environmental and Leadership Factors, 1960–1973." Unpublished thesis, Western Michigan University.

Gurdon, C. 1985. "A Preliminary Assessment of the Distribution of Non-Hydrocarbon Minerals in Libya." In *Planning and Development in Modern Libya*, edited by M. M. Buru, S. M. Ghanem, and K. S. McLachlan, 178–93. Wisbech, UK: Menas Press.

Habib, H. (1975) *Politics and Government of Revolutionary Libya*. Ottawa: Le Cercle du Livre de France.

Haley, R. 1984. *Qaddafi and the United States since 1969*. New York: Praeger Publishers.

Harris, Lillian Craig. 1987. *Libya: Qadhafi's Revolution and the Modern State*. Boulder, CO: Westview Press.

Hasan, Y. (1985) "The Historical Roots of Afro-Arab Relations." In *The Arabs and Africa*, edited by Khair El-Din Haseeb, 27–57. London: Croom Helm and Centre for Arab Unity Studies.

Hodges, Tony. 1983. *Western Sahara: The Roots of a Desert War*. Westport, CT: Lawrence Hill and Company.

Hottinger, Arnold. 1981. "L'Expansionnisme Libyen: Machrek, Maghreb et Afrique Noire." *Politique Etrangère* 46, no. 1 (March):137–49.

Howe, John. 1981. "Qadhafi and Africa." *Africa*, no. 115 (May):16–17.

Ismael, T. 1974. "Africa and the Middle East." In *The Middle East in World Politics*, edited by T. Y. Ismael, 162–80. Syracuse: Syracuse University Press.

Laipson, E. 1983. "U.S. Policy in Northern Africa." *American-Arab Affairs*, no. 6 (Fall):48–58.

Lanne, Bernard. 1982. *Tchad-Libye: La Querelle des Frontières*. Paris: Editions Karthala.

Legum, Colin. 1982. "The Middle East Dimension." In *International Politics in Southern Africa*, edited by G. M. Carter and P. O'Meara, 115–21. Bloomington: Indiana University Press.

Lemarchand, René. 1984. "Chad: The Road to Partition." *Current History* 83, no. 491 (March):113–16.
Libyan Arab Republic. 1973. *The Revolution of 1st September: The Fourth Anniversary*. Benghazi: Ministry of Information and Culture.
Mattes, Hanspeter. 1987. "Libya's Economic Relations as an Instrument of Foreign Policy." In *The Economic Development of Libya*, edited by Bichara Khader and Bashir el-Wifati, 81–123. London: Croom Helm.
Mertz, R., and P. Mertz. 1983. *Arab Aid to Sub-Saharan Africa*. Munich: Chr. Kaiser Verlag.
Nasser, G. 1955. *Egypt's Liberation: The Philosophy of the Revolution*. Washington: Public Affairs Press.
Nelson, H. 1979. *Libya: A Country Study*. Washington: The American University.
Neuberger, Benjamin. 1982. *Involvement, Invasion and Withdrawal: Qadhafi's Libya and Chad, 1969–1981*. Occasional Papers no. 83. Tel Aviv: The Shiloah Center for Middle Eastern and African Studies.
Otayek, René. 1987. *La politique Africaine de la Libya (1969–1985)*. Paris: Editions Karthala.
Parker, Richard. 1984. *North Africa: Regional Tensions and Strategic Concerns*. New York: Praeger.
Qadhafi, Moammar. 1975. *Discourses*. Valletta, Malta: Adam Publishers.
Robinson, Pearl T. 1987. "Playing the Arab Card: Niger and Chad's Ambivalent Relations with Libya." In *African Security Issues: Sovereignty, Stability and Solidarity*, edited by Bruce Arlinghaus, 171–84. Boulder, CO: Westview Press.
Rondos, Alex. 1985. "Civil War and Foreign Intervention in Chad." *Current History* 84, no. 502 (May):209–12, 232.
St John, Ronald B. 1983. "The Ideology of Mu'ammar al-Qadhafi: Theory and Practice." *International Journal of Middle East Studies* 15, no. 4 (November):471–90.
———. 1986. "Terrorism and Libyan Foreign Policy, 1981–1986." *The World Today* 42, no. 7 (July):111–15.
———. 1987 *Qadhafi's World Design: Libyan Foreign Policy, 1969–1987*. London: Saqi Books.
Shembesh, A. 1975. "The Analysis of Libya's Foreign Policy: 1962–1973. A Study of the Impact of Environmental and Leadership Factors." Unpublished dissertation, Emory University.
Thompson, Virginia, and Richard Adloff. 1981. *Conflict in Chad*. London: C. Hurst and Company.
Wright, Claudia. 1981–82. "Libya and the West: Headlong into Confrontation?" *International Affairs* 58, no. 1 (Winter):13–41.
Wright, John. 1982. *Libya: A Modern History*. Baltimore: The Johns Hopkins University Press.
Yost, David. 1983. "French Policy in Chad and the Libyan Challenge." *Orbis* 21, no. 1 (Winter):965–97.

VIII.

QADHAFI AND THE ORGANIZATION OF AFRICAN UNITY

Jean-Emmanuel Pondi

Except for a brief period of harmony, from 1969 to 1972, diplomatic relations between Muammar Qadhafi's Libya and the Organization of African Unity (OAU) have been nothing short of tumultuous. Qadhafi's own actions within and outside the OAU, while providing abundant proof of his disdain for the conventional rules and responsibilities of international behavior, have set the stage for the gradual isolation, and ultimately the virtual ostracism of the Libyan Jamahiriya—but not without confronting the OAU with acute political crises.

As a diplomatic arena the OAU has both hampered and facilitated Libyan policies, yet the dominant trend has clearly been in the direction of mutual obstruction rather than facilitation. On the one hand the OAU has provided Qadhafi with an international forum for the projection of his doctrine, an institutional setting for whipping up support for his policies, and a wealth of behind-the-scenes opportunities for cutting deals and winning votes. Yet the limitations placed on Qadhafi's ambitions through the OAU machinery cannot be overlooked, any more than the threats posed to the survival of the organization by Libyan obstructionism.

Before turning to a more sustained discussion of the Libyan-OAU nexus, attention must be paid to the norms and values of the OAU: Qadhafi's growing disregard for the normative framework of the OAU is a commentary on the basic contradictions between his thoroughly unconventional approach to regional unity and the set of procedures and institutional norms set forth in the OAU Charter.

Qadhafi and the OAU: Conflicting Norms and Orientations

Created on May 25, 1963, in Addis Ababa, the OAU can best be viewed as a compromise between "unionists" and "statists" (see note 3), between two distinctive schools of thought separated by the different emphases each placed on the significance of state sovereignty. Today, with its fifty member-states it is the world's largest regional organization. Four basic substantive norms regulate the interactions of its member-states; the extent to which they are binding upon them goes far in explaining its remarkable staying power (Zartman 1984, 28). These four norms are as follows:

(1) Intra-system solutions to African problems are preferred over extra-system solutions, whenever possible [Art. XIX].

(2) The successor state is the basic sovereign, inviolable, legitimizing unit of African politics [Art. III (3)].

(3) Wars of conquest are not an acceptable policy alternative, and colonial boundaries are sacred unless changed by popular consent expressed in referenda [Art. III].

(4) All available means will be used to achieve the manifest destiny of the OAU system, that is, to remove white minority governments wherever they exist on the continent [Art. II].

These four norms have held firm over the past two decades, and the legal restraints thereby imposed upon most member-states explain the longevity and relative effectiveness of the organization.

Given the low level of institutionalization of the OAU, the personal philosophies of its constituent members are bound to influence the course and character of their interactions. To properly grasp Libya's relationship with the OAU, therefore, something must be said of Qadhafi's ideology in the context of the OAU's norms and values.

Arab nationalism is the central element of Qadhafi's ideology (St John 1983, 471). Like Nasser, whom he greatly admired as a youngster and subsequently sought to emulate, Qadhafi's brand of nationalism is rooted in a deep appreciation of, and respect for, Arab history and culture. From this vantage point the Arabic-speaking world is inseparable from the "Arab nation." In the colonel's eyes, Libya is the center, the vanguard, and the hope of Arab nationalism. As the standard bearer of pan-Arabism, Libya must assume its responsibilities in the fight against Israel and its Zionist allies (including the United States) and lend moral and material support to any camp that stands in opposition to Israeli interests. By extension, Qadhafi visualizes himself as the spokesman of the Arab nation.

Qadhafi's third imperative, next to pan-Arabism and anti-Zionism, is to encourage the birth of a world-wide, Tripoli-centered, Islamic community, beginning with the creation of a sense of unity among African Muslims. Because he views the Arab nation as the product of an age-old civilization based on a universally accepted religious message, Qadhafi feels that he has the right as well as the duty to act as the vehicle of Islam. Only Islam can lead humanity out of darkness into the light (St John 1983, 476).

Incorporating Qadhafi's messianic view of history into the normative framework of the OAU proved to be an immensely frustrating experience for both. At least three overlapping chronological stages can be identified in the evolution of OAU-Libyan relations between 1969 and 1986. Following a period of relative harmony between 1969 and 1972, mutual distrust increasingly set the tone of Libyan-OAU relations during the next four years, forcing Qadhafi into a position of growing isolation within the OAU. Finally, from 1979 to the present, Qadhafi's Libya attracted universal resentment, to the point where it found itself practically ostracized by the vast majority of OAU members.

The Era of Harmony: 1969–1972

Opting for caution and thus preferring to adopt a "wait-and-see" attitude toward the week-old regime in Tripoli, participants in the OAU Summit of September 6, 1969 in Addis Ababa made no mention in their resolutions of the Qadhafi-led Revolutionary Command Council (RCC) military takeover. In subsequent months, however, following a series of judicious diplomatic and political initiatives, the new rulers of Libya were able to present a highly attractive image to their fellow African heads of state.

Upon seizing power in 1969, Qadhafi and the RCC were quick to ally themselves with Gamal Abdel Nasser's Egypt. The alliance brought handsome dividends to Tripoli. At the time, Egypt enjoyed the unanimous and unconditional support of the OAU members,[1] much of this sympathy reflecting a sense of shock over her defeat and loss of territory during the 1967 Six Day War against Israel. Moreover, whatever his political shortcomings, Nasser, along with Ghana's Kwame Nkrumah, stood as the foremost proponent of pan-Africanism; and the key role played by Egypt in the creation of the OAU could hardly be ignored. Thus Qadhafi's association with Egypt did much to cast him in a favorable light in the eyes of most OAU member-states.

Furthermore, Qadhafi's early domestic policies, most of them designed to assert Libyan sovereignty and independence from the West, won him the envy and admiration of those OAU member-states that wished to do likewise. On March 28 and June 11, 1970, Britain and the United States were formally requested to evacuate the Al Adem and the Wheelus air base. The lease agreements signed under the previous Libyan regime had expired and would not be renewed. On October 7, 1970, Italian-owned assets were confiscated by the new military rulers. To properly celebrate his decision to expel all remnants of neocolonialists, June 11 and October 7 were officially proclaimed national holidays (St John 1983, 474).

Scarcely two weeks after taking power, the RCC issued a decree requiring foreign banks to form Libyan joint stock companies with at least 51 percent of their shares owned by Tripoli. Qadhafi's courageous (or perhaps reckless, by the standards of that time) nationalistic policies, so strikingly reminiscent of Nasser's during the 1956 Suez crisis received tacit OAU support; his initiative, at any rate, did not come under fire from any of the OAU members. Finally, and quite aside from the significance of these moves, there was something inherently appealing about an austere twenty-seven-year-old Bedouin head of state who, despite Libya's growing oil wealth, insisted on spending his nights in a desert tent.

The young colonel took full advantage of his growing popularity among OAU members to work toward an increased diplomatic isolation of Israel. It is worth remembering in this connection that, from 1960 onward, Israel entered into a series of cooperation agreements with a number of African states: in 1960 with Mali, Upper Volta (now Burkina Faso), and Madagascar; in 1961 with Dahomey (now Benin); in 1962 with the Ivory Coast, Uganda, Gabon, Sierra Leone, Rwanda, Cameroon, Gambia, and Burundi; in 1963 with Nigeria and Tanzania; in 1964 with Togo and Chad; and in 1965 with Kenya (Mazrui 1975, 729). To reduce and ultimately eliminate the Israeli presence from the continent thus became a key priority on Qadhafi's foreign policy agenda. But perhaps the main reason for the atmosphere of relative serenity surrounding the relations between Qadhafi and the OAU in the 1969–72 period was that most of his attention was devoted to the promotion of pan-Arabism; only secondary attention was paid to pan-Africanism as a long-term foreign policy objective. On December 27, 1969, Qadhafi signed the Tripoli Charter with President Gaafar al Nimeiry of Sudan and President Gamal Abdel Nasser of Egypt, and two years later, in September 1971, the short-lived Federation of Arab Republics came into existence, consisting of Libya, Egypt (under Anwar el Sadat), and Syria (Deeb 1986, 156).

Following Nasser's death in 1970, however, Egypt rapidly emerged as the principal stumbling block on the road to pan-Arab unity. Sadat's diplomatic overture to the United States, coupled with his decision to reverse the trend toward socialism initiated under Nasser, could not but greatly irritate the Libyan leader. If Sadat's rapprochement with Israel's strongest supporter in the Middle East was seen as little short of a treasonable act, equally offensive were the implications of his domestic policies—the latter tantamount to a desecration of Nasser's heroic image. Calling his Libyan colleague "a vicious criminal, 100 per cent sick and possessed of the demon," Sadat made it plain that he had run out of patience with Qadhafi's claim to moral leadership and unpredictable meddling in Egyptian affairs (Ogunbadejo 1986, 35). Similarly, Sudan's Gaafar Nimeiry's diagnosis of his Libyan counterpart as "a split personality—both evil" was a clear indication of the sharp deterioration of Libyan-Sudanese relations, following Tripoli's unsolicited interference in the affairs of the Sudan (Ogunbadejo 1986, 35).

Faced with these ominous threats to pan-Arab unity, Qadhafi increasingly turned to pan-Islamism as an alternative tack, in an effort to check Israel's diplomatic inroad into Africa and widen the scope of his influence in the OAU. Determined to capitalize upon his oil wealth, Qadhafi correctly saw that he stood a far better chance to influence the behavior of the OAU than that of the Arab League, where, compared to Saudi Arabia, for instance, Libya carried relatively little weight.

Not until 1972 did Qadhafi begin to issue repeated calls for the destabilization of "unfaithful" and pro-Zionist African regimes; yet the direction in which he was about to move had already become clear in his 1970 speech before the International Conference for the Propagation of Islam, in Tripoli, in which he called for a *jihad* (holy war) against infidels in Palestine, Eritrea, and Zanzibar. From 1972 on, the Libyan leader's crusading spirit showed a blissful indifference to the norm of sovereignty enshrined in the OAU Charter. This relentlessly truculent style marks the beginning of Libya's growing marginalization in the pan-African organization.

The Trend Toward Marginalization: 1972–1978

A remarkable feature of the 1972–1978 period is the extent to which the steady deterioration in Libyan-OAU relations has tended to coincide with the realization of one of Qadhafi's foremost foreign policy objectives: the isolation of Israel on the African continent. However, Israel's increasing isolation in Africa occurred in spite of, rather than because of, Qadhafi's actions.

Credit must be given to Qadhafi for initiating a series of diplomatic breaks between African states (beginning with Uganda, Chad, and Niger) and Israel that precipitated further ruptures between 1972 and 1973 (*Jerusalem Papers on Peace Problems* 1980, 34). From Libya, Uganda's President Idi Amin sought not only financial aid (denied him by his Israeli allies when his intention to mount a military offensive against Tanzania became clear), but also a new alignment to end his political isolation in Africa. The long-standing diplomatic relations between Kampala and Tel Aviv were abruptly severed one month after Amin's return from a trip to Libya in February 1972, a move that can hardly be said to be coincidental, although this interpretation is disputed by some scholars (Mazrui 1975, 727).

The circumstances under which Chad and Israel closed their respective embassies owed much to Qadhafi's diplomacy. In August 1971, Chad's President François Tombalbaye broke off relations with Libya after accusing Qadhafi of supporting Muslim insurgents and instigating revolutionary plots in N'Djamena. In April 1972, President Hamani Diori of Niger offered to act as a mediator between Libya and Chad and eventually succeeded in persuading them to resume diplomatic relations. As part of the bargain, Qadhafi offered to withdraw support from the *Front de Libération National du Tchad* (Frolinat) and provide Chad with financial aid, but only if Chad agreed to break off relations with Israel. In hopes of choking the rebellion by drying up its main source of external support, President Tombalbaye agreed to the Libyan offer and Chad severed relations with Israel on November 28, 1972 (*ACR* 1972–73, B519; *ACR* 1974–75, B568).

For his part, while serving as a mediator in the Libya-Chad dispute, President Hamani Diori agreed to reconsider his Libyan policy. In the 1960s Diori's closest ally in West Africa was Felix Houphouet Boigny of the Ivory Coast, at a time when Diori's relations with his Arab neighbors were strained, especially since Algeria harbored his political rival, Djibo Bakary. In the 1970s, however, Niger's relations with the Ivory Coast cooled considerably and Diori sought to cultivate better relations with the Arabs to the north, hoping that Algeria and Libya, in addition to providing Niger with financial help, would withdraw their support from Diori's domestic opposition (*ACR* 1973–74, B718). On January 4, 1973, after more than a decade of friendly relations, Niger severed relations with Israel.

That Qadhafi's African diplomacy was instrumental in precipitating the break-off of diplomatic relations between Israel on the one hand and Uganda, Chad, and Niger on the other can scarcely be denied. But contrary to the colonel's claims, the subsequent further isolation of Israel in Africa, although conforming to Qadhafi's wishes, occurred in spite of his tactlessness and his increasing marginalization in the OAU. Events at the OAU Addis Ababa summit of May 1973 lend credence to this judgment.

The Arab diplomatic victory against Israel at the Addis Ababa summit was all the more remarkable in view of Qadhafi's attempts to prevent its convening. A few weeks before the summit conference, the Libyan leader sent cables to all African heads of state and governments, urging them to boycott the meeting unless the venue was changed to Cairo, Egypt, or unless Ethiopia immediately severed diplomatic relations with Israel and closed the Israeli Embassy in Addis Ababa. No one heeded Libya's boycott call, and every OAU member-state (including Libya) sent a delegation to the Addis Ababa Conference (Akinsanya 1976, 523).

At the summit, it was not Qadhafi but Algerian President Houari Boumedienne who, by skillfully linking the Palestinian and South African issues, persuaded most of the OAU members to side with the Arab cause. Boumedienne passionately and convincingly explained that "Africa cannot adopt one attitude toward colonialism in Southern Africa and a completely different stand towards Zionist colonization in Northern Africa." He called on all African heads of state to sever diplomatic relations with Israel as "a concrete act of African unity" (Akinsanya 1976, 523). In contrast, Qadhafi's reckless attacks on Ethiopia infuriated many black African leaders and embarrassed his African Arab colleagues.

Following Boumedienne's speech, the OAU Resolution on the Middle East Problem, which reaffirmed support for the territorial integrity of Egypt, was unanimously adopted and signed on May 29, 1973. When war broke out in October 1973, twenty-seven member-states reacted strongly by breaking diplomatic relations with Israel as a reaffirmation of the stand taken five months earlier during the annual pan-African summit conference.

Further evidence of Libya's declining influence came at the organization's fifteenth summit in Khartoum, Sudan, in July 1978. On that occasion, Qadhafi forcefully called on all OAU member-states to break all diplomatic ties with Egypt, after Sadat's historic visit to Israel. Not a single African state followed Qadhafi's advice.

Several factors account for Qadhafi's dwindling esteem within the OAU during the 1972–1978 period. Among the most prominent were his overt disregard of, and open contempt for, the organization's basic norms and values, and his ill-advised choice of political allies (and adversaries) in the African diplomatic arena. As early as 1971, the new Libyan regime began its long-standing habit of breaching the cardinal OAU rule of non-interference in the domestic affairs of neighboring member-states. In September of that year, the Libyan RCC reviewed events in Chad and reached the conclusion that Tombalbaye's government was oppressing its own people, particularly Muslims, in addition to discriminating against all elements of Arab origin and acting as an agent of Zionism. Qadhafi thus felt he had no choice but to recognize the Frolinat, and promptly authorized the opening of an office for the rebel movement in Tripoli (*ACR* 1972–73, 843). In May 1973, following a secret deal with Tombalbaye, Libya occupied an area of twenty-seven thousand square miles—the so-called Aouzou Strip—in the northwestern part of Chad.

Qadhafi's concern for allegedly persecuted Muslims spread further when, in an October 1973 speech at Sabrata in Libya, he announced that his country was ready to send arms to his Guinean religious brothers. In the course of the following years, such initiatives became a trademark of Qadhafi's leadership; by making a mockery of a fundamental OAU norm, Libya found itself increasingly isolated.

His poor choice of African allies contributed in no small way to Qadhafi's diplomatic isolation. In his determination to counter Israeli advances in Africa, Qadhafi did not hesitate to join hands with "Field Marshall" Idi Amin Dada of Uganda, the self-declared "Conqueror of the British Empire." Even by African standards, where scrupulous respect for individual human rights is not always obvious, Idi Amin's regime distinguished itself as one of the most ruthless in Africa's post-colonial history.[2] If there can be little question that the Ugandan dictator was genuinely despised by most of his peers, it is equally plain that Qadhafi's association with, and support for, Idi Amin could not but profoundly sully Libya's image in the OAU.

Qadhafi's unfortunate selection of opponents in the OAU (Egypt, Ethiopia, and Tanzania, to name only the most prominent) has likewise contributed to Libya's waning influence. Egypt is considered the most pan-African of the Arab states (with the possible exception of Algeria under Boumedienne) and has generally enjoyed widespread respect in the OAU, over and above the esteem which Nasser earned for himself for his role in the creation of the organization. Qadhafi's unsuccessful attempt to ostracize Egypt after her rapprochement with Israel during the Khartoum summit of 1978 testified to Egypt's standing in the OAU, and served as yet another reminder of the organization's impatience with Libya.

Like Egypt, Ethiopia played a central role in the creation of the OAU and even drafted the organization's compromise charter.[3] With her two thousand years of history, Ethiopia (like Egypt) is a source of legitimate pride in a continent culturally and physically mutilated by European colonialization. It is a measure of Ethiopia's standing within the OAU that Qadhafi's call for the boycott of the 1973 Addis Ababa summit was ignored by all African countries.

Julius K. Nyerere was at the time one of the most articulate and highly respected figures in the OAU. Qadhafi's opposition to Nyerere and support for Amin, a man not known for the brillance of his intellect, was bound to reflect badly on Libya. In 1972, Qadhafi unexpectedly attacked the rulers of Tanzania for having "liquidated all the Muslims in Zanzibar" (*Jerusalem Papers* 1980, 27), even though Nyerere himself had nothing to do with the 1964 Zanzibar revolution, in which the ruling Arab elites were overthrown by Africans who were themselves of Muslim origins.

Finally, no chronicle of the years between 1972 and 1978 would be complete without mentioning the increasing interaction between pan-African and pan-Arab identities. In 1974, with nearly half of the Arab League membership belonging to the OAU, two of the organization's major functions came into focus. By then the OAU provided an arena in which the Arabs could politically influence black Africans. It also had evolved into an institution through which black Africans could seek economic concessions from Arab members (Mazrui 1975, 739). There is little doubt that during the 1970s, the Arabs attempted to exercise greater political influence in the OAU. The 1974 Mogadishu summit conference (in predominantly Muslim Somalia) elected President Siad Barre as the organization's chairman for that year, as it is customary for the host country's head of state to hold that position. Somalia and Zambia each unsuccessfully presented a candidate of their choice for the position of Secretary General; in the end a Cameroonian, William Eteki Mboumoua, was elected as a compromise candidate (Mazrui 1975, 740).

OAU member-states tried to cope as best they could with the rising costs of petroleum imports and manufactured products while suffering severe losses of revenue from the sale of their primary commodities. At their Algiers summit of November 1973, Arab heads of state responded positively to the OAU request to impose an oil embargo on South Africa and Rhodesia. They announced the establishment of an Arab Bank for Industrial and Agricultural Development in Africa, with an initial capital of $231 million, and an Arab economic organization with a total capital of $446 million, to provide loans and technical assistance to African states (Akinsanya 1976, 525).

Expecting Libyan support, many African leaders turned to Tripoli for help.[4] At the end of 1975, the international financial reserves of Libya stood at $2,053 million. Her reported commitments in Africa amounted to $565.64 million in 1974 and $297.65 million in the first half of 1975 (Penrose 1976, 279). Actual disbursements were much lower, however, at $341.95 million and $206.25 million, respectively. Furthermore, 69 percent of Libyan aid consisted of reimbursable loans, granted on a more restrictive basis. Qadhafi's economic aid policies did not win him many friends in the OAU and helped to further isolate him.

At least two views have emerged regarding the increased Arab role in African affairs in the 1970s. The more pessimistic is best captured by Kum Buo's suggestion that "Afro-Arab friendship, if it exists at all, is on paper one which thrives mainly during diplomatic encounters." His assessment rests on the notion that since the "barbaric [early Arab] slave raids in Africa, a mutual distrust has characterized the coexistence between black and Arab Africans" (Kum Buo 1975, 46). He concludes that an accident of geography is hardly sufficient to provide a basis for genuine African-Arab friendship, let alone political and economic solidarity. Ali Mazrui articulates a second, more optimistic view of the same relationship. In his opinion, "since 1973, the Middle East and Africa have edged a little closer towards becoming a single international subsystem" in a mutually satisfying, though sometimes strained, relationship (Mazrui 1975, 740).

Given Qadhafi's often patronizing economic and political attitudes and religious zeal, and especially his outright contempt for non-Muslim "unfaithfuls," it is a safe assumption that in 1978 most OAU member-states probably identified more closely with Kum Buo's analysis than with Mazrui's (see Dunton in this volume). This sentiment is worth bearing in mind as we now turn to the third phase in the Libyan-OAU relations, a period in which isolation quickly turned into ostracism.

Libya Ostracized: 1979–1986

In 1979, Qadhafi's position in sub-Saharan Africa was considerably weakened when one of his most reliable allies, Idi Amin Dada, was ousted from power by Tanzanian forces. At the Addis Ababa summit of July 1979, Nyerere explained that the war between his country and Uganda had been caused by the Ugandan army's aggression against Tanzania and Amin's claim to have annexed part of Tanzanian territory (Cervenka and Legum 1981). Although the Tanzanian army's action clearly violated one of the OAU's rules (the inviolability of member-states' frontiers), dislike of Idi Amin ran so high that most of the organization's membership was willing to overlook the incident and breathe a sign of relief at Amin's departure. For Libya, however, no such respite was as yet forthcoming.

From 1980 on, Qadhafi's activities in Chad once again became a major source of preoccupation for most African leaders (see Lemarchand in this volume).[5] The turning point came in December 1980 with the full-scale intervention of Libyan armed forces on behalf of Goukouni Oueddeye's faction during the battle of N'Djamena. That an Islamic Legion made up of Arab and African "volunteers" trained in and by Libya could so brazenly violate Chadian sovereignty came as a shock to most OAU members. Equally unsettling (in both senses), assassination squads were said to have been sent by Qadhafi to liquidate those political leaders in Chad who opposed Libya's intervention (Cooley 1981, 75). The handwriting on the wall could not have been clearer: no African leader could claim immunity from Qadhafi's unpredictable wrath.

In January 1981, a special OAU conference was convened, during which Libya's proposed merger with Goukouni Oueddeye's Chad was unanimously condemned and withdrawal of all Libyan forces from Chad urgently requested (Cooley 1981, 76; Kelley 1986, 50). Coming at a time when most African leaders viewed with grave concern his efforts to destabilize the governments of Sudan, Egypt, and Tunisia, Qadhafi's push into Chad further intensified their anxieties. Libyan meddling in the domestic affairs of African states (more often than not in the name of Islamic brotherhood) constituted a clear-cut case of subversion, hence a violation of Article III of the OAU Charter. Exasperated by Libyan actions, Senegal, Gambia, and Ghana severed their diplomatic relations with Tripoli in 1980. By 1981 tensions between Qadhafi and most of the other OAU states had escalated to the point where the Libyan leader preferred to remain in Tripoli rather than confront his peers at the organization's eighteenth summit in Nairobi.

The full measure of Qadhafi's isolation in the OAU came a year later. In 1982, for the first time, the organization came to the brink of disintegration over three main disputes: (1) disagreements over who claimed legitimate authority in Chad; (2) divergences over the admission into the OAU of the Saharawi Democratic Arab Republic (SDAR), with Morocco insisting on its historic claim to the former Spanish territory; (3) and most important, perhaps, disaccords over the designation of Tripoli as the site for the 1982 OAU summit.

Something in the nature of a radical versus moderate cleavage crystallized around each set of issues. Thus it was against the wishes of the so-called "moderates" in the OAU that Qadhafi in 1982 insisted on seating Goukouni Oueddeye's "rebel" faction at the forthcoming Tripoli meeting in lieu of the official delegation (headed by Hissene Habre) invited by the OAU Secretary General (Ogunbadejo 1986, 49). Much the same line-up emerged out of the debate over the choice of Tripoli as a venue for the organization's nineteenth summit.

> All the "radical" states, particularly "socialist" Ethiopia, Congo, Benin, Angola, Zimbabwe and Mozambique, stood solidly by Qadhafi. Led by President Samora Machel, these regimes militantly urged the Libyan leader to ignore the OAU rule on the needed quorum and go ahead with the Summit. The logic behind this line of argument was that all the member-states that boycotted Tripoli could, if they wished, form their own "reactionary" continental organization. (Ogunbadejo 1986, 52)

Fortunately, Nyerere's strong opposition to this rash scheme prevented its implementation and saved the OAU from splitting down the middle. At any rate, after two unsuccessful attempts to meet the required two-thirds quorum for holding the Tripoli summit, the incumbent chairman, Daniel arap Moi, decided to move its venue to Addis Ababa for 1983.

The 1982 crisis prompted many African leaders to lay blame for the organization's troubles on "incessant Arab quarrelling," specifically on Qadhafi. President Mobutu of Zaire, for instance, advocated the creation of a "League of Black African States" (Poli 1985, 32). There is no reason to assume, however, that such an organization would foster greater intra-African unity.

The Western Sahara's "Gordian knot" was finally cut in November 1984 when Mohammed Abdel Aziz, president of the Saharoui Arab Democratic Republic, took his seat at that year's OAU summit in Addis Ababa. In protest, the Moroccan delegation left Africa Hall and withdrew from the OAU, the first effective resignation of a member-state since 1963.

Apparently unaffected by his 1982 debacle in the OAU, Qadhafi's crusading spirit gathered fresh momentum in 1984 and 1985, with disastrous effect on his OAU standing. During a visit to Rwanda and Burundi (two of Zaire's neighbors) in 1985, the Libyan leader openly sought to engage the small Muslim population of these countries in a plan to overthrow Mobutu, the president of Zaire (*ACR*, 1984–85, A128). Denouncing Mobutu as "a Zionist agent" Qadhafi reverted to his favorite pitch: "You must incite Muslims in Zaire and urge them to engage in the *jihad* so that Mobutu may be toppled" (*ACR* 1984–85, A128).

The extent of Qadhafi's ostracism became obvious when, following the April 15, 1986, U.S. raid on Libya, very few if any expressions of sympathy were officially voiced by African states (Soudan 1986, A53). Apart from the unconvincing communique published by the OAU Secretary General Ide Oumarou, which merely condemned the American offensive in Libya, only Burkina Faso and Sudan manifested support for Qadhafi. From Kinshasa to Dakar, from Bangui to Abidjan, silence, if not jubilation, was the predominant mood. The African press only reproduced news agency dispatches on the Libyan situation, often without comment (Soudan 1986).

Qadhafi, to be sure, is not irredeemably unpopular throughout Africa. His revolutionary brand of politics holds an emotional appeal for many a student radical. Following the American attacks on Tripoli and Bengazi, some students in Togolese and Cameroonian universities overtly expressed their indignation over the aggression perpetrated by the Reagan administration (Soudan 1986, A53). Yet such signs of support are expressive of little more than a diffuse sense of opposition to incumbent regimes, and have little effect on the policies of the OAU.

In short, Qadhafi's insistence on pursuing his twin objectives of promoting regional unity while opposing Israeli advances in Africa, regardless of the costs, has resulted in his near ostracism from the mainstream of intra-African cooperation. Difficult though it is to predict Qadhafi's future contribution to the OAU's fortunes, there is little to suggest a decisive alteration of the current trend toward further isolation. Faced with major economic difficulties on the home front,[6] Qadhafi's patronage policies are bound to suffer, leaving him with fewer inducements to attract the sympathies or commitments of the poorer members of the OAU. By the same token, it would be surprising if Libya's diminishing economic capabilities did not force him to reduce the scale of his external involvements and thus remove some of the more contentious issues from the agenda of the organization. Finally, with the spectacular and decisive routing of the Libyan forces in northern Chad, it is a question whether the costs of Libyan adventurism will not cause the colonel to engage in a fundamental reappraisal of his foreign policy options. One thing, at any rate, is clear: After the formidable impediments posed to the OAU by Qadhafi's vindictiveness, that the organization was able to survive the many crises thrust upon it from Tripoli is perhaps not the least of its achievements.

NOTES

1. See the OAU Resolution on the Middle East unanimously condemning Israel's annexation of Egyptian territory and requesting the restitution of this land to Egypt. AHG/Res. 53(V) of September 1968, in *Africa Contemporary Record* (*ACR*) 1970–71, C3.

2. Between 1971 and 1979, an estimated three hundred thousand Ugandans were killed under Amin's reign of terror. For a detailed account of the Amin years, see Henry Kyemba 1977.

3. In 1963, the future evolution of Africa was seen from two different perspectives: The "unionists," which included Ghana, Egypt, Guinea, and Mali, defended the view that common continental structures should be established. These would include a common market, currency, customs union, and continental government. The "statists," who included Nigeria, the Ivory Coast, Ethiopia, and Senegal, advocated the creation of regional (and mainly economic) organizations as a first step toward an eventual continental amalgamation that would preserve the individual sovereignty of each state. The latter was the dominant view in independent Africa, as reflected by the OAU Charter.

4. In 1974, the presidents of Liberia, Mauritania, and Guinea paid visits to Tripoli. (Nigeria and Gabon visited as well, but not for economic reasons.) Economic agreements were concluded with Rwanda, Zaire, Liberia, Niger, Somalia, Chad, and Mali. In that same period, Qadhafi paid visits to Somalia, Uganda, Chad, Niger, and Guinea. See *ACR* 1974–75, B64.

5. In November 1981, the OAU sent a peace-keeping force into Chad, consisting of troops from Nigeria, Senegal, and Zaire. Unable to fulfill their mandate, mainly for lack of financial means, the OAU force withdrew in June 1981 (*ACR* 1981–82, A86).

6. While in 1980 Libya earned $22 billion from its oil sales, in 1986, oil industry experts predicted earnings of only $4 billion.

REFERENCES

Africa Contemporary Record (ACR). 1969–70, 1972–73, 1974–75. Exeter: Africa Research Limited.

Akinsanya, Adepup. 1976. "The Afro-Arab Alliance: Dream or Reality." *African Affairs* 75, no. 301 (October):511–29.

Cervenka, Zdenek, and Colin Legum. 1981. "The OAU in 1979." *ACR*, 1979–1980:A58-A71.

Cooley, John K. 1981. "The Libyan Menace." *Foreign Policy*, 42 (Spring):74–93.

Deeb, Mary-Jane. 1986. "Qadhafi's Calculated Risks." *SAIS Review* 6, no. 2 (Summer–Fall):151–62.

Jerusalem Papers on Peace Problems. 1980. Jerusalem: The Hebrew University.

Kelley, M. P. 1986. *A State in Disarray: Conditions of Chad's Survival*. Boulder, CO: Westview Press.

Kum Buo, S. 1975. "The Illusion of Afro-Arab Solidarity." *Africa Report*. September–October:2–5.

Kyemba, Henry. 1977. *A State of Blood*. New York: Grosset and Dunlap.

Mazrui, A. 1975. "Black Africa and the Arabs." *Foreign Affairs* 53, no. 4 (July):725–42.

Ogunbadejo, Oye. 1986. "Qaddafi and Africa's International Relations." *The Journal of Modern African Studies* 24, no. 1:33–68.

Penrose, Edith. 1976. "Africa and the Oil Revolution" *African Affairs*, no. 300 (July):277–83.

Poli, F. 1985. "Pour ou Contre la 'Ligue des Etats Noirs.' " *Jeune Afrique*, no. 1284–1285 (August 14–21).

St John, R. B. 1983. "The Ideology of Muammar al Qadhafi: Theory and Practice." *International Journal of Middle East Studies* 15, no. 4 (November):471–90.

Soudan, F. 1986. "Après le raid U.S.: Des réactions voisines du 'degré zéro'." *Jeune Afrique*, no. 1322 (May 7).

Zartman, William. 1984. "The OAU in the African State System: Interaction and Evaluation." In *The OAU After Twenty Years*, edited by Yassin El-Ayouty and I. William Zartman, 13–44. New York: Praeger Publishers.

IX.

BLACK AFRICANS IN LIBYA AND LIBYAN IMAGES OF BLACK AFRICA

Chris Dunton

On the main street in Benghazi a large poster of Qadhafi immediately captures public attention: the stern, charismatic image of the man is easily recognizable behind the dark glasses; behind the poster stands a statue of Nasser, arm stretched upward to wave at an imaginary crowd. The juxtaposition establishes the intellectual origins of Libya's 1969 revolution: to this day the Libyan experiment in revolutionary change retains a strong element of Nasserite nationalism. A few hundred meters down the road from Qadhafi and the Nasser memorial stands the sports stadium, and here Libya's sign-makers turn to the south; across the main entrance the boarding reads: *Africa for Africans: L'Afrique aux Africains.*[1]

The cultural nexus between Libya and black Africa is a central element in Qadhafi's use of political symbols and, indeed, a central theme of his public discourse. How far this image is shared and internalized by Libyans and by black Africans is an entirely different matter. It raises fundamental questions about the domestic and external bases of support of Libyan policies, and focuses attention on a range of constraints that has gone generally unnoticed in the contemporary literature on Libya.

Do Libyans see themselves unequivocally as members of the Arab nation, or do their identities extend to sub-Saharan Africa? Does the maxim *Africa for Africans* form a real component in their social consciousness, or is it only a projection of the will of the present regime? Conversely, how do African students and workers in Libya perceive Qadhafi's pronouncements and policies with regard to Black Africa? In short, is there any significant cultural interaction or empathy between the peoples of Libya and those of sub-Saharan Africa, and if so, how is this likely to affect the success of Qadhafi's foreign policy objectives?

Before coming to grips with these questions something must be said of the Libyan regime's projection of its role in Africa through the media and various official publications. There follows a discussion of how this role fits in with, or deviates from, the standard image that Libyan students have of sub-Saharan Africa. We next consider how the presence of a black minority among Libyan citizens might affect Libyan images of Africa, and conclude with an inquiry into the experience of sub-Saharan students in Libya.

One important caveat must be entered at the outset, however. Much of what follows reflects certain limitations of space and time. The materials on which I have based my analysis were collected from late 1983 to July 1986, during which period I taught at Gar Younis (Benghazi) University. Comments from Libyan and sub-Saharan students were gathered systematically; some of the remaining material is, however, based on casual, isolated interviews, and any conclusions drawn from it must remain tentative.

Libya's Projection of Its Role in Africa

Whatever part sub-Saharan Africa may play in the consciousness of most Libyans, the regime appears to be in no doubt as to the leadership role Libya should pursue on the continent. Apart from Qadhafi's well-documented and invariably controversial position on African issues, the projection of Libya's Pan-African Policy is easily discernible on occasions such as the Pan-African Youth Festival of 1983 and in the provision of hundreds of scholarships for African students at universities and colleges. It can be read, too, from key speeches by Qadhafi and from Libyan publications like *New Africa* and *Rissalat al Jihad*,[2] which provide significant insights into the regime's articulation of its role on the continent.

The first issue of *New Africa* appeared in mid-1984. Published at first in Vienna, its editorship remains, technically, anonymous, though style and content pin its origins down—more decisively in later issues—to Libya. Significantly, the standard of production is very high, apart from sporadic mistranslations in the English and French editions and the occasional bizarre factual error. The journal's cover is glossy and durable, and page layout is consistently attractive. In places the emphasis on layout—on bold visual statement—overrides other considerations. In one issue a full-page feature on the withdrawal of French troops from Chad comprises a dramatic photo, some imaginative titling—and a mere four hundred words of reading matter. But then, the point of the page is not to offer an inclusive or explanatory account of the Chad crisis; its intention is to state a particular policy toward the war, in the unambiguous terms of a wall-poster (*New Africa*, November 1984).

There are more substantial items: each issue carries material on aid projects and their deficiencies, on world banking, on drought and famine crises. The breadth of concern here is impressive and reflects, perhaps, Libya's own dynamism in agricultural development. Other pieces do seem meager. In the second issue, a three-page article on the Republic of Benin does nothing more than reprint a few hundred words of basic data from a world gazetteer (*New Africa*, August 1984). The journal's attractive design and its general avoidance of indepth material suggest a phase of public relations' publishing where the need to put forward an attractive product supersedes a commitment to any specific content.

As for Libya's own role: in the early issues there is little direct reference to the Jamahiriya. There is a generally radical orientation and a concentration of articles on "friendly" states: Burkina Faso, Benin, Ghana. In later issues, there is more: an article on an agricultural project near Benghazi; a statement of faith in Libyan policy on Chad, which is projected as aiming to free the continent "from foreign intervention in the internal affairs of African countries" (*New Africa*, October 1985). One article addresses the role of the French language and culture in Senegal, with a view to rebuking Senghor's attacks on the influence of Arab culture in his country. As the *New Africa* author points out, the official status of French in the country hardly begins to reflect its broad irrelevance to the bulk of the population, and Senghor's absorption in things French does render him in some senses a marginal figure. The article goes on to discuss the issue of the Arabic language, pointing out that for the Muslim 80 percent of Senegal's population, after all, Arabic might surely seem more relevant than French. What is striking is that nowhere does the article mention any language other than Arabic and French. The argument appears conceived in the spirit of a struggle for influence. One camp pitches in against the other and neither Fulfulbe, Serer, nor Wolof (first language for 40 percent of Senegalese and understood by many more) register in the account (*New Africa*, October 1985).

Elsewhere, the pact between Libya and Morocco—which in an earlier issue had been heralded as "the first of a series of victories for the benefit of all the people of the African continent," representing a "thrust of life to the Organization of African Unity"—is now described as a realization of "Arab-African Unity," as "a new approach which interests the life of both Arabs and Africans," (*New Africa*, November 1984, October 1985). The impulse toward unification, the drive against imposed divisions, is attractive, of course, and potentially of great significance. What spoils the pitch here is public knowledge of the accounting act that led Morocco and Libya into the accord (Libyan withdrawal of support for the Saharawi African Democratic Republic [SADR]; Libyan reliance on a Moroccan labor force, and so on),[3] and public awareness of the frailty of successive Libyan attempts since the early 1980s at union with its Arab neighbors (see Tessler, in this volume).[4]

New Africa's description of the Libyan-Moroccan accord as a boost for the OAU appears even more tenuous in the light of Morocco's subsequent withdrawal—and Libya's nonwithdrawal—from the organization and, indeed, with the subsequent dissolution of the accord in 1986 after Shimon Peres's visit to Rabat. What is interesting here is the confidence with which the agreement is held forward as a model for the OAU—as a pointer toward possible unification among other African states ("a new approach which interests the lives of both Arabs and Africans"). Libya, characteristically, thrusts itself center-stage as political innovator; under Qadhafi, Libya is concerned to place itself in close focus, and external factors sometimes recede right out of the field of vision.

This tendency is even more conspicuous in articles published in the journal *Rissalat al Jihad*. Here, in the coverage of African affairs, eulogies on Qadhafi's role tend to exclude all other considerations: witness the following comments on his visit to Rwanda and Burundi in 1985:

> The African masses in general consider [Qadhafi] as the hero thanks to whom Africa will realize its hopes and its ambitions. For the African masses, in their entirety, he is simply a son of the African continent, a revolutionary born from the people of a small country in the north of the continent, but a man who does not hesitate to defy the colonialist forces and their vile lackeys. All see in him the hero of Africa and the pillar of the African peoples in their struggle and their movement towards liberation. (*Rissalat al Jihad*, September 1985, 33)

> The dream of Africans had come true when they saw the Muslim Revolutionary who carried the pickaxe on their behalf to destroy the heritage of imperialism. . . . The Muslim revolutionary *explained* to the Africans that the continent of Africa suffers from problems inherited from the imperialistic actions of France, Britain, Belgium and Italy. (*Rissalat al Jihad*, January 1986, 70; my emphasis)

A visit later in the same year to Ghana is reported in much the same way, the article noting "the historical link between the North and South of the continent"—and then referring to Qadhafi's visit as "the cultural hope coming from the North" (*Rissalat al Jihad*, January 1986,

20). The report on a visit to Senegal concentrates, like the others, on eulogy and on recording Qadhafi's policy statements (especially on Chad). Nothing specifically Senegalese merits a mention, except the people in the streets, "expressing in their cheers and signs their pride with the Muslim African revolutionary" (*Rissalat al Jihad*, January 1986, 11).[5]

In November 1984 Qadhafi made a marathon speech to the Department of Political Science at the University of Gar Younis on the subject of neocolonialism.[6] Throughout, he referred to the nonexistence of a valid—that is, properly analytical—literature on colonialism and on the "vacuum" prone to be filled by foreign influence and interests after independence. Western writing on the subject was cited and attacked for its bias. Nowhere in the speech was there any recognition of the considerable body of acute and methodical analysis of colonialism and postcolonial developments that has come over the last few decades from Africa itself, as well as from the Caribbean and Indian regions and elsewhere. Hence ultimately, perhaps, the eulogies in the *Rissalat* on Qadhafi's role, and hence the heady emphasis on proselytizing: Qadhafi's initiative shines all the more brightly because of this general unawareness—or at least proclivity to overlook—the whole history of political engagement in other parts of the continent.

Libyan Students' Perspectives on Sub-Saharan Africa

The regime, then, confidently projects the notion that Libya is, by historical necessity, intimately engaged in Africa's political destiny and, moreover, that it sustains a leadership role on the continent.

Yet no such belief is evident among the Libyan people at large. As far as Qadhafi's political initiatives in Africa are concerned, there is widespread skepticism as to their value or their relevance. Expenditure on foreign causes is resented, especially now that there is domestic retrenchment. On this subject there is a very marked, widespread concurrence of opinion; one recorded comment, from a taxi driver, stands for many: "We have oil, as big as the sea, we should have everything. But what do we spend the money on? On foreigners, on Palestine and on Chad. But, really, that is none of our business."[7]

Qadhafi's refusal to admit the presence of Libyan forces in Chad has created a grotesque situation in which real, expressed anxiety on the part of ordinary Libyans contrasts with official silence on the subject: a situation that must be even more acute at the time of writing (April 1987), with heavy Libyan losses as Habré's forces occupy the north.[8]

At the university, lecturers tried not to fail students reading preliminary courses, since ejection from the university would mean conscription, and that, in the end, might mean service in Chad. A Libyan secondary-school student described to me a training-course he and his mates had been sent on near Kufra and the death of one of his friends from heat exhaustion.[9] Again, the burden of what he was saying was clear: that Libya's overriding concerns were domestic ones and that Chad had nothing to do with them.

Resentment of Libya's involvement in Chad is general and bitter. This is so despite a real anxiety about the extent and implications of French and U.S. influence in the region. The antipathy Libyans have toward external interference in their own affairs—and the fact that this is not simply a rhetorical invention of Qadhafi's but is rooted in their own recent history—

appears generally underestimated in the West. Nonetheless, the loss of lives and resources in Chad far outweighs for most Libyans any disquiet at the activities of Habré's Western allies.

Qadhafi's initiatives in Africa are viewed with skepticism at best and with real resentment when, as in the case of Chad, Libya is seen to squander its own resources. The question remains whether Libyans do feel any marked political or cultural affinity between their own country and those of sub-Saharan Africa. Libyans committed to the regime or to its apparatus (for instance, students from the revolutionary committees) respond to that question with bland statements of shared interest and solidarity. It is part of the given. Outside that group, what one registers time and time again is the defensiveness of Libyan attitudes—defensiveness in the most literal sense: their preoccupation lies with resistance to external influence on Libya itself and with resentment of internal pressures brought to bear on family and group as the Libyan state apparatus becomes more and more oppressive. The lived and felt experience—as opposed to official expressions of Libyan identity and role—does not easily accommodate engagement on a continental scale.

Teaching African literature courses at the university provided an opportunity to look more closely at Libyan responses to African culture.[10] The anticolonial literature made a definite impact. Novels dealing with Cameroon under French colonial rule, poems from Angola and Mozambique, and recent South African poetry, all provoked shock and anger. The classes registered a direct, effective empathy with the victims—hapless or self-defeating—of colonial regimes and of apartheid. Here again was a reminder that, whatever Libya's actual cultural isolation from sub-Saharan Africa, Libyans' aversion to external interference in their own affairs can generate an associative sympathy.

Much the same conclusion emerges from students' reactions to *The River Between*, by Kenyan writer Ngugi wa Thiong'o. Ngugi's depiction of the transformative effect of British colonial rule on Gikuyu society interested Libyan students and moved them. They would follow up specific points by referring to their parents' stories of conditions under the Italians. Even if the parallels were not precise, the wish to make them suggested that these texts had taken hold—and that there was developing awareness here of common or related experiences. This was particularly evident when we read Fanon's *The Wretched of the Earth*: when we discussed the growth (and under the colonial regime, cultivation) of anti-Arab sentiment among black Africans and of white racism among Arabs. Again the students related this to their own experience: to the stigmatization of blacks by their parents, or to their awareness of Mussolini's exploitation of racist attitudes among Libyans during the Ethiopian campaign. Ngugi's novel dramatizes the damage colonial rule inflicted on the organizing structures of Gikuyu society by focusing on missionary opposition to circumcision rites. As it happens, the practice of one culture here coincides with another, and there was no problem for Libyan students in taking this theme up, in empathizing with Gikuyu efforts to safeguard their culture.[11] But when we passed from Ngugi to the Senegalese Birago Diop, whose poetry offered very little in common with the culture of the Libyan students, the reaction was very different. In poems like "Breath" and "Viaticum," Diop evokes belief in, say, the role of ancestors or describes an animist ceremony, such as a mother's prayers over her son before he sets out on a voyage, in meticulous detail. The very loading of detail in this way acts as an assertion of a pre-Islamic culture. Nothing here was very accessible to my students, and their reaction—however guarded—was one of ridicule and distaste.[12]

Moving away from course-work, what kind of awareness did the Libyan students have of African affairs in general? In 1985 and again in 1986 I asked groups of students to complete questionnaires ranging over African politics, geography, and history and over Libyan-African and Arab-African relations. Their answers showed, except in certain areas, a massive un-awareness of the continent and its affairs. It was interesting to see which areas produced more accurate answers, and there were some intriguing biases in information. Just over half the students in both surveys were able to answer the question "Who was Idi Amin?" But in early 1986, when Nelson Mandela was much in the news, only a third knew who he was, and only 15 percent had heard of Desmond Tutu. Although Ghana has close diplomatic relations with Libya only 20 percent of students could name Jerry Rawlings as the country's present leader. Ghana's People's Democratic Committees (PDCs) bear a superficial resem-blance to Libya's Popular Committees, but a question asking what form of government Ghana had at present produced an even mix of replies: multi-party democracy; popular committees; military dictatorship. What kind of government Nigeria might enjoy seemed equally a mystery; only one student out of fifty was able to name Buhari as head of state (correct at the time). Only one in ten students could name the capital of Ghana. The capital of Chad should have been more familiar, and 50 percent got it right. But only one in ten knew where the head-quarters of the OAU were situated, and only the same proportion could name Morocco as the country that withdrew from the OAU in 1985 (uncertainty over the OAU is surprising, given the controversy over Qadhafi's chairmanship a few years previously, and given Libya's conspicuous unwillingness to support Morocco's withdrawal).

Some answers proved more accurate. Questions designed to yield impressions of Lagos provoked references to overcrowding, violence, limits to opportunities, unequal distribution of wealth, and people being "not of the same expression" (language, culture)—an emotive point. Another strong area was the answers to the question "Why do you think countries like the U.S.A. and Great Britain support South Africa so strongly?" which cited "material exploitation" and "strategic position." Asked which countries south of the Sahara, if any, have a large Muslim population, most students were able to cite Nigeria and Senegal.

One question that produced an interesting response was "Which countries in Africa or which parts of Africa suffered in 1985 from famine and drought?" Among other answers, mostly accurate, 65 percent cited Sudan—but only 20 percent mentioned Ethiopia. Why was this? Did perhaps news from Libyan sources tend to downplay the extent of the crisis in Ethiopia or, during Nimieri's rule—which was fiercely opposed by Qadhafi—emphasize the problem of Sudan?

The most accurate response came to the question "Do any African countries have diplomatic relations with Israel? If so, which?" Here the local interest is obvious. Most students mentioned South Africa and Zaire, with a few references to Liberia (some references to Ethiopia and Sudan on the 1985 questionnaire might have reflected a muddled awareness of the Falasha airlift, in the news at the time).

"How helpful are the majority of African states in supporting the Arab cause against the Israeli occupation of Palestine?" There was a somber response here: 60 percent of the students answered "helpful in word alone" and 25 percent said "not helpful at all"; only 15 percent gave a more positive answer. The next question—"How helpful is the Arab League in sup-porting the struggle against apartheid in South Africa?"—was edited out when the ques-tionnaire was vetted.

Black Libyans: Migrant Workers

There is general disaffection among the Libyan people with regard to Qadhafi's African adventures, and for all the empathy generated by a common heritage in Islam there is little evidence that Libyans sense any profound cultural and political identity between themselves and the peoples of sub-Saharan Africa. As the data collected from Libyan students suggests, there is, indeed, little familiarity with the realities of social and political life in the bulk of the continent.

Not that Libyans have no personal contact with black Africans, among their own citizens or as foreigners. The black diaspora, after all, has extended into Libya over hundreds of years, and any record of Libyan images of black Africa must take this into account. Libya's own nationals include a substantial minority of West African origin, especially prominent in the south of the country, the Fezzan. In discussing the origins of this population with Libyans or Arabs or those of other origin, demography becomes a subject of controversy. Trade flourished from northern West Africa, through the southern Sahel and the Fezzan and to the coast, right up until colonization.[13] Important commodities here included gold and ivory and salt (the latter traded from north to south). Part of the trans-Saharan trade, however, dealt in domestic slaves, and embarrassment over this issue—or a refusal to admit a history of slave-trading—constitutes a real obstacle in discussing demographic shift in Libya.[14]

The official Libyan line on slavery and the Arab world is quite clear. "The Arab countries are a natural extension to the African continent. The African Arabs, or those who carried the indulgent message of Islam, were the first to effectively oppose slavery as inhumane and unnatural"; the claim that Arabs were involved in the trade at all is a mischievous invention of the West, made "in order to divide the Arabs from their brothers and sisters who live in the African continent" (*New Africa*, November 1984). Some Libyans, however, are prepared to reject this interpretation and even to argue that it is damaging, not just because it denies the past, but because this denial may be seen elsewhere as a betrayal of trust. "If a West African sees," one Libyan told me, "that we can't admit that part of our historical relationship, what is he going to think of the relationship between our countries now?"[15] A Hausa-speaking Libyan indicated the site of a slave market in the Fezzan and offered me a pair of shackles as souvenir. He said that the Arabs' nervousness over the slave trade was entirely transparent, a bad joke; what was problematic was the relationship between Libya and the rest of the continent now.[16] Both speeches touched upon the same dual problems, that is, that African fears of Libya exerting a control-relationship are intensified by Libyan duplicity over the kind of role it envisages for itself.

In addition to Libyan citizens of sub-Saharan origin the country has, until recently, hosted a large number of migrant workers from Sudan, Mali, Niger, and Ghana. Included among them are economic refugees drawn to Libya during the drought or, in less drastic cases, where subsistence living would be available in the home country, by the attraction of foreign-exchange earnings. Large groups of workers have been brought into Libya under intergovernmental contract agreement, from Asian as well as African countries. Hundreds of thousands of others came into the country from Sudan and West Africa on an informal basis—some trekking into Fezzan from as far as Ghana.[17] Many of these sub-Saharan migrants have now, in fact, been expelled.[18] Prior to that they had become dominant in certain areas such as vehicle-repair (the Ghanaians a prominent group here) and formed the biggest source of farm labor in the Fezzan.

Outside the town center in Sebha in early 1985 there were still large camps where new arrivals would be allocated tents. Inside the town, the post office and the bank acted as gathering points, where workers would wait to be hired. Visiting farms in central Fezzan, I was told by one young farm-owner that there was a minimum wage fixed by the government. He paid the most senior of his workers 150 dinars (about 450 U.S. dollars) a month. There was a strong sense of the men being delimited in his eyes by their status as workers. "They have no reason to be here, they only come because they want the money." Another farm-owner, whose land was worked by a Malian, complained bitterly that when he was not at hand to supervise, the Malian would not get up until ten o'clock in the morning. I asked him how he knew this. "My friends telephone me."

Yet the charge of insufficient loyalties leveled at Sahelian migrant workers was made in a context in which their Libyan employers' loyalties were themselves fractured and compromised. In this region there were both privately-owned farmland (on which the migrants worked) and the communally-held *masruhe*. Provision for the latter was impressive, in terms of the agricultural technology that had been organized to create it out of the desert, but in places it seemed like a structure imposed on traditional methods of labor organization, and it was neglected in comparison with private farms.

The Libyan response to foreign labor is complicated and reflects contradictions inherent in Libyan society. There is, for instance, a constant thrust against the continuing presence of foreign labor—a resentment of the drain this creates on Libyan foreign exchange holdings—which is expressed again and again in popular committee meetings. Qadhafi himself is eager to remind Libyan nationals how damaging to the economy the presence of such a large foreign labor force has proven. But the very fact that he has had to reiterate the point over so many years lends it a poignant irony.[19] The presence of large numbers of migrant workers signifies a deep distaste among Libyans for manual labor: it is one of the respects in which Libya most closely approaches the standard image of the Arab *rentier* state. Qadhafi's difficulty over the foreign labor question connotes the refusal of a people to adapt their concept of the status of the manual worker to the precepts of the Third Universal Theory; the maxim "partners not wage workers" hardly jibes with the disinclination of many Libyans to perform the work that would enable them to displace foreign wage earners.

There is an Arab proverb that states "you can't spit and lick." Both Libyans and their migrant workers are forced into disproving this. Migrant workers face hardship and discrimination in Libya, but they achieve a standard of living that drought and chronic recession deny them at home. However grudgingly, they continue to enter the country, and some of those expelled seek to return; as recently as January 1987 the Libyan authorities have indicated to the Ghanaian government their disquiet over the number of Ghanaian citizens entering the country illegally. For their part, those Libyans who are not in a position to hire migrant workers resent their presence and yet require the consumer products and the service facilities provided by the work they perform (in the private, labor-hiring section, of course, the attitude to the foreign work force is much more pragmatic). The more farmland is neglected and the more difficult it becomes to find a mechanic, the more evident become contradictions in Libyan attitudes toward labor and toward foreign laborers.[20]

What is also evident is that Libyan attitudes toward black Africans are integrally related to their attitudes toward labor. There is no simple, demeaning equivalence here: there are other major factors involved. The concept of brotherhood in Islam has commanding influence and certainly should not be dismissed as rhetoric. But there is a tension here, and the identification of blacks with the notion of the labor force is deep-rooted. If there is among Libyans considerable skepticism regarding Qadhafi's identification of Libya's political aspirations with those of sub-Saharan Africa, then this is surely connected—at however subliminal a level—with a habit of mind that doubts the cultural legitimacy of labor and that tends to associate labor with blacks.

The Experience of Sub-Saharan Students in Libya

The response to Libya from the rest of the continent is varied, ranging from a wholesale adherence to the negative mythification encouraged by the West, to an acknowledgment of Libya as role-model, whether in the spheres of welfarism or popular democracy or the Islamic revival. Among conservative governments the Libyan regime is unequivocally seen as being subversive, yet there are conflicting views as to the degree to which its activities are ideologically coherent, consistent, or opportunistic.[21] And radically different responses can be expected of different socio-ethnic sectors within any given African state.

In some respects Libya has the potential to stand as a role model. The welfare and service system is enthusiastically publicized by the regime. The country's rapid development of housing programs, local clinic facilities, road, water, and electricity services are all impressive—indeed, the scale of new housing development is staggering.[22] Commitment is the key term here, since the point of Libya's publicity is not to demonstrate what can be done with oil-wealth so much as what can be done with the will to maintain absolute control over that wealth and to spend it where it matters.

The attractiveness of wealth has opened up a new range of relationships between Libya and its poorer African neighbors. As we have seen, Libya, like Nigeria in the 1970s, has absorbed large numbers of migrant workers; again, as with Nigeria, the expulsion of these workers during a period of declining oil revenues has led to a palpable, albeit diplomatically contained, tension between Libya and other African states.

In the political sphere, Libya presents its revolution and its political system as a model, with Qadhafi's Third Universal Theory and system of popular committees put forward, with varying degrees of earnestness, as ideal alternatives to nonrepresentative government. In terms of international relations Libya forcefully rejects the idea of intercontinental dependence and argues that African states must wrench themselves away from the oppressive influence of the West.[23] But this must be done according to prescription.

All of these perspectives were acknowledged by sub-Saharan students at Gar Younis University. There was nothing but praise for the regime's commitment to welfarism; at the same time there was a general concern—in some cases acute frustration—that the regime's radical orientation was so delimited by mixed motivations and opportunism and by its overriding insensitivity to the need to seek a dialogue with sub-Saharan African states rather than to attempt to act as their revolutionary mentor.

Further, unlike their colleagues at home, whose views on Libya are restricted to media coverage, these students had had years of personal interaction with Libyans and therefore provided a source of information on the Libyan response to black foreign nationals living in the country. It is true their situation was marginal; it would have been worthwhile to have spoken in like detail with African manual workers in the city. Again, therefore, any conclusions drawn from their comments should be tentative.

During the period 1983–86 there were several dozen sub-Saharan students at Gar Younis, drawn from a wide range of countries, the largest groups being from Eritrea, Ghana, Mali, and Uganda.[24] They were reading a variety of subjects, favorites being economics, sociology, law, and Arabic. They had come to Libya through various channels, though the ones I interviewed were all on Libyan government scholarships. One had deliberately worked his way into a job with a Moslem Council in his own country so as to be on hand when any scholarship offer came along. One Ghanaian student had been selected by the Moslem community in which he lived to go abroad to study Arabic, after a visit to his town by a (Ghanaian) Islamic Call student from Tripoli. When I asked him what had encouraged him to come all the way to Libya, he explained: "My community needed an Arabic teacher. But I had a personal reason, too. I wanted to leave the technical school I was in. And I could see no other way."

They formed a discrete, identifiable group, living in a separate foreign student hostel, together with Palestinian and Chinese students and others (the decision to live together as an African students' group was their own). They mixed hardly at all with the Libyan students. When I asked whether students from Anglo- and Francophone countries fell into separate groups, I was told this did happen—it was thought to be unavoidable—but not to the extent of its being rigidly restrictive. It was true everyone regretted the leaving of the Malian lecturer, some years before, who had done a good deal to bring all students together socially. But in any case, the English/French language obstacle didn't seem to loom too large; one student from the Gambia, for instance, had always been more at home in Arabic than in English, and the African students generally used Arabic when they were talking among themselves.

Many of them had had problems when they first arrived in Libya. It was a common experience for their previous secondary education to be under-assessed by the Libyan Ministry of Education and for them to be subjected to unnecessarily elaborate predegree courses. One fairly mature student, who really only required an Arabic course at pre-university level, had been sent to one of Libya's Foreign Institutes on arrival to take his schooling all over again. He remembered walking into the classroom on his first day and being asked to visualize a pile of oranges. He was then asked if there were four oranges and he took one away, how many would be left? Surely no need at this stage, he thought, to keep on counting oranges. But there seemed little choice except to stay with the course. Meanwhile he took a part-time job in the town, to get some money together, "just in case it rained."

"How did you feel?" I asked him. "It sounds like you were having a very difficult time."

"Yes, but then I was the one who had come to Libya looking for something. So I had to get through."

"What did you do for company?"

"I shared a room with my countrymen. I listened a lot to the radio in my room. Sure, I was very lonely."

This student, and others, faced considerable difficulty winning recognition from the Libyan authorities of their actual educational standing. One way or another, by the time he reached university he had wasted three years on redundant courses.

The experience of another student was striking in a different way. He had been sponsored to learn Arabic, but, after completing his predegree course at the Benghazi Foreign Institute (in effect, a secondary school), had entered the university to read economics.

"Wasn't it difficult to transfer?"

"No, once you've gone through the Foreign Institute you don't need a scholarship for university. You apply directly to any faculty and the faculty will send to the ministry for approval."

"The system seems very open."

"Yes, well there's a reason for that, they are keen for foreign students to learn through Arabic—and maybe also they want to foster political sympathies."

"Does that weigh heavily on you; are you put under any pressure [to express political commitment]?"

"No, not really. You can take it or leave it. And we do get our education."[25]

I asked each student interviewed whether there was any likelihood that any of the sub-Saharan students were fostered at Gar Younis specifically as dissidents, active or passive, toward their own regimes. This was considered only a marginal possibility, even in the case of students whose governments were wary of the Libyans. It was stressed that the primary motivation for being in Libya was a personal one and that if graduation from Libya drew these students into an awkward political conjuncture, then that was considered an irritating but superable by-product of the process of gaining qualifications.

Despite all the difficulties they faced, most of the students ended by admitting the final result, the degree, made the long haul worthwhile. One Ghanaian student said "I have to be sincere. I've acquired a lot." Other students, however—for instance, those from Uganda and Guinea—who had been unable to enter university in their own countries because of domestic political problems were disparaging about the calibre of the Libyan degree.

For too many African students in the United States or in Europe adaptation, incorporation, and isolation prove either untenable or difficult to bear. To a large extent this seems to hold true in Libya.

I asked whether they felt themselves isolated. One Ugandan explained that back at home he had broken away from his family while still young and had learned to look after himself. "I knew when I got there I had to push on. I'm used to it." But other students had come to Libya directly from a village community or small town, where they had had a unitary up-bringing; they were making a simultaneous transition from village to metropolis and from home to a foreign country. Some were clearly unhappy, including one young Malian who seemed permanently at a loss. "It's difficult for him," one of his friends told me, "to choose between options. He doesn't know how to identify problems, let alone how to solve them. So he's always looking for guidance."

There had been an attempt by the African Students Society to set up a cultural committee, to promote an awareness among the students of their situation. But the university's General Students' Committee had expressed a fear that some kind of aberrant political forum was being established and the African Students Society folded.

"Was it actually ordered to close?"

"No. It died the death of non-cooperation."

I asked the students who they spent their time with. The answer was never, it seemed, with Libyan students.

"I used to spend my weekends with Ghanaian workers in the town, until they were sent out of the country."

One student commented thoughtfully and at length on the difficulty Libyan students faced in coming to terms with the sub-Saharans. How were the Libyans to recognize what experience they shared and what was apart from them?—they found it difficult to draw close and to acknowledge apartness simultaneously. Another student said: "We will say confidently that Libya is part of Africa, while it is the Libyan students who have trouble in saying this and meaning it." There was a general—and sophisticated—recognition that the problems faced in trying to form relationships with Libyan students were symptomatic of the problems the Libyans faced in negotiating their own sense of identity and in projecting this in social exchange: a situation that was equally marked in relations between individual Libyans and Europeans.

At one point I asked a group of the sub-Saharan students to take part in an oral questionnaire about their experience in Libya. A few of the answers (taken from different students) follow:

**"My impression is the African students here cope very well with what are often difficult circumstances. Is this so?"

"Mostly, yes. But university life here is very unstable and so adjustment is difficult. There were constant interruptions, for popular committee meetings, for days—and, latterly, whole semesters—reserved for production, or during crises [such as the U.S. raid]. For students who develop personal problems there is the very big difficulty that the university has no way of coping with them. There is no proper counseling."

**"Do Libyan students talk with you about the political situation in this country?"

"We can't have any free discussion."

**"How do you think the average Libyan thinks of you, as an African?"

"He knows where he wants the African. In the back seat of his car." Another student: "That's unjust. But they are happiest when they are meeting you on common ground, like when you are talking together in Islam. Always it's a question how do they cope with you."

**"How do you see the status of African labor here? For instance, farm workers, mechanics, and so on."

"Look at the way the students treat the kitchen staff." (At that time all Tunisian workers had been expelled, and the majority of kitchen staff were Sudanese).

"Well, what do you think of that?"

"It's appalling."

I asked, if one of the most important maxims of Qadhafi's revolution did not state, "Partners not Wage Workers"? "After all, there is this drive toward breaking down the idea that work is disreputable, of breaking down the master-servant relationship."

"Good, but do you think it's working? Go and stand in line in the cafeteria and see how the students address the kitchen staff. To them they are nothing more than servants and that is very low."

**"What about Libya's relations with other African countries—about Libya's involvement in African affairs?"

"Put it this way, I myself can't just stand up and say I support Everton or Liverpool. You will ask me why do I support this or that team? If the Libyans support African interests, all well and good. But how do they see these interests? I always ask, on what grounds?"

**"How do you feel you are placed in the lecture room?"

"I know I'm ahead of any Libyan student there."

Another student: "Libyan staff and students demonstrate all the time their belief in their own superiority. We know that this is unfounded, but it seems there's nothing we can say or do to change it."

Another student: "I've been in a class of students for three years now and I have next to no contact with any of them."

"Do you think this is a situation peculiar to Libya?"

"No, not at all. It's a big problem all over." (We had in fact just been listening to BBC radio reports of disquiet amongst African students in Chinese universities.)

**"Going back to your country, what prejudices will you face as a Libyan-trained student?"

"There may be some prejudice. It's my responsibility to combat that."

I asked all of them whether in the end they felt the years in Libya had been worthwhile. All of them said yes. Even if a Libyan university degree might look a little flimsy elsewhere in Africa.

"It's not what I'd hoped for," said one student. "But once I got here I had to push on."

Conclusion

Libya's involvement in the affairs of sub-Saharan Africa embraces commerce, religion, political intrigue,[26] and military intervention. The most significant of these initiatives has proven to be the military opposition to Habré's regime in Chad. Certainly this seems likely to be decisive in establishing a "final verdict" among other African governments on Qadhafi's policies on the continent. It has also had a considerable impact on Qadhafi's domestic standing. Popular opposition to the intervention built up within Libya during the 1980s has certainly been intensified by the military defeats of early 1987. From outside the country, however, it is difficult to judge exactly how damaging popular rejection of the Chad policy will be to the regime. Despite all recent crises, and despite widespread disgust at public executions and other visible tokens of domestic political repression, Qadhafi does maintain a degree of support, predicated on a recognition—however strained this may now be—of his success in transforming the living conditions of the majority of his people. Whether this debt of loyalty will survive an increasingly acute sense of Qadhafi as a liability is for the moment unclear. If specific interventions in African affairs have lacked general popular support, so too has the rhetoric that informs these. There has been a sustained effort on the part of Qadhafi and the Libyan media and information services to articulate a leadership role for Libya on the continent. The terms in which this drive is expressed are themselves suspect, frequently exposing an unawareness of the specific situation of other African states and communities and a bizarre amnesia vis-à-vis sub-Saharan Africa's own long history of anticolonial struggle and radical thought.

Further, whatever effective pan-African role one might like to envisage for a radical North African state, Qadhafi's projection of Libya as being integrally related to the continent as a whole and as being therefore a revolutionary mentor, concerned with the political destiny of the continent, relates only very obliquely to the Libyan people's sense of their own culturo-political identity. In so far as there is any tangible cognition among Libyans generally of sub-

Saharan Africa and of its people, this has come in recent years mainly through the involvement in Chad and through contact with migrant workers—a strained and unhappy relationship.

There is, in short, a considerable gap between collective representations (among, for instance, both black African and Libyan students) and public discourse in Libya. This must suggest at the broadest level, as well as in terms of specific interventions, a lack of support at home for Qadhafi's insistence on the cultural nexus between Libya and sub-Saharan Africa.

NOTES

1. Some of the material included in this chapter has appeared previously in *West Africa* (September 1, 1986):1820–22; (September 8, 1986):1873–74; (September 15, 1986): 1918–19.

2. *Rissalat al Jihad* is a journal on religious and political affairs, published monthly by the Islamic Call Society in Tripoli, in Arabic, French, and English editions. It is distributed throughout Africa—generally through the offices of the Libyan People's Bureaux—and is on sale in Libya. *New Africa* is a monthly journal, now published in Rome, in bilingual editions (Arabic-English, Arabic-French).

3. Official publications can prove an acute embarrassment where political priorities shift rapidly. The government-sponsored Atlas of Libya—prepared shortly before the Libyan-Morocco accord—boldly shows the SADR as a separate political entity. Turning back to 1972 and a Third Anniversary volume for Qadhafi's revolution, there are references to the "hireling king of Morocco and his feudalistic class that tyrannize over the Arab people." One of the heroes of this volume is Sadat, photographed signing the tripartite accord between Libya, Syria, and Egypt. (Perhaps, however, the charge of inconsistency should be directed at Sadat, not Qadhafi?)

4. There is however, more than one way of looking at this; beyond the flailing and floundering and acts of gross cynicism such as the abandonment of the SADR and of the anti-Hassan Moroccan opposition, it is possible to interpret Qadhafi's approach, as Mirella Bianco does, as one in which intransigence is actually a merit. "It matters little," argues Bianco, "if these combinations, constantly formed and dissolved, encounter trouble. Sooner or later, Qadhafi thinks, he will succeed in finding that first nucleus; he will succeed above all, precisely by that intransigence which makes the process slower, in making certain that this nucleus, fashioned without ambiguity, shall be lasting" (Bianco 1975, 126).

5. For further information, see specifically, *Rissalat al Jihad*, no. 36 (September 1985):33; no. 40 (January 1986):11, 20, 70.

6. At the time of writing (April 1987) the speech remains unpublished. References here and later are to a draft of the translation of the speech, which I was asked to help prepare.

7. This conversation took place, ironically, in the forecourt of Benghazi's magnificent and provocatively named Aouzou Hotel.

8. The London *Observer* cites as many as thirty-six hundred Libyans killed in the assault on Ouadi-Doum and seven hundred taken prisoner, and goes on to speculate that as a result of this debacle "Qadhafi's own position at home may now be seriously at risk" (*Observer*, April 5, 1987, 15).

9. Interview in Benghazi, June 1985.

10. The written literature of Africa constitutes high, or privileged, culture; but it also permits access to the continent's culture in a broader sense—in, for instance, its documentation of social activity.

11. Ngugi's dual response to Christianity—unambiguous opposition to missionary activity and to the divisive effect proselytizing had on Gikuyu society, combined with a desire to vindicate Christ's teaching and to work this into the novel's symbolic scheme—also appealed to the class. It happened to mesh quite neatly with Qadhafi's stand on Christianity—a stand that most Libyans respond to, and that combines fierce opposition to proselytizing (the "crusader Christianity" condemned in the journal *Rissalat al Jihad*)with stated respect for the religion *per se* and tolerance of the church within Libya.

12. A large part of Diop's intention here was to present a defense against the overbearing influence of

French colonial culture; this was a major strategy in West African writing in the 1930s. Libyan students were unimpressed by Diop's failure to make his case by reference to Islam.

13. Trade was a significant factor in the history of West African empires from Mali and Songhai onward—indeed, the major determining factor in the growth and development of certain political entities, such as the Kanem-Bornu kingdom (forming part of present-day northern Nigeria). Given the emphasis placed on European colonization in the West, one tends to forget sometimes how the trans-Saharan trade persisted into the present century; for a vivid illustration of this north-south relationship, see a letter written by Libyan traders from Ghadames living in Kano to the new Sultan of Sokoto and dating from 1902, the year before the British seizure of Sokoto (Backwell 1969, 49–50).

14. The one frankly racist comment I heard from a Libyan came when I told a friend I wanted to visit Ghat. He told me it was a dirty place, because it was full of blacks, who spoke Hausa rather than Arabic. When I asked how blacks came to be in Ghat in the first place, my friend began to overcompensate, withdrawing all objections to going there. What is significant here is not so much the racism but the defensiveness about racism these comments reveal. (His reference to Hausa is, again, interesting as a signal of disaffection, but it is misleading. Even in the southwest of the country, where Hausa is spoken and understood, its position is marginal. Students whose parents speak the language will not necessarily speak it themselves. Tamaschek—the language of the Tuareg—is more prominent. There is a striking, tangible indication of this in parts of the Fezzan, where to walk into the *jebel*, the rock mountain, is to enter a diary or memo-pad, the rock face being scored with names, dates, and messages in Tifina, the Tamaschek script.)

15. Interview with Libyan staff member at Gar Younis University, November 1985.

16. Hotel-worker interviewed October 1985, a few weeks prior to the comments recorded above.

17. As an indicator of Libya's reliance on foreign labor, consider the following: Figures from 1980 cite 58 percent of "ordinary [i.e. non-professional] workers" in the country as being non-Libyan (Zayd 1982, 167). Over the last decade there have been considerable influxes of migrant workers (for instance, during the drought) as well as large-scale expulsions (of Egyptians, Tunisians, and most recently, Sahelians). In such an unstable situation statistics are bound to be approximate, but the proportion of foreign to indigenous manual workers has always been high. Birks and Sinclair gave a breakdown of migrant workers by nationality, which cites only twenty-two hundred (0.4 percent) as being of "African and Other" origin in 1980 (Birks and Sinclair 1984, 271). This figure had increased considerably by the mid-1980s. For a recent interview-based article on West African migrant workers who have entered Libya on foot through the Sahara, see K. K. Kwasitsu, "Through Mungo Park," *West Africa* (Sept. 21, 1987):1844–48.

18. A series of expulsions of sub-Saharan workers began in the summer of 1985 (prior to that, other groups had been ordered home, for instance, Egyptian farm workers in 1984). A large number of Ghanaian school teachers hired through Libyan-Ghanaian governmental cooperation had their contracts abrogated early in 1986 when English and French language teaching was canceled in the schools. The expulsion led to at least a temporary straining of relationships between, for example, the Libyan and Mauritanian governments.

19. Speeches from the early 1970s comment on the marginality of Libyan Arab society (a "non-productive, consumer society"), on "the lack of manpower" to cultivate land, and so on (see Hai 1982, 60–62). On November 2, 1984, addressing political science staff and students at Gar Younis University, Qadhafi criticized Libyan society for its nonproductivity with characteristic vehemence: "During the colonial period and under Idriss a Contessa, an old Italian lady, owned the (present-day) 7th of October farm and ran all the quarries that stretched from Tripoli to Zawia near the sea. . . . After the revolution we snatched the quarries from the Contessa and liberated the farms. We freed the Mediterranean coast from Tripoli to Zawia. . . . The quarries are now disused, the farm deteriorates. They are in need of a Contessa, who will rule and insult you" (unpublished transcript, by the author).

20. I found the extent to which the withdrawal of foreign labor had affected the maintenance of farms difficult to judge. Evidence ranged from farms in the Benghazi region that had fallen into total disuse since the exodus of Egyptian workers and which would not be reestablished unless foreign labor were reintroduced, to farms around Tripoli and Sabraatha that were worked (highly productively) by Libyan farm-owners and their families (although here other projects—such as private house-building—had been stalled by the forced withdrawal of Tunisian workers). I didn't visit the Fezzan after the mass expulsion of Sahelian workers and do not have any clear idea about the current state of the private and communal farms I had seen there.

21. Desmond Davies claims, "There has always been a pattern behind Libya's campaign of destabilization

and subversion" (Davies 1985, 14). The problem is, surely, that the pattern is more multistranded than is sometimes assumed; it is not, for instance, simply predicated on support for Islamic revivalism. The problem of assessing continuity in Libyan policy has exercised the patience of radical as well as conservative governments. Certainly any claim that Libya's engagement in African affairs is ideologically pure would be contested by the Eritreans and the Saharawis, whose respective causes have been supported and neglected by the Libyans according to shifts in relationships with Ethiopia and Morocco. See Alison Perry's telling report on a congress of Saharawi women after Libya's signing of the accord with Morocco: "While the Saharawi people gave all the delegates an enthusiastic reception, with much nationalistic slogan-shouting, the only sign of disapproval was when the Libyan delegate started shouting Libyan slogans from the congress platform. The Saharawi people sat quietly, unresponsive" (Perry 1985, 724).

22. In the five years before the revolution, government construction programs had been conspicuously unsuccessful in meeting the need for new housing. From 1969 to 1974 contracts were signed to build 160,781 housing units; figures for later years show a steady increase (Zayd 1982, 122–23). Even those sub-Saharans living in Libya who were most hostile to the regime would preface their criticism with an acknowledgment of the scale of this achievement.

23. Hence Qadhafi's furious denunciation of Francophone and Anglophone African countries at the 1986 Non-Aligned Summit as being "poodles" of France and Britain.

24. Composition varies dramatically over a period of time. Referring to 1977–78, H. P. Mattes records one hundred students from sub-Saharan Africa at Gar Younis. Eighteen of these were Nigerian and twenty were Senegalese. Mattes cites the largest singular group (twenty-four) as being from Eritrea, then as later (Mattes 1984, 150). All students whose comments are recorded here were interviewed shortly before they completed their courses and left Libya. (I am grateful to them for the amount of time they gave up for these interviews.) Some of the most potentially interesting material—for instance, that relating to the experience of Ugandan students in Libya during the last year of Amin's rule—I have not included because it remained uncorroborated. I have not included any material gathered from Eritrean students, whose position in Libya is a peculiarly difficult one, many of them having come to Libya for secondary schooling at a time when Libya supported the Etritrean liberation movement, and who have since seen Libya's rapprochement with the Ethiopians after the installation of the Mengistu government.

25. All students at the university, Libyan and foreign, were required to read courses in Third Universal Theory. Beyond this, there seemed little overt pressure on a foreigner to conform politically. It would be possible, say, for a foreign student to sail through the university, gaining his degree, and to remain privately totally opposed to Qadhafi's political philosophy.

26. Commercial involvement includes the establishment of joint companies such as the Libyan-Beninois BELIMINE (mining), BELIPECHE (fisheries), and SABLI (animal products). Religious proselytizing is carried out through, for instance, the offices of the Islamic Call Society. Both activities have a political dimension in that they maintain a broad base for Libya's aspiration toward a leadership role.

REFERENCES

Backwell, H. F. 1969. *The Occupation of Hausaland, 1900–1904*. London: Frank Cass.

Bianco, Mirella. 1975. *Gadafi, Voice from the Desert*. London: Longman.

Birks, Stace, and Clive Sinclair. 1984. "Libya: Problems of a *Rentier* State." In *North Africa: Contemporary Politics and Economic Development*, edited by Richard Lawless and Allan Findlay, 241–75. London: Croom Helm.

Davies, Desmond. 1985. "Libya following a predictable pattern," *Africa Now* (April):14.

Hai, Tahsin Abdul. 1982. *Power and Revolution*. Tripoli, English edition.

Kwasitsu, K. K. 1987. "Through Mungo Park." *West Africa* (Sept. 21):1844–48.

Mattes, H. P. 1984. *Al-Dawda al-Islamiya: Die Innere Islamische Mission Libyens, Historisch-politischer Kontext, Interne, Struktur. Regionale Auspregung am Beispiel Afrikas*. Hamburg: Deutsches Orient Institut.

New Africa. 1984. "French troops leave Chad," no. 5 (November):21.

———. 1984. "The Arabic–African Unity," no. 5 (November):24–27.
———. 1985. "Senegal and the Arabic language," no. 7 (October):26.
———. 1985. "The Anniversary of the Unity," no. 7 (October):2–3.
The Observer. 1987. 5 (April):15.
Perry, Alison. 1985. "The Women Behind the War." *West Africa*, (April):722–25.
Rissalat al Jihad. 1985. No. 36 (September):33.
———. 1986. No. 40 (January):11, 20, 70.
Zayd, Mohammed. 1982. *Economic Transformation in the Jamahiriya.* Tripoli, English edition.

Conclusion

ON COMPARING REGIONAL HEGEMONS
LIBYA AND SOUTH AFRICA

René Lemarchand

Time and again through the previous chapters it is the singularity of the Libyan policy mold that impresses itself upon our mental retina. On closer inspection, however, the Libyan case reveals certain definite points of resemblance with another, though far more formidable, regional hegemon—South Africa. For all the qualifications that immediately spring to mind (of which more in a moment) the parallel is no less convincing for being paradoxical.

At opposite poles of the African continent two major crisis areas have indeed captured public attention, one centering on South Africa, the other on Libya. Behind their "fearful symmetry" a curious paradox emerges: no other two states in the continent offer a more palpable contrast from the standpoint of their state systems, ideological underpinnings, and perceived security interests, yet both aspire to regional hegemony, and in their efforts to achieve preeminence they have pursued remarkably similar strategies. The parallel is even more compelling when one reflects on the inability of the two interested superpowers to rein in the excesses of their reluctant allies. Nowhere are the limitations of crisis prevention more cruelly apparent than in the loss of regional initiative suffered by Washington and Moscow at both ends of the continent.

The convergent strategies pursued by Libya and South Africa call into question the significance of ideology as a reference point for sorting our friends and enemies: How is one to reconcile the conventional orthodoxies of the Reagan doctrine with its growing irrelevance to the dynamics of regional conflicts? Where, exactly, do these conflicts fit into the modes of discourse generated by cold war rivalries? But perhaps the really critical issue is the demonstrable incapacity of the global powers to manage regional convulsions. If the dangers of local brushfires getting out of hand are transparent, so is the inability of the global fire-fighters to bring them under control. Conditions of "low intensity warfare"—to use the reassuring phrase coined to describe regional anarchy—may thus signal the advent of a far more dangerous phase in the international relations of Africa, in which regional actors are able to project their military capabilities with relative impunity.

Beyond the ironies of their convergent strategies, the cases of Libya and South Africa provide a convenient point of entry into the emergent pattern of subregional power relationships in the continent. The essence of the new power realities is well captured by Foltz's observation that the continent has become "the setting for the acting out of rivalries between neighboring African states," thus signaling a major shift of intra-African politics "away from issues based on extra-continental influence and heritage toward those based on regional power realities" (Foltz 1981, 95). Seen in these terms the cases at hand bring into focus a critical aspect of superpower politics. Whether in the name of military advantage, strategic convenience, or trade benefits, both of the superpowers have provided their African allies with the resources needed to stoke up the fires of local insurgencies, only to realize their utter impotence in the face of expanding confrontations.

Preliminary Caveats

To begin with the obvious: South Africa is an embattled polity, whose enduring commitment to white supremacy lies at the root of the domestic and international threats posed to its political survival; Libya is an expansionist state, inspired by a sense of historic mission, bent upon carrying into effect its own vision of pan-Arab unity. The main liability facing South Africa arises from a home-grown liberation movement whose branches ramify into neighboring states; it is Libya, on the other hand, that throws its weight behind "liberation movements" and thus poses a mortal danger to its neighbors. In one case the pursuit of the national interest dictates strategies aimed at political survival; in the other it is identified with an expansionist drive destined to vindicate a historic mission.

The geopolitics of dependency suggest another obvious contrast. There is no counterpart anywhere in the continent for the extent of economic and infrastructural dependency of Zimbabwe, Mozambique, Lesotho, Botswana, and Swaziland on South Africa. Nothing like the stranglehold exercised by Pretoria on its black-ruled neighbors through its control of the regional transportation grid, labor market, and trade flows ever materialized between Libya and its neighbors. The political leverage available to South Africa by virtue of its dominant economic position in the region is richly documented and requires little elaboration (Hanlon 1986a, 1986b, 1987; Maasdorp 1985; Rotberg 1985), except to note that by comparison Libya's oil wealth, though by no means inconsequential, carries very different implications. It is one thing to use oil money to orchestrate political destabilization or buy off hit squads, and quite another to threaten established governments with economic strangulation unless specific demands are met.

Equally noteworthy are their different modes of insertion into the world economy. Both depend for capital accumulation on their linkages with the core areas of the world economy, but the constraints arising from this relationship are by no means evenly distributed. Libya remains in many ways a classic peripheral area overwhelmingly dependent on petroleum exports. South Africa, on the other hand, was able over the last fifty years to alter its position in the world economy in a way that greatly lessened its dependence on core areas, thus giving it a degree of autarky unmatched by Libya. The lessening of South Africa's dependence on the world capitalist economy has gone hand in hand with the reinforcement of regional linkages with its neighbors, a pattern for which there is evidently no equivalent in Libya. Colonial rule in Southern Africa has decisively strengthened regional interdependence to the advantage of South Africa; the effect of colonial rule in Libya and the Sahel has been precisely the opposite, that is, to disrupt the patterns of interdependence established through the precolonial trade routes ramifying from Tripoli into Chad, Niger, and the Sudan.

Given such obvious and irreducible differences between them, their disposition to embark on basically similar strategies in dealing with their neighbors is all the more intriguing. Symmetry, of course, does not imply perfect identity. The theme of regional hegemony admits of many variations, and these are nowhere more evident than at the level of perception and performance. The egregious failure of Libyan policies stands in obvious contrast to the relative success achieved by Pretoria in pursuing basically similar policies. Once this is said, there emerges an unmistakable pattern of convergence out of the combination of long-term goals and short-run strategies pursued by each state.

The Quest for Regional Hegemony: The Diplomatic Dimension

Though inspired by radically different logics—a pan-Arab revolutionary logic in one case, and anti-revolutionary regional logic in the other—the achievement of regional hegemony remains to this day the paramount long-term objective of South African and Libyan policies. Hegemony, in this context, does not imply a static relationship. Whether conceptualized as "satellization" or "the unity of Arabic-speaking peoples," hegemony allows for varying degrees of control and forms of influence, from which force is not to be excluded. Especially in point here is Hedley Bull's definition of hegemony as a relationship in which "there is resort to force, but this is not habitual and uninhibited but occasional and reluctant." A hegemonic state, adds Bull, "is prepared to violate the rights of sovereignty, equality and independence enjoyed by the lesser states, . . . it does not disregard them: it recognizes that these might exist, and justifies violation of them by appeal to some specific overriding principles" (Bull 1977, 215).

This formulation, pointing to "respect for norms but occasional resort to force when other means fail" (Keal 1986, 141), is crucial to an understanding of the strategies employed by each state to alter the structure of their regional environments. At first, primary reliance was placed on diplomacy and respect for norms, but as diplomacy proved unavailing, recourse to force loomed increasingly large in their foreign policy arsenal. By the early 1980s both states practiced the dismal art of political destabilization on an extensive scale and with utter disrespect for the norms of sovereignty and independence.

The formulas initially devised by Libya and South Africa to assert their hegemonic claims are best understood as an extension of their domestic policies. Just as the Homelands system provided South Africa with the inspiration for its unfulfilled Constellation of Southern African States (CONSAS), the rather nebulous, pseudo-participatory concept of Jamahiriya, or State of the Masses, was intended to serve as the foundation stone for Libyan efforts at regional unification.

Until 1980 the CONSAS scheme was seen by Pretoria as central to its security needs. First introduced by P. W. Botha in 1978, in response to the growing assertiveness of the Frontline States and in anticipation of Zimbabwe's independence, CONSAS was intended to promote South African hegemony through the economic, military, and political satellization of its neighbors, while at the same time providing a basis for the *de facto* recognition of the Homelands (Evans 1986, 3). Drawn into Pretoria's orbit by the gravitational pull of its economic and military power, the Front-line States would thus be reduced to the status of client states, not unlike the Homelands in relation to their white patron. The strategic benefits expected of the CONSAS formula, as Robert Price perceptively notes, were essentially four: (1) "to lock Pretoria's neighbors ever more firmly into the South African economic system"; (2) to encourage "the indirect recognition, at least by some African states, of the independence and sovereignty of the South African homelands-cum-states"; (3) "to split the countries of tropical Africa on the issue of relations with Pretoria, making it more difficult to coordinate support for black liberation movements"; and (4) "to create an environment conducive to a rap-prochement between South Africa and the West, and on Pretoria's terms" (Price 1985, 69). To protect its security interests through diplomatic bargaining and in the process strengthen its leverage over its neighbors, such, in brief, was the primary concern of South African diplomacy until 1980.

Libya, like South Africa, seeks to achieve a basic reordering of existing regional conditions, but on a far more drastic scale. The aim is nothing short of the total elimination of territorial boundaries inherited from European colonization. Only then can the ultimate vision become reality, and bring into effect the political and cultural unification of Arabic-speaking com-munities in the Maghreb and Sahelian regions. For Qadhafi Arabo-Islamic unity is the "secure frame and final image of the struggle of the Arab Nation" (Ogunbadejo 1983, 157). It is indeed the only way to protect the Arab people against its enemies, among whom Israel and the United States are given pride of place. Rather than satellization, which maintains existing international boundaries while seeking to alter interstate relations to the advantage of hege-monic power, agreements, mergers, or federations have been the standard diplomatic in-struments used by Qadhafi to achieve regional hegemony (see Burgat in this volume). The consistency with which unification schemes have been attempted, from the Benghazi treaty of 1971 to the Oujda accords of 1984, is only paralleled by the brevity of their existence. Between 1971 and 1984 no less than six unification agreements were concluded between Libya and its neighbors; all of them have now virtually sunk into oblivion.

In neither case has diplomacy proved equal to the task. The turning point, for South Africa, was the decision of the Front-line states in 1979 to counter the CONSAS scheme by the creation of their own regional organization, the Southern African Development Coordination Con-ference (SADCC). The independence of Zimbabwe in 1980 gave the latter instant credibility: as M. Evans notes, "apart from South Africa, Zimbabwe possessed the strongest economy and transport system and potentially was the anvil upon which any SADCC would be forged" (Evans 1986, 2). With Zimbabwe opting out of the South African orbit, CONSAS lost is *raison d'être*: "The collapse of CONSAS, the strengthening of the Front-line States by the membership of Zimbabwe and the ability of the Front-line diplomatic coalition to found SADCC, repre-sented for South Africa the most shattering regional political defeat since the foundation of the modern Afrikaner Republic in 1961" (Evans 1986, 2).

Libyan diplomacy under Qadhafi reveals a similarly dismal record. None of the four bilateral merger agreements concluded between 1972 and 1980 ever went beyond the drafting stage. Egypt's move to the West after the Yom Kippur War disqualified it once and for all from any partnership with Tripoli, and as the latter, *faute de mieux*, turned to Tunisia in 1974, further obstacles arose on the path to unification. The Djerba treaty never got off the ground, and is only exceeded for the brevity of its life-span by the Chadian-Libyan unification agreement of 1981. Qadhafi's quest for Arab unity remains as elusive as it was in the days of the Tripoli Charter (1969).

The failure of diplomacy thus led to a major reassessment of regional policies in Pretoria and Tripoli, and ultimately to a combination of military and political initiatives designed to orchestrate a wide range of destabilization strategies. From 1980 onward Libya and South Africa shared the dubious distinction of practicing state terrorism more frequently and brazenly that any other state in the continent.

The Shift to Force: The Politics of Destabilization

As a global strategy to keep neighboring states in line—or on their knees—destabilization covers a wide range of tactics: intervention of ground forces and air-borne units, surgical air strikes against specific targets, occupation of strategic border areas, recruitment of mercenaries, military and logistical backing of opposition factions, political and financial support of individual dissidents, assassination or kidnapping of recalcitrant clients or perceived enemies, radio propaganda, expulsion of foreign workers identified with unfriendly regimes—all of these and more have been employed at one time or another by Pretoria and Tripoli in coming to terms with their neighbors.

The choice of tactics has not been random. It reflects a careful consideration of how domestic and international factors are likely to affect the vulnerability of the target state. And just as the choice of political, military, or economic weapons, or a combination thereof, is in part dictated by the structure of opportunities in existence at any given time, so also are tactical retreats to the bargaining table. Recourse to force does not automatically rule out bargaining and negotiation. The latter may turn out to be the only sensible course where destabilization has exhausted the range of options available to the target state, or where the intervention of third parties threatens to decisively raise the costs of destabilization. As the cases of Chad and Angola plainly demonstrate, the use of force has taken place in an environment in which interested third parties have a major stake in the outcome of regional conflicts: the Cubans in Angola, like the French in Chad, have significantly altered the regional parameters of destabilization.

Broadly speaking three major areas of convergence emerge from the record of destabilization of Libya and South Africa: each state has engaged in outright aggression against its neighbors—Libya against Chad, and South Africa against Angola (to which must be added the commando strikes mounted against African National Congress [ANC] bases in Harare, Lusaka, and Gaborone in 1986, and in Maputo and Maseru in 1982); each state has made a sustained effort to destabilize its neighbors through proxies; and they both have made remarkably short shrift of their international obligations under the terms of specific agreements: Tripoli's violation of the Franco-Libyan mutual withdrawal accords in November 1984 is paralleled by Pretoria's failure to honor its obligations under the terms of the 1984 Nkomati and Lusaka accords, with Mozambique and Angola respectively.

The parallelism extends to the seemingly inexorable process of escalation triggered by specific events in the political arena of neighboring states. Angola and Chad provide graphic examples of how changing circumstances led from one form of involvement to another, each time raising stakes while creating new justifications for intervention.

This is hardly the place for a sustained discussion of South African involvement in Angola. Suffice it to note, to begin with, that Pretoria's motives for intervention have undergone fundamental changes over time. Until 1975 cross-border raids into Angola were specifically aimed at South West Africa Peoples' Organization (SWAPO) guerillas and took the form of hot pursuit operations mounted from Namibia. The independence of Angola in November 1975 was the signal for a full-scale offensive of the South African Defense Forces (SADF) against the combined forces of the Popular Movement for the Liberation of Angola (MPLA) and Cuban auxiliaries, in hopes that a similar offensive would be called by the National Front for the Liberation of Angola (FNLA), with U.S. logistical and military support, and thus usher the collapse of the Cuban and Soviet-backed MPLA government in Luanda. The failure of the FNLA strike to materialize, coupled with the decision of the United States Senate in December 1975 to ban all aid to anti-MPLA factions, eventually caused the SADF to withdraw. Yet in 1981 another major invasion took place (Operation Protea), this time aimed at removing Soviet Sam-missile sites. By then South Africa's policy of "pro-active defense" had become inextricably tied up with a policy of massive military, logistical, and economic support to its client faction, Jonas Savimbi's Union for the Total Independence of Angola (UNITA).

As much as the absence of clear political objectives (short of destabilization), the most striking aspect of Pretoria's involvement in Angola is the improvised character of its responses. Changing perceptions of threats and opportunities have resulted in cross-border raids, full-scale invasions, air strikes against Soviet missile sites, and rescue missions on behalf of UNITA. Whether these add up to anything like a coherent policy is open to debate (Geldenhuys 1984, 79). At best they are ad hoc responses to changing circumstances; at worst, they tend to create their own contradictions. By pushing the MPLA ever more tightly into the Cuban/Soviet embrace, South African policies have created their own justification for further destabilization as well as new obstacles in the way of the realization of this objective. And by making UNITA ever more dependent on Pretoria's military support, Savimbi's credibility appears all the more questionable in the minds of African nationalists.

Much the same pattern of improvisation and contradiction emerges from the story of Libyan involvement in Chad. Between the take-over of the Aouzou strip in 1973 to the full-scale invasion mounted on behalf of the *Gouvernement d'Union Nationale Transitoire* (GUNT) "rebels" a decade later, Libyan policies ran a wide gamut. The motives for occupying Aouzou were both strategic and political. To secure a border area of considerable strategic significance to Libya, and in so doing fill the vacuum left by the withdrawal of the Chadian forces in the face of the victories scored by the *Front de Libération National Tchadien* (Frolinat), these, in brief, were the prime motives behind Qadhafi's move into Aouzou—a move made all the more tempting by the sympathies then evinced by the local populations for the Libyan leader. Ironically, the Libyan takeover of Aouzou became the source of profound disagreements among Frolinat leaders, thus forcing new options upon Qadhafi. Not only did Qadhafi find it politically expedient to throw his weight behind the pro-Libyan faction, headed by Goukouni Oueddeye, against its rival, headed by Hissene Habre, but as factional competition picked up momentum, Libyan involvement on behalf of Goukouni increased correspondingly.

What began as a limited territorial occupation (not unlike the occupation of border areas between Namibia and Angola by the SADF) soon developed into a more extensive penetration of northern Chad by Libyan army units backed up by the Islamic Legion (the Libyan counterpart of the South African Buffalo battalion, made up of dissidents from the Chipenda faction of the MPLA and various other African recruits). In December 1980 a full-scale invasion was launched on behalf of Goukouni Oueddeye, culminating in the capture of the capital city, Ndjamena. In a sequence of events strikingly reminiscent of what happened in Angola, Libyan forces withdrew shortly thereafter (at the request of Goukouni, and under French pressure), only to launch a massive offensive against the Habre government in the summer of 1983, which in turn prompted a large-scale intervention of French armed forces (the so-called Sting-Ray Operation, involving the deployment of some three thousand troops along the sixteenth parallel). Now controlling approximately the entire northern half of Chad, and fully backed by the Libyan army, the dependence of the GUNT on Tripoli tended to approximate that of UNITA on Pretoria. The analogy extends to the supportive role played by third parties, with the French providing the Habre government with security guarantees very similar to those extended by Cuba to the MPLA government in Luanda.

Reflecting on the motives behind South Africa's intervention in Angola, Geldenhuys raises the following questions:

> Was it South Africa's intention to drive the Cubans out of Angola, thus freeing the country from a communist presence? . . . Or did South Africa want to help the anticommunist forces to hold their own against the MPLA, and thus promote the chances of a government of national unity (as envisaged in the Alvor and Nakuru Agreements)? Or was it Pretoria's intention to help set up a separate UNITA controlled state in southern Angola—one freed of SWAPO? (Geldenhuys 1984, 79)

"In the event," adds Geldenhuys, "not one of these possible objectives was achieved."

Similar queries, and much the same conclusion, arise when one seeks to elucidate Qadhafi's motives in Chad. Was it his intention to drive the French out of Chad, and thus clear the way for a GUNT regime in Ndjamena? Or was the ultimate goal to pave the way for a government of national unity (as appeared to be the case during the abortive Kano and Lagos conferences in 1979–80)? Or was it to carve out a Libyan sphere of influence in northern Chad? Or should the short-lived Chadian-Libyan merger, in January 1981, be viewed as a prefiguration of future attempts at regional unification? There are no clear answers to these questions, only informed guesses about Libyan perceptions of what might have seemed an appropriate course of action at any given juncture.

One thing, however, is clear: destabilization involves a great deal more than the random application of force by direct or indirect means; it also brings into play a variety of pressures and incentives, including economic sanctions and the careful manipulation of surrogate forces. On both counts Pretoria's performance emerges as the more impressive, and its effects on the target states immensely more devastating.

The Strategic Uses of Economic Muscle

To dwell as we have on the similarities between the Libyan and South African quest for regional hegemony is not meant to obscure certain abiding differences in their strategic capabilities. As noted earlier, the structure of regional economic dependence on South Africa is without parallel anywhere in the continent, and so, also, is the extent of political leverage arising from Pretoria's economic grip over the region. The range of economic pressures available to Libya seems puny by comparison. Thus, none of the measures advocated by Geldenhuys in 1981 in support of Pretoria's strategic objectives (all of which were subsequently put into effect) are available to Tripoli—"manipulating the availability of railway trucks or berthing facilities in harbors . . . restrictions on the amount of goods that may be exported via South Africa, and deliberate delays at order posts" (cited in Hanlon 1986a, 219). In short, Pretoria's neighbors are directly and profoundly vulnerable to its economic muscle; Tripoli's neighbors are only marginally sensitive to the withdrawal of its economic benefits, the latter exclusively derived from its huge petroleum resources.

The devastating impact of Pretoria's economic destabilization strategy is dramatically evident in the crises and disruptions visited upon its neighbors from 1982 to 1986.

The most telling manifestation of its economic supremacy occurred in January 1986, when, following a twenty-day blockade of Lesotho, the government of Chief Lebua Jonathan was promptly overthrown by the military and replaced by a more pliant (i.e., pro-South African) team headed by General Justin Lekhanya. The utter dependence of Botswana, Lesotho, and Swaziland (the so called BLS states) on Pretoria suggests that the Maseru scenario could be reenacted any time in Gaborone or Mbabane (Hanlon 1987, 107–29).

Though neither Mozambique nor Zimbabwe shares the hostage status of the BLS states, their concerted efforts to reduce their economic dependence on South Africa have been repeatedly thwarted by sabotage operations against port facilities, oil depots, and rail links, conducted by the South African–backed Mozambican National Resistance Movement (MNR). Pretoria's determination to deny access to alternative regional transportation nets received dramatic confirmation with the blowing up of the Beira oil depot in December 1982. Widespread economic dislocations followed, reaching far beyond the immediate site of the sabotage operation (Hanlon 1987, 131–50). The result was to deprive Zimbabwe of a two-month oil supply (valued at $12 million). As was reported at the time, "white morale plummeted; travel was impossible, cars were abandoned, factories closed, power cuts became frequent and Harare appealed to the world for help. . . . South Africa had made its point" (Jenkins 1983, 21). The point, however, was made again and again as subsequent MNR raids interrupted traffic on the Beira-Harare rail link. As for the total economic losses suffered by Mozambique through "South African aggression and economic destabilization," these were officially estimated by Maputo in February 1984 at $4 billion, that is "three times Mozambique's total indebtedness to the West" (St. Jorre 1984, 3).

If the case of Lesotho provides a textbook example of how South Africa can use its economic muscle to bring about political destabilization, the plight of Mozambique is a tragic illustration of the reverse phenomenon: it shows how destabilization through proxies can usher economic chaos on a major scale within and beyond the boundaries of the target state. Nor are the social costs any less horrendous. According to a recently published UNICEF report, Angola and Mozambique claim the world's highest mortality rates: 325 deaths for each 1,000 children less than five years of age; 45 percent of the total deaths of children under five, or 140,000 a year, are said to be caused by war and economic destabilization (*New York Times*, February 19, 1987).

The Libyan economic armory seems singularly ineffective by comparison. Vital as they are to Qadhafi's destabilization strategies, oil resources are no substitute for the array of economic pressures available to Pretoria, ranging from the destruction or manipulation of rail links and port facilities to the actual or threatened expulsion of migrant workers. Thus, nothing like the compromise forced out of Maputo through the Nkomati accords in 1984—since then repeatedly violated by Pretoria—could conceivably be imposed by Libya on any of its neighbors. In February 1984 Mozambique had no other choice but to sue for peace. For any of Libya's neighbors to be driven to this extremity is unthinkable. Sensitive though they are to economic pressures, their vulnerability to Libyan sanctions is minimal. Qadhafi's decision in 1985 to expel some thirty thousand Tunisian workers, in retaliation for Tunisia's harboring of Libyan dissidents, was little more than an irritant; the plight of four hundred thousand Mozambicans reported to face starvation in 1987 can only be described as an unprecedented human tragedy.

South Africa's grip on regional infrastructures offers a range of compliance mechanisms that are simply not available to Tripoli; but perhaps the most effective of such mechanisms stems from its ability to manipulate surrogates on a scale and with a degree of efficiency unmatched by Libya.

Limits of Factional Sponsorship

Behind each pattern of regional interference lies the spectrum of opportunities and dangers associated with opposition movements in neighboring states. These movements cover a wide gamut, ranging on the South African side from the almost extinct Lesotho Liberation Army, to the large-scale insurrections spearheaded by the MNR and UNITA, and, on the Libyan side, from the more or less inchoate *groupuscules* of Malian and Nigerian dissidents to the more enduring (though now defunct) GUNT rebellion in northern Chad. In dealing with this mixed bag of presumptive clients both states have had to grapple with the same knotty issues: how best to foster internal cohesion within their respective surrogate forces, how to work out mutually acceptable relationships between patron and proxy, and make sure the latter receives appropriate logistical, military, and diplomatic support. On each of these dimensions South Africa emerges as the more adept in handling the ambivalence of the patron-client nexus, but for reasons that are not entirely of its own design.

The framing of viable patron-proxy partnerships has been directly affected by the contextual roots of local insurgencies. The critical significance of ethnicity is nowhere more evident than in the sharply divergent trends exhibited by "rebel" forces in Chad and Angola. Unlike the GUNT factions, whose tendency to fragment is only matched by their disposition to quarrel, UNITA shows a far greater degree of internal cohesion, enjoying as it does the solid support of the Ovimbundu, the largest ethnic aggregate in Angola, and the crucial advantage of a skilled charismatic leader, Jonas Savimbi, whose popularity extends to the more conservative precincts of the Reagan administration. Plagued by incessant splits, tiffs, and misunderstandings, the GUNT, on the other hand, has tended to replicate within its ranks the pattern of segmentary opposition or structured anarchy familiar to students of northern Chadian societies.

Although there is no equivalent in Mozambique for the sheer fractiousness of Sahelian societies, ethnic dissentions and factional in-fighting have afflicted the MNR with disabilities quite similar to those suffered by the GUNT: bitter struggles for leadership positions, chronic factional disputes and ethnic rivalries, the latter centering on competition among Shona, Makonde, and Makwa elements. Here again the contrast with UNITA is striking and carries implications that go far beyond the realm of structural dissimilarities. Just as the internal handicaps of the GUNT have greatly contributed to its dependence on Libya, the MNR remains to this day overwhelmingly dependent on Pretoria.

The constraints on the policy choices available to Pretoria and Tripoli are in part a reflection of the debilitating splits and leadership crises suffered by their client factions and in part the result of the uncertainties inherent in the patron-client relationship. The patron-client relationship draws each partner into a nexus of reciprocal manipulation whose outcomes are often unpredictable. In time the proxy may end up forcing upon the patron-state options that the latter had not anticipated, thus setting the stage for a process of escalation which neither patron nor proxy can fully control. Or else circumstance may dictate policy shifts on the part of the patron that the client faction, or a segment thereof, is unprepared to accept, thus generating new sources of conflict between patron and client and, indeed, among client factions (as happened in Chad on several occasions). Patron-client interactions thus tend to generate their own complex dialectics, sometimes ensnaring each partner into a catch-22 situation, from which neither can extricate itself without major costs (as the case of Chad again demonstrates), and sometimes resulting in a modus vivendi in which tensions are kept within manageable bonds (as in Angola).

The cases of Chad and Angola are at opposite poles on the continuum of attraction and repulsion present in every patron-client relationship. If Libyan insistence on a close subordination of its GUNT allies stands in sharp contrast with South African sensitivity to the autonomist claims of UNITA, equally striking is the divergence between the internal convulsions suffered by the GUNT and the growing political strength and military capabilities displayed by UNITA.

Despite major changes over time in Libyan policies the dominant trend has been to transform the GUNT into a vehicle of Libyan cultural and political expansion. By trying to convert his allies into satellites, Qadhafi paved the way for countless discords and defections. His subsequent efforts to play one faction against another proved unavailing. The crunch came in late 1986, when the bulk of the GUNT forces suddenly switched sides and turned against Libyan troops and the consistently "loyalist" *Conseil Démocratique Révolutionnaire* (CDR). What had initially begun as a war by proxy transformed itself almost overnight into a head-on confrontation between Libyans and Chadians.

The Angolan insurgency reveals an entirely different pattern. Rather than a loose assemblage of disparate factions, UNITA must be seen for what it is, a cohesive, disciplined and largely self-sustaining force, buttressed by regular units and guerilla fighters numbering approximately forty thousand and claiming effective control over nearly one-third of Angola's territory. Crucial as it is to its persistence as a viable political and military organization, Pretoria's backing never developed into a rigid tutelage relationship. Not only is such eventuality made unnecessary by the convergence of strategic objectives between proxy and patron, but it is thoroughly incompatible with Pretoria's claims on behalf of UNITA, that is, that it is an autonomous movement with considerable local support. Such claims are difficult to dismiss. Although the imprint of South Africa is everywhere visible in the so-called "liberated areas"—from "soft drinks, soap and cigarettes to trucks, weapons and gasoline" (Ottaway and Tyler 1986)—there is also ample proof of indigenous political support for Savimbi, even beyond the Ovimbundu perimeter.

UNITA's preferential clientage relationship with South Africa has resulted in a modus vivendi from which each partner draws maximum benefits: in return for Pretoria's protection and continued economic, military, and logistical assistance, UNITA can be relied on to carry on the fight against the Luanda government; and as long as the resulting threats to its security make it imperative for Luanda to seek the protection of Cuban mercenaries, U.S. efforts to link a phased withdrawal of all foreign troops from Angola to a timetable for Namibian independence will be in vain. The extension of the Reagan doctrine to Angola, dramatized by the shipment of U.S. Stinger missiles to UNITA (via Zaire), is the most tangible proof of the diplomatic gains achieved by Pretoria through its skillful handling of clientage relations—from Jumba to Washington, and from Washington to Kinshasa.

Unlike UNITA, whose origins are traceable to its struggle against Portuguese rule, the MNR claims a more ambiguous pedigree: its roots lie in the widespread disaffection caused by the egregious ineptitude of the socialist reforms initiated by the Frelimo government, but its subsequent growth was nurtured by the intelligence services of what was then Rhodesia (Fauvet 1984, 115). The nascent and deeply fractured anti-Frelimo insurrection was indeed promptly "recuperated" by the Rhodesian Central Intelligence Organization (CIO), then headed by Ken Flowers, and converted into a tool of Rhodesian armed activities, directed against both the Maputo authorities and the Zimbabwe African National Union (ZANU). A mixed assemblage of former Pide agents and Portuguese settlers and businessmen joined hands with Rhodesian officials to hammer out a basic command structure, and after Mugabe came to power, in 1980, the MNR directorate was "flown to Pretoria, lock, stock and radio station" (Jenkins 1983, 20). As is now widely recognized, the MNR is "financed and armed by the SADF and given logistical support in the form of training, command and control equipment, helicopter transport and special operations" (Jenkins 1983, 21). Even by Libyan standards the degree of satellization achieved by South Africa appears unprecedented.

The Portuguese settler connection continued to permeate the MNR, adding a strong settler-African tension to the inter-African strains that have repeatedly hampered the emergence of a unified command structure. Despite South African hopes that the MNR would evolve into something approximating the UNITA—"something which, in the final analysis, was under Pretoria's control, but which had an international projection and image of its own" (Fauvet 1984, 117)—the resulting pattern of internal fragmentation suggests a state of affairs closer to the pre-1986 GUNT, with the additional handicap of a white settler connection, which further lessens its credibility. Furthermore, the degree of grass-roots anarchy that prevails in MNR-dominated areas appears to even surpass the standards of disorganization set by Chadian "rebels," reminiscent in many ways of the social banditry that flourished on the Mozambican-Rhodesian border at the turn of the century. As has been noted, "many of the (MNR) recruits join up because that is the simplest way to survive. If a young man is on the verge of starvation, joining the MNR and thereby receiving a weapon with which to steal food is an attractive option" (Gunn 1986, 10). Whether looked at from the standpoint of its external dependence, internal divisions, or overall structural disorganization, the MNR stands as a rather unique phenomenon in the morphology of foreign-linked factionalism.

Where the South African sponsorship differs most conspicuously from that of Libya is in

178 The Green and the Black

the diversity of external linkages it has been able to broker between its client factions and other interested parties. By consistently posing as the standard-bearer of a world-wide anti-communist crusade, and by imparting to its surrogates the image of dedicated fighters against the spread of Afro-Marxist influence in the continent, Pretoria is in a privileged position to mobilize the support of a wide range of self-proclaimed anti-communist forces on behalf of its African clients. Pressuring the Reagan administration into throwing its weight (and Stinger missiles) behind UNITA required little effort considering the preexisting sympathies of die-hard, conservative Republicans for Savimbi, whose charismatic appeal in Washington is never more mesmerizing than when he lambasts Soviet imperialism in Angola; yet it clearly stands as the single most important achievement of South African diplomacy on behalf of its Angolan client. All the more so, indeed, in view of the apparent ease with which Washington was able subsequently to enlist Mobutu's cooperation in facilitating the shipment of U.S. military assistance to UNITA. Saudi Arabia, for its part, contributed some $15 million worth of military hardware to "anti-Communists in Angola." The range of external clientage relations brokered through Pretoria is by no means limited to Washington, Riyadh, and Kinshasa. A mere look at the variety of states that have shown their active sympathy and support for the MNR is enough to suggest the extent of Pretoria's diplomatic leverage within and beyond the African continent:

> In a rather bizarre coincidence Israel and Saudi Arabia, protagonists in the Middle East, are also providing assistance to the MNR guerrillas. While the Israelis train the guerrillas in Malawi, the Saudis and other conservative Arabs extend financial assistance under the pretext of supporting the minority Muslim population in Mozambique. Malawi, South Africa's only trusted ally among African nations, serves as a major route for the MNR. The tiny nation of Comoros Islands, which has become a sanctuary for mercenaries, is also being used as a launching ground for MNR attacks into Nampula, Inhambana and Cabo Delgado provinces. (Cheru 1986, 35)

There is no common measure between Pretoria's adeptness at "subcontracting" its patronage to its ideological allies in the United States, Europe, the Middle East, and Africa, and Libya's very limited ability to mobilize the forces of Islam on behalf of its African clients. And while Pretoria is in no way to be described as Washington's client, any more than Libya can be said to be Moscow's proxy, it is nonetheless clear that the former has been decidedly more successful in enlisting U.S. support on behalf of its African surrogates, notably UNITA, than Libya in securing Soviet diplomatic support and military assistance for its African allies.

The very success of factional sponsorship, however, confronts the sponsor with self-imposed limitations, and here Libya fares no better than South Africa. For when the time comes to operate a transfer of power to the winning faction, as must surely happen when opponents become incumbents, a very different set of relationships comes into being, with the destabilizer more often than not cast in the role of protector. Simon Jenkins tersely captures the essence of the dilemma: "Backing insurgents in the mountains or in the bushveld is chicken-feed compared to backing them in power" (Jenkins 1983, 25). The wisdom of this statement was driven home to Qadhafi with compelling force in early 1981, when, after contributing decisively to Goukouni Oueddeye's capture of Ndjamena, the GUNT leader proved utterly unsympathetic to Qadhafi's merger attempt and proceeded to request the immediate withdrawal of Libyan forces, only to turn once again to Tripoli after being driven out of power. The costs of supporting recalcitrant or ineffective regimes faced with renewed insurgency are likewise anticipated by Pretoria, which is why Botha has shown little inclination to further extend its backing to the MNR to the point where it would have no other option but to back it in Maputo. It is one thing to manipulate a proxy *qua* opponent, and quite another to restructure the clientage relation within the framework of a state system.

The Limits and Contradictions of Superpower Involvement

The ironies and contradictions of superpower involvement in regional conflicts are nowhere more cruelly revealed than in the sequence of events that followed in the wake of the U.S. raid on Tripoli and Benghazi on April 14, 1986. Not only did the raid fail to achieve its cardinal objective—killing Qadhafi—but it gave Pretoria the pretext it needed to launch similar strikes against ANC bases in Zimbabwe, Zambia, and Botswana. Thus, early on May 19 crack commando units of the SADF launched a series of coordinated attacks against ANC headquarters in Harare (Zimbabwe), Lusaka (Zambia), and Gaberone (Botswana), causing considerable material destruction and scores of human casualties. Despite Washington's vigorous condemnation of the attacks, Africans could not fail to note the "relevance" of the U.S. raid on Libya to similar moves by Pretoria against its neighbors; nor could they fail to read into these events irrefutable proof of the failure of "constructive engagement."

The U.S. strike on Libya did more than provide a model for Pretoria. It also brought to light the limits of superpower influence on their presumptive allies. Just as the U.S. raid elicited little more than a pro forma condemnation from the Soviets, the South African strikes against the ANC underscored the innocuousness of the U.S. response to a move that clearly ran counter to U.S. interests in the region. Besides demonstrating the inability or unwillingness of the superpowers to effectively restrain—or protect—their regional allies, what emerges from these events is a serious questioning of the simplistic and all-too-prevalent notion of a symmetry of dependence of South Africa on the United States and of Libya on the USSR.

The asymmetries in this case are reasonably clear and require little elaboration. Libyan dependence on Moscow is exclusively military; South African dependence on Washington is anything but military, and is matched by a reverse (though often vastly exaggerated) pattern of dependency of the United States on South African strategic minerals for which there is no equivalent in the Moscow-Tripoli axis. Moreover, while the United States has consistently refrained from including Pretoria on its list of recipients of U.S. military aid, this restriction does not apply to Pretoria's proxy in Angola. Precisely the reverse situation obtains with regard to Libyan-Soviet relations: At no time have any of Tripoli's surrogates, in Chad or elsewhere, received direct military assistance from the USSR. Finally, and despite profound disagreements within the Soviet hierarchy about how best to deal with African issues (Albright 1987), one would be hard put to find in the record of Soviet policies toward Libya anything comparable to the uncertainties, discords, and contradictions that continue to plague U.S. policies toward South Africa.[1] That the phenomenon happens to be firmly rooted in the extreme vulnerability of U.S. foreign policies to conflicting domestic pressures and interests does not make it any less relevant.[2]

If there is any parallelism in superpower behavior, it lies in the common distaste displayed by Washington and Moscow toward the domestic politics of their respective allies in southern and northern Africa. For if apartheid is indeed anathema to virtually every shade of opinion in the U.S. domestic spectrum, the least that can be said is that the kind of socialism that has taken root in Libya is difficult to reconcile with even the most flexible tenets of Marxism-Leninism. Seen through the prism of the Kremlin's orthodoxy Qadhafi is, at best, an "idealist"; at worst a "Muslim fanatic." There is a parallelism of sorts, as well, in the willingness of each superpower to overlook these incompatibilities for the sake of a common stand on global policy issues. Just as there is a fundamental coincidence of views between the USSR and Libya on most issues regarding the Middle East, equally striking is the degree of harmony between Washington and Pretoria on East-West issues. Both have consistently shared the same visceral hostility toward the Soviet positions; and both have gone on record as adhering to double standards whenever East-West issues spill over into African arenas. As Jerry Hough pertinently notes, "America's use of France as a proxy in African activities is taken for granted—in fact, the only complaint was about French reluctance to intervene in Chad—but the Soviet Union has no right to use Cuba as its proxy in Africa." Nor are such double standards limited to Africa. Again to quote from Hough: "It is simply asserted as self-evident that sovereign Nicaragua—1,000 miles from US shores—cannot be allowed to accept Soviet MIG-21s, while the US must be able to send the equivalent of much more advanced MIG-29s to Pakistan, which virtually borders on the Soviet Union" (Hough 1986, 3).

It is perhaps a commentary on the limits of superpower behavior in the continent that such coincidence of views on global issues tends to evaporate when confronted with more narrow, inter-African issues. Superpower allegiance operates at the global level, but the strategic benefits of African alliances with the superpowers are invested at the regional level, and with consequences that are seldom anticipated, much less approved, by the senior partners. Libyan adventurism in Chad is one example; others include Pretoria's violation of the Nkomati/Lusaka accords, its clandestine support for the MNR, the 1986 SADF strikes against ANC bases in Zimbabwe, Zambia, and Botswana, followed on April 25, 1987, by yet another attack on Zambia. In each case the dominant theme is the inability of the superpowers to restrain the aggressive interference of their African allies in the affairs of their neighbors. As Zaki Laidi conclusively shows, in a broader context, "all the evidence points to the fact that the super-powers are in a position to determine the rhythm and intensity but not the direction of inter-African relations" (Laidi 1986, 280).

In short, if the concept of state autonomy has any meaning in contemporary Africa it is primarily in relation to its external environment that it can best be analyzed. And it is at this level as well that the parallel between Libya and South Africa appears to be most compelling, if not entirely reassuring.

NOTES

1. Note for example the striking inconsistencies of the voting record of the U.S. House of Representatives in September 1986. As Pauline Baker notes, "in a little noticed move on September 17, the US House of Representatives refused to cut off the CIA covert military aid program for Savimbi. Two weeks later, the House voted to override President Reagan's veto of economic sanctions against South Africa. Taken together these votes pointed the US in diametrically opposite directions, signalling moral opposition to and strategic support for the apartheid state" (Baker 1987, 196).

2. In the aftermath of the Iran-Contra scam there is little to add to the list of bizarre initiatives associated with the "privatization" of U.S. foreign policy, with the exception of the Libyan caper cut by Edwin Wilson and Frank Terpil in 1976. Thanks to their CIA connections and private contacts both men were able to organize the shipment of twenty-one tons of C-4 explosive to Tripoli in cans labeled as oil-drilling mud; for $8 million a year Wilson agreed to provide Qadhafi with spare parts for his fleet of American-made C-130 transport planes. Furthermore, Wilson "entered into an agreement to provide veterans of the US Special Forces, Green Berets, to train (Libyan) commando teams. The Libyans paid $100,000 per Green Beret; Wilson in turn recruited each of them for half as much" (Maas 1986, 38). A similar scenario developing within the precincts of the KGB opens up some fascinating areas of speculation for writers of science fiction.

REFERENCES

Albright, David. 1987. "Four Soviet Views of Africa." CSIS *Africa Notes*, no. 72 (May 9):1–4.

Baker, Pauline. 1987. "United States Policy in Southern Africa." *Current History* 86, no. 520 (May):193–96.

Bull, Hedley. 1977. *The Anarchical Society*. London and New York: Columbia University Press.

Cheru, Fantu. 1986. "The Politics of Desperation: Mozambique and Nkomati." *Transafrica Forum* 3, no. 3 (Spring):29–48.

Evans, M. 1986. *The Front-Line States, South Africa and Southern African Security: Military Prospects and Perspectives*. Zimbabwe: University of Zimbabwe Publications.

Fauvet, Paul. 1984. "Roots of Counter-revolution: The Mozambique National Resistance." *Review of African Political Economy*, no. 29:108–21.

Foltz, William J. 1981. "US National Interest in Africa." In *The National Interest of the United States*, edited by Prosser Gifford, 93–103. Washington, D.C.: University Press of America.

Geldenhuys, Deon. 1984. *The Diplomacy of Isolation: South African Foreign Policy Making*. New York: St. Martin's Press.

Gunn, Gillian. 1986. "Mozambique After Machel." CSIS *Notes*, no. 67 (December 29):1–11.

Hanlon, Joseph. 1986a. "Conflict and Dependence in Southern Africa." In *Third World Affairs 1985*. London: Third World Foundation for Social and Economic Studies.

———. 1986b. *Apartheid's Second Front*. New York: Penguin Books.

———. 1987. *Beggar Your Neighbors: Apartheid Power in Southern Africa*. Bloomington: Indiana University Press.

Hough, Jerry. 1986. *The Struggle for the Third World*. Washington D.C.: The Brookings Institute.

Jenkins, Simon. 1983. "Destabilization in Southern Africa." *The Economist*, (July 16):19–28.

Keal, Paul. 1986. "On Influence and Spheres of Influence." In *Dominant Powers and Subordinate States*, edited by Jan Triska, 124–44. Durham: Duke University Press.

Laidi, Zaki. 1986. *Les Contraintes d'une Rivalité: Les Superpuissances et l'Afrique*. Paris: La Découverte.

Maas, Peter. 1986. "Selling Out." *The New York Times Magazine*, (April 13):26–41.

Maasdorp, Gavin. 1985. "Squaring up to Economic Dominance: Regional Patterns." In *South Africa and Its Neighbors*, edited by Robert Rotberg et al., 91–136. Lexington, MA: Lexington Books.

New York Times. 1987. (February 1):19.

Ogunbadejo, Oye. 1983. "Qadhafi's North African Design." *International Security* 8, no. 1 (Summer):154–78.

Ottaway, David, and Patrick Tyler. 1986. "Angola Girds for a Battle." *International Herald Tribune*, July 28.

Price, Robert M. 1985. "Creating New Political Realities: Pretoria's Drive for Regional Hegemony." In *African Crisis Areas*, edited by G. Bender, J. S. Coleman, and R. L. Sklar, 64–88. Berkeley and Los Angeles: The University of California Press.

Rotberg, Robert. 1985. "South Africa in Its Region: Hegemony and Vulnerability." In *South Africa and Its Neighbors*, edited by R. Rotberg et al., 1–13. Lexington, MA: Lexington Books.

St. Jorre, John de. 1984. "Destabilization and Dialogue: South Africa's Emergence as a Regional Superpower." CSIS *Notes*, no. 26 (April 17):1–7.

CONTRIBUTORS

François Burgat taught in the Law Faculty of the University of Constantine from 1973 to 1980. He is currently a research associate at the Centre National de la Recherche Scientifique in Aix-en-Provence. He has written extensively on issues of political development in North Africa and has contributed articles to *L'Annuaire d'Afrique du Nord*, *Maghreb-Machreq*, *Grand Maghreb*, and *Les Cahiers de l'Orient*.

Mary-Jane Deeb is assistant professorial lecturer at George Washington University. She has worked for USAID and various UN organizations and has published a number of articles on social and political problems in the Middle East. She is coauthor with Marius K. Deeb of *Libya since the Revolution: Aspects of Social and Political Development*.

Chris Dunton has taught African literature at the Universities of Sokoto, Nigeria, and Gar Younis, Libya. Publications include *Wole Soyinka's Three Short Plays* and *The Novels of Ferdinand Oyono* (forthcoming). He writes regularly for *West Africa* magazine.

William J. Foltz is professor of political science at Yale University and director of The Yale Center for International and Area Studies. A specialist in Africa's politics and international relations, his recent work includes editing *Arms and the Africans: Military Influences on Africa's International Relations*.

E. G. H. Joffé is consultant-editor for the Middle East and North Africa at Economist Publications and research associate at the Centre for Middle East Studies in the School of Oriental and African Studies of London University. He has numerous publications dealing with the Middle East and North Africa and is currently engaged in a study of Libya and in a joint study of the Gulf War with Dr. K. S. McLachlan of London University.

René Lemarchand is professor of political science at the University of Florida and former director of the Center for African Studies. He is the author of *Political Awakening in the Congo* and *Rwanda and Burundi* (for which he received the Herskovits Award in 1971), editor of *African Kingships in Perspective, American Policies in Southern Africa: The Stakes and the Stance*, and coeditor, with S. N. Eisenstadt, of *Patronage, Clientelism and Political Development*.

Jean-Emmanuel Pondi was a visiting research fellow with the African Studies Program at the Johns Hopkins University School of Advanced International Studies (SAIS) in 1986. He now teaches international politics at the International Relations Institute of Cameroon (IRIC), University of Yaounde. His latest article on African international relations appeared in the December 1986 issue of *SAIS Review*.

Ronald Bruce St John has had considerable experience with Libya, having worked there over a four-year period. Specializing in the foreign policies of developing states, he has authored over three dozen books, articles, and reviews. His most recent publication is *Qadhafi's World Design: Libyan Foreign Policy, 1969–1987*.

Mark Tessler, coeditor of the Indiana University Press series in which this volume appears, is professor of political science at the University of Wisconsin-Milwaukee. Among his recent publications are *Political Elites in Arab North Africa* and *The Evaluation and Application of Survey Research in the Arab World*. He has also written extensively on North Africa and the Middle East for the Universities Field Staff International.

INDEX